Liberty, Justice and Equality

To those men and women
for whom liberty, justice and equality
are more than just rhetorical exhortations
to be made on the Fourth of July

LIBERTY, JUSTICE AND EQUALITY

*How These Constitutional Guarantees
Have Been Shaped by United States
Supreme Court Decisions Since 1789*

by
James E. Leahy

McFarland & Company, Inc., Publishers
Jefferson, North Carolina, and London

British Library Cataloguing-in-Publication data are available

Library of Congress Cataloguing-in-Publication Data

Leahy, James E., 1919–
    Liberty, justice and equality : how these constitutional
guarantees have been shaped by United States Supreme Court decisions
since 1789 / by James E. Leahy.
        p. cm.
    Includes bibliographical references and index.
    ISBN 0-89950-742-5 (lib. bdg. : 50# alk. paper) ∞
        1. Civil rights – United States – History.   2. Due process of law –
United States – History.   3. Equality before the law – United States –
History.   I. Title.
    KF4749.L4   1992
    342.73'085 – dc20
    [347.30285]   92-50308
                                                                                              CIP

©1992 James E. Leahy. All rights reserved

Manufactured in the United States of America

McFarland & Company, Inc., Publishers
Box 611, Jefferson, North Carolina 28640

Contents

Preface

Our history abounds with references to the ideals of liberty, justice, and equality. In declaring our independence from Great Britain we announced to all the world that we believed "that all men are created equal; that they are endowed, by their Creator with certain unalienable rights; that among these are life, liberty, and the pursuit of happiness." Further, when it came time to create a government for this new and independent country, the framers of the Constitution wanted it clearly understood that among the goals of this government, as stated in the preamble, was the establishment of "justice."

It has been the task of the Supreme Court throughout our history to give meaning to these ideals within our constitutional system, a task that the justices have performed well, with some notable exceptions.

Liberty

Liberty, in the abstract, depends upon one's point of view. President Abraham Lincoln expressed that thought when in a speech given in April 1864, he stated:

> The world has never had a good definition of the word liberty. And the American people just now are much in want of one. We all declare for liberty; but in using the same word we do not mean the same thing. With some, the word liberty may mean for each man to do as he pleases with himself and the product of his labor; while with others the same word may mean for some men to do as they please with other men and the product of other men's labor.[1]

John Stuart Mill, on the other hand, had a very simplistic idea of liberty: "Liberty consists in doing what one desires." And further:

"The individual is not accountable to society for his actions, insofar as these concern the interests of no person but himself."[2]

Justice Felix Frankfurter was of the opinion that liberty was found in fair procedures: "The history of liberty has largely been the history of the observance of procedural safeguards."[3]

Justice Frankfurter was surely correct in noting that it is in the strict observance of procedural rules within our constitutional system that our liberty is protected. But to confine the definition of liberty to the adherence to proper procedures is much too limiting. Liberty encompasses much more than that, as Justice Louis D. Brandeis pointed out when he wrote that the Founding Fathers

> sought to protect Americans in their beliefs, their thoughts, their emotions and their sensations. They conferred, as against the Government, the right to be let alone — the most comprehensive of rights and the right most valued by civilized men.[4]

The Supreme Court, while recognizing the importance of procedural safeguards, has also given a more expansive meaning to the liberty that is protected by the due process clauses of the Fifth and Fourteenth amendments. The justices have held that there are certain substantive rights within the meaning of the word *liberty*. These include the right of parents to control the education of their children, the right to marry and have children, and the right of families to live together. Liberty also includes the right of a woman to make the choice whether to have children, the right of children and prisoners to be free from undeserved punishment, and the right of the mentally ill to have minimally adequate care and treatment during confinement.

Justice

Defining *justice* is somewhat more elusive. An old Latin saying defines legal justice "as the art of the good and the fair."[5] The embodiment of justice in the Constitution is in the phrase "due process of law" found in the Fifth and Fourteenth amendments. Justice Frankfurter thought that "due process is that which comports with the deepest notions of what is fair and right and just."[6] And for Chief Justice Earl Warren, whether justice would be done was to be found in the answer to the question "Is it fair?"[7]

The authors of the Bill of Rights, of course, were concerned about justice being done, especially to those accused of crimes, as the Fourth, Fifth, Sixth, and Eighth amendments clearly indicate. These amendments give protection against unreasonable searches and seizures, double jeopardy, and self-incrimination. They guarantee due process, a speedy public trial, to be confronted by witnesses against oneself, to have compulsory process to secure witnesses for one's defense, and a right to counsel. And there is a prohibition against cruel and unusual punishment.

But whether government actions are fair goes much further than just protecting persons accused of crime. As Justice Frankfurter pointed out, fair procedure is essential. And this is true when governmental action affects a person's life, liberty, or property.

Justice also requires a just result from governmental action, whether that action is a finding that a person is disloyal or a security risk, should be deported, or be interned, as many Japanese Americans were during World War II.

Equality

The dictionary definition of *equality* is simply the "state or instance of being equal." That hardly defines the equality contemplated in the statement "all men are created equal" in the Declaration of Independence. And that statement was surely meant to be more comprehensive than that written by Anatole France when he wrote: "The law, in its majestic equality, forbids the rich as well as the poor to sleep under bridges, to beg in the streets, and to steal bread."[8]

We have attempted to secure equal treatment for all persons by including in the Fourteenth Amendment the guarantee that "no State shall . . . deny to any person within its jurisdiction the equal protection of the laws." And the Supreme Court has interpreted the due process clause of the Fifth Amendment to require the same kind of equal treatment from the federal government. In giving this statement a more precise meaning, the Supreme Court has written that "it may be said generally that the equal protection clause means that the rights of all persons must rest upon the same rule under similar circumstances."[9] But that does not mean that government can never treat people differently, for the Court has also held that "unless a classification trammels fundamental personal rights or is drawn upon inherently suspect distinctions such as race, religion, or alienage, our decisions presume the constitutionality of the statutory discriminations and require only that the classification challenged be rationally related to a legitimate state interest."[10]

In implementing the concept of equal protection, the justices use different approaches when dealing with dissimilar kinds of classifications. For example, when government treats people differently because of their race, national origin, or alien status, the justices examine such classifications with the utmost care and most often find them unconstitutional as a denial of equal protection. Sometimes government makes distinctions that effect a fundamental right, such as placing restrictions on the right to marry, to travel, or to vote for some people but not others. The justices will also examine such categorizations to see whether the government has a compelling reason for making them. Only then will they be deemed constitutional.

Government giving different treatment to one sex or taking action that affects illegitimate children differently than legitimate children will also cause the Court to examine the disparate treatment carefully.

Finally, for the great majority of classifications made by government that do not deal with any of the above, the justices still require that the different treatment have some rational connection to the goals to be accomplished by the government's classification.

The mere fact that the concepts of liberty, justice, and equality are deeply ingrained in our society and explicitly expressed in the Constitution, however, does not mean that they are absolutes. The extent to which these ideals actually affect our lives is entirely dependent upon the justices when they are called upon to choose between upholding our constitutional rights or concluding that our rights must yield to valid governmental interests.

This book examines how the guarantees of liberty, justice, and equality have developed by decisions of the Court since the United States began in 1789. The focus will be on the people involved in that evolution, petitioners and judges, and upon the response of the justices.

We enjoy more liberty, have greater justice, and receive more equal treatment from government than any other people. We must not forget, however, that "the condition upon which God hath given liberty to man is eternal vigilance; which condition if he break, servitude is at once the consequence of his crime and the punishment of his guilt."[11]

CHAPTER 1

Liberty

> While this Court has not attempted to define with exact-
> ness the liberty thus guaranteed, the term has received
> much consideration and some of the included things
> have been definitely stated. Without doubt, it denotes
> not merely freedom from bodily restraint but also the
> right of the individual to contract, to engage in any of the
> common occupations of life, to acquire useful knowl-
> edge, to marry, establish a home and bring up children,
> to worship God according to the dictates of his own con-
> science, and generally to enjoy those privileges long
> recognized at common law as essential to the orderly
> pursuit of happiness by free men.
> —*Meyer v. Nebraska*, 262 U.S. 390, 399 (1923)

The Prophets, Socrates, President Lincoln, and Others

> And proclaim liberty throughout all of the land unto all the in-
> habitants thereof.*

References to liberty go back a long way and can be found in numerous speeches and writings. The above words, for example, can be found in Leviticus, the third book of Moses, and are related there as words spoken by the Lord to Moses.

The Greek philosopher Aristotle said: "The basis of a demo-cratic state is liberty."[1] And we all remember what that great Ameri-can patriot Patrick Henry said: "Forbid it, Almighty God. I know not what course others may take, but as for me, give me liberty or give me death!"[2]

Benjamin Franklin warned the country at the time: "They that

Leviticus, 25.10.

1

can give up essential liberty to obtain a little temporary safety deserve neither liberty nor safety."[3]

But it is as true today as it was when President Lincoln said it. "The world has never had a good definition of the word liberty." While the world may not need a good definition of liberty, the people of the United States surely need to know its meaning because it is one of those precious rights guaranteed to them by the Fifth and Fourteenth Amendments to the Constitution, both of which provide that no person shall be deprived of "life, liberty, or property, without due process of law."

A search for the roots of the meaning of this constitutional liberty leaves much to be desired. When the English barons forced the Magna Carta from King John in 1215, Article 39 read: "No freeman shall be captured or imprisoned or disseised or outlawed or exiled or in any way destroyed, nor will we go against him or send against him, except by the lawful judgment of his peers or by the law of the land." The liberty to be protected by Article 39, however, seems to have been confined to freedom from physical restraint. And this is how Sir William Blackstone understood it, as his *Commentaries* on the law indicate: "This personal liberty consists in the power of locomotion, of changing situation, or removing one's person to whatsoever place one's own inclination may direct; without imprisonment or restraint, unless by due course of law."[4]

If this were the meaning of the personal liberty promised by the Constitution, it would give little protection for the many other freedoms free people ought to enjoy. And we can be thankful that over the years the Supreme Court, the ultimate interpreter of the Constitution, has not adopted such a narrow constriction of our constitutional liberty.

Untold number of statements appear in Supreme Court opinions with regard to liberty. For example, the Court has written that "due process is the primary and indispensable foundation of individual freedom. It is the basic and essential term in the social compact which defines the rights of the individual and delimits the powers which the state may exercise."[5]

And further, as stated by Justice Stephen J. Field:

> By the term "liberty," as used in the provision, something more is meant than mere freedom from physical restraint or the bounds of a prison. It means freedom to go where one may choose, and to act in such manner, not inconsistent with the equal rights of others, as

his judgment may dictate for the promotion of his happiness; that is, to pursue such callings and avocations as may be most suitable to develop his capacities, and give to them their highest enjoyment.[6]

What follows in this chapter is an examination of the Court's development of the constitutional liberty envisioned by Justice Field and stated by the Court in the *Meyer* case quoted above.

Even though our judges, and ultimately the justices of the Supreme Court, should be an "impenetrable bulwark" protecting our liberty, as contemplated by James Madison,[7] we ought to heed the warning of Judge Learned Hand:

> I often wonder whether we do not rest our hopes too much upon constitutions, upon laws and upon courts. These are false hopes; believe me, these are false hopes. Liberty lies in the hearts of men and women; when it dies there, no constitution, no law, no court can save it; no constitution, no law, no court can do much to help it. While it lies there it needs no constitution, no law, no courts to save it.[8]

Parents' Right to Rear Their Children

> The Act . . . unreasonably interferes with the liberty of parents and guardians to direct the upbringing and education of [their] children.*

On May 25, 1920, Robert T. Meyer, a teacher in Zion Parochial School, Hamilton County, Nebraska, taught biblical stories to ten-year-old Raymond Parpart in the German language. Despite his argument that his teaching served two purposes — teaching of a foreign language together with stories from the Bible — he was convicted of violating a state law prohibiting "the teaching in any private, denominational, parochial or public school, of any modern language, other than English."[9]

Against an argument that the conviction violated his religious freedom, the Nebraska Supreme Court affirmed the judgment, with two justices dissenting. The U.S. Supreme Court reversed, with justices Oliver W. Holmes, Jr., and George Sutherland dissenting.

In an opinion written by Justice James C. McReynolds, the Court stated that "the problem for our determination is whether the statute as construed and applied unreasonably infringes the liberty

---

Pierce v. Society of Sisters, 268 U.S. 510, 534–535 (1925).

guaranteed to . . . [Meyer] by the Fourteenth Amendment. 'No State shall . . . deprive any person of life, liberty, or property, without due process of law.'"

Justice McReynolds concluded that this case involved two interests that were protected by the Fourteenth Amendment — the right of Meyer to teach and the right of Raymond's parents to control what he was taught. Of these two interests, the justice wrote, "His right thus to teach and the right of parents to engage him so to instruct their children, we think, are within the liberty of the Amendment."

Nebraska asserted that the purpose of the law "was to promote civic development by inhibiting training and education in the immature in foreign tongues and ideals before they could learn English and acquire American ideals." To this, Justice McReynolds responded, "The state may do much, go very far, indeed, in order to improve the quality of its citizens, physically, mentally and morally, . . . but the individual has certain fundamental rights which must be respected." Further: "No emergency has arisen which renders knowledge by a child of some language other than English so clearly harmful as to justify its inhibition with the consequent infringement of rights long freely enjoyed."

Justice Holmes thought that the only issue before the Court was whether the law unreasonably deprived teachers of a liberty interest. He concluded that it did not and wrote that if the law "is reasonable it is not an undue restriction of the liberty either of teacher or scholar."

Parents' liberty interest in rearing their children found its way into the judicial system again when the Society of Sisters of the Holy Name of Jesus and Mary brought an action against Walter M. Pierce, governor of Oregon, contesting the validity of an Oregon law "requiring children between 8 and 16 years of age to attend public schools."[10] The Society of Sisters operated schools and colleges as well as maintaining orphanages in Oregon.

Judge Charles E. Wolverton, acting for the federal District Court for Oregon, issued an injunction barring the governor and other officials from enforcing the law. In so doing, Judge Wolverton recognized that "the absolute right of these schools to teach in the grammar grades . . . and the right of the parents to engage them to instruct their children, we think, is within the liberty of the Fourteenth Amendment." The Supreme Court unanimously agreed.

Justice McReynolds again wrote the opinion for the Court. He first pointed out that the result of the enforcement of the law against the Sisters would be the complete destruction of their schools. But even more important was the effect the law had on the rights of the parents. "The Act unreasonably interferes with the liberty of parents and guardians to direct the upbringing and education of children under their control."[11]

Even though the Court has recognized that parental control of children is a liberty interest entitled to constitutional protection, it is not an absolute interest and is therefore subject to being restricted when governmental interests are sufficently great.

Sarah Prince found that to be true when she permitted her nine-year-old niece, Betty M. Simmons, to distribute religious literature on a street in Brockton, Massachusetts. The Massachusetts Supreme Judicial Court described Betty's activities:

> Both [Sarah Prince and Betty M. Simmons] belonged to a religious sect known as "Jehovah's Witnesses" and as such regarded themselves as "ordained ministers" of God. Betty carried a "magazine bag" on which was printed "Watchtower explains the Theocratic Government" "5 [cents] a copy." In the bag were copies of the religious publications "Watchtower" and "Consolation." Betty held up a copy of each in her hand. She testified that she was "taking contributions" of five cents for each magazine, or more "if people should give more"; that she was not selling them; that on that night she did not receive any contributions or give any magazines away; that when she had received "contributions" she gave all the money to . . . [Sarah]; and that . . . [Sarah] had given her the bag and the magazines.[12]

Sarah Prince was convicted of violating a state law that made it unlawful for anyone to furnish any article of merchandise, including magazines, to any minor who intends to sell the merchandise on any street or in a public place. On appeal to the Supreme Court, Prince's conviction was upheld with four justices dissenting. Prince made two arguments why the Massachusetts decision should be reversed. Her first argument "rests squarely on freedom of religion under the First Amendment, applied by the Fourteenth Amendment to the states. She buttresses this foundation, however, with a claim of parental right as secured by the due process clause of the latter Amendment."[13]

> Thus, two claimed liberties are at stake. One is the parent's to bring up a child in the way he should go, which for appellant [Prince]

means to teach him the tenets and practices of their faith. The other freedom is the child's to observe these; and among them is "to preach the gospel . . . by public distribution" of "Watchtower" and "Consolation," in conformity with the scripture: "A little child shall lead them."

Justice Wiley B. Rutledge, writing for the majority, acknowledged the difficult task this case presented by noting that "to make accommodation between these freedoms and an exercise of state authority always is delicate." And with reference to the rights of parents, he stated, "It is cardinal with us that the custody, care and nurture of the child resides first in the parents, whose primary function and freedom include preparation for obligations the state can neither supply nor hinder." But Justice Rutledge then pointed out that the rights of parents are not beyond state regulation in the public interest, and the state does so in many ways. "Acting to guard the general interest in youth's well being, the state as *parens patriae* may restrict the parent's control by requiring school attendance, regulating or prohibiting the child's labor and in many other ways." Recognizing also the the state may exercise greater control over children than adults, the justice concluded for the majority that Prince's right to have her niece distribute religious literature must give way to the state's interest in the well-being of the child.

Justice Frank Murphy, in dissent, argued that "this attempt by the state of Massachusetts to prohibit a child from exercising her constitutional right to practice her religion on the public streets cannot, in my opinion, be sustained."

While Sarah Prince's right to control the religious upbringing of her niece, Betty, was subordinated to the authority of the state to protect the welfare of children, Jonas Yoder, Wallace Miller, and Adin Yutzy fared better in their quarrel with Wisconsin's compulsory school attendance law.

Yoder and Miller were members of the Old Order Amish religion, and Yutzy belonged to the Conservative Amish Mennonite Church.

> The tenets of the Old Order Amish communities generally, [are] that their children's attendance at high school, public or private, was contrary to the Amish religion and way of life. They believed that by sending their children to high school, they would not only expose themselves to the danger of the censure of the church community, but . . . also endanger their own salvation and that of their children.[14]

Because they refused to send their children to school beyond the eighth grade, Yoder, Miller, and Yutzy were convicted of violating school attendance laws. The Wisconsin Supreme Court reversed, concluding that the application of these laws to the Amish would be a violation of their right to free exercise of religion. The U.S. Supreme Court agreed, with Justice William O. Douglas dissenting in part and justices Lewis F. Powell and William H. Rehnquist not participating.

Chief Justice Warren Burger, who authored the Court's opinion, discussed the Amish way of life:

> A related feature of Old Order Amish communities is their devotion to a life in harmony with nature and the soil, as exemplified by the simple life of the early Christian era that continued in America during much of our early national life. Amish beliefs require members of the community to make their living by farming or closely related activities. Broadly speaking, the Old Order Amish religion pervades and determines the entire mode of life of its adherents.

Based upon their religious beliefs and their way of life, Yoder, Miller, and Yutzy argued for not only their rights under the free exercise clause of the First Amendment but also their rights as parents in the word *liberty* of the due process clause.

The chief justice acknowledged that the rights of the Amish parents were an important factor in the Court's decision. "The history and culture of Western civilization reflect a strong tradition of parental concern for the nurture and upbringing of their children. This primary role of the parents in the upbringing of their children is now established beyond debate as an enduring American tradition."

Wisconsin argued, as Massachusetts had in *Prince*, that it had a substantial interest in the education of children and especially the Amish children because those who leave the Amish community would be ill equipped to make their way in the world with only an eighth-grade education. The Court did not buy this argument, however, being of the opinion that the education of those children did not stop with their formal education in school. "Not only do the Amish," the chief justice responded, "accept the necessity for formal schooling through the eighth grade level, but continue to provide what has been characterized by the undisputed testimony of expert educators as an 'ideal' vocational education for their education of their children in the adolescent years."

Weighing the right to free exercise of religion and the liberty right of these parents against the interests of the state in the education of its children led the chief justice to conclude that "in this case the Amish have introduced persuasive evidence undermining the arguments the State has advanced to support its claims in terms of the welfare of the child and society as a whole."

Justice Byron R. White restricted his concurrence to the free exercise of religion rights of the Amish families because he did not think that standing alone, their parental rights would outweigh the educational interests of the state. The decision in the *Society of Sisters* case he asserted, "lends no support to the contention that parents may replace state educational requirements with their own idiosyncratic views of what knowledge a child needs to be a productive and happy member of society."

The majority's decision was faulty, Justice Douglas believed, because it did not take into consideration the rights of the children. "On this important and vital matter of education" he argued, "I think the children should be entitled to be heard. While the parents, absent dissent, normally speak for the entire family, the education of the child is a matter on which the child will often have decided views. He may want to be a pianist or an astronaut or an oceanographer. To do so he will have to break from the Amish tradition." Further: "It is the student's judgment, not his parents', that is essential if we are to give full meaning to what we have said about the Bill of Rights and of the right of students to be masters of their own destiny."

The Biological Connection Between Parent and Child

> Parental rights do not spring full-blown from the biological connection between parent and child. They require relationships that are more enduring.*

Do unwed fathers have a protectable liberty interest in the children they sire out of wedlock? That was the question before the Court in *Stanley v. Illinois*.[15]

> Joan Stanley lived with Peter Stanley intermittently for 18 years, during which time they had three children. When Joan Stanley died, Peter Stanley lost not only her but also his children. Under Illinois

---

Justice Potter Stewart dissenting in Caban v. Mohammed, 441 U.S. 380, 397 (1979).

law, the children of unwed fathers become wards of the State upon the death of the mother.

Shortly after Joan Stanley's death, the Stanley children were declared wards of the state in a proceeding before Judge John P. McGury and placed with court-appointed guardians. Peter Stanley appealed, but the Illinois Supreme Court affirmed, holding that "Stanley could properly be separated from his children upon proof of the single fact that he and the dead mother had not been married. Stanley's actual fitness as a father was irrelevant."

Stanley appealed to the U.S. Supreme Court, which reversed in an opinion authored by Justice White. The justice first focused on Stanley's interest as a father and noted that "the private interest here, that of a man in the children he has sired and raised, undeniably warrants deference and, absent a powerful countervailing interest, protection."

Taking note of the Court's prior cases which established parental rights as within the meaning of liberty, Justice White pointed out that the law has not "refused to recognize those family relationships unlegitimized by a marriage ceremony." Stanley, therefore, had a constitutional liberty interest in retaining the custody of his children.

The state, on the other hand, asserted its interest in the mental and physical welfare and protection of the children. The Court accepted those as legitimate interests but was unable to see how separating children from *fit* parents served those goals. "Indeed," Justice White argued, "if Stanley is a fit father, the State spites its own articulated goals when it needlessly separates him from his family."

> It may be, as the State insists, that most unmarried fathers are unsuitable and neglectful parents. It may also be that Stanley is such a parent and that his children should be placed in other hands. But all unmarried fathers are not in this category; some are wholly suited to have custody of their children.

The majority thus concluded that Stanley's parental interest in his children entitled him to a hearing on the question of his fitness to retain custody.

Stanley also argued that the equal protection clause was violated because unwed fathers were treated differently than wedded fathers, who were entitled to a hearing before they were found unfit. The majority agreed, and that was another reason for reversing the Illinois court's decision. Chief Justice Burger and Justice Harry Blackmun disagreed and dissented, arguing that the question of the violation of Stanley's due process liberty interest was not raised in the Illinois courts and that there was no violation of equal protection in this case.

The liberty interest of a parent in one's children, however, cannot be sustained on the biological link alone, especially when that relates to unwed fathers. Some recognition of the child and commitment to parenthood by the father is essential before the parental relationship is entitled to constitutional protection. Six justices agreed to that principle over the strong opposition of three dissenters. The question before the justices, as stated by Justice John Paul Stevens, was "whether New York has sufficiently protected an unmarried father's inchoate relationship with a child whom he has never supported and rarely seen in two years since her birth."[16] While there was some disagreement between the majority and the dissenters over the relationship and contacts between the father and the child, some facts were not in dispute. Jonathan Lehr and Lorraine Robertson lived together for about two years until Jessica was born, but not thereafter. Although Jonathan visited Lorraine and Jessica in the hospital, his name did not appear on the birth certificate. From the time Lorraine left the hospital and for about two years thereafter, she concealed her whereabouts until Jonathan was able to locate her with the help of a detective agency. By that time, Lorraine had married Richard Robertson.

Shortly thereafter, the Robertsons filed for adoption of Jessica, which the family court granted. When Jonathan learned of this, he filed a petition to have the adoption set aside on the grounds that as Jessica's father he was entitled to notice of the adoption proceedings. Judge Hugh R. Elwyn denied the petition, and his decision was affirmed by two New York appellate courts. At the time of the adoption, New York law provided that putative fathers could be assured of receiving notice in adoption proceedings simply by sending a postcard to a central registry. Jonathan had not done this.

Jonathan's legal argument was "that a putative father's actual or potential relationship with a child born out of wedlock is an interest in liberty which may not be destroyed without due process of law; . . . therefore he had a constitutional right to prior notice and an opportunity to be heard before he was deprived of that interest."

In spite of the disagreement between the majority and the

dissenters over how much effort Jonathan had made to establish and have contact with Jessica, the real issue separating them was whether the biological link alone was enough to protect the parental interest.

The majority recognized that its prior decisions had established a liberty interest in parental control of children, including unwed fathers who demonstrate "a full commitment to the responsibilities of parenthood by 'com[ing] forward to participate in the rearing of his child.'" But Justice Stevens pointed out that "the mere existence of a biological link does not merit equivalent constitutional protection."

> The significance of the biological connection is that it offers the natural father an opportunity that no other male possesses to develop a relationship with his offspring. If he grasps that opportunity and accepts some measure of responsibility for the child's future, he may enjoy the blessings of the parent-child relationship and make uniquely valuable contributions to the child's development. If he fails to do so, the Federal Constitution will not automatically compel a State to listen to his opinion of where the child's best interests lie.

In this case Jonathan could have grasped the opportunity simply by mailing the postcard to the registry. "The possibility," Justice Stevens noted, "that he may have failed to do so because of his ignorance of the law cannot be sufficient reason for criticizing the law itself."

For the dissenters, Jonathan's contact with Jessica was not relevant in determining whether he had a protectable liberty interest in Jessica's future. "As Jessica's biological father," Justice White asserted, "Lehr either had an interest protected by the Constitution or he did not."

> The "biological connection" is itself a relationship that creates a protected interest. Thus the "nature" of the interest is the parent-child relationship; how well developed that relationship has become goes to its "weight," not its "nature." Whether Lehr's interest is entitled to constitutional protection does not entail a searching inquiry into the quality of the relationship but a simple determination of the *fact* that the relationship exists — a fact that even the majority agrees must be assumed to be established.

Further, the dissenters could find no state interest that was served by not giving notice to Lehr.

Marriage and Family Life

> This Court has long recognized that freedom of personal choice in
> matters of marriage and family life is one of the liberties protected
> by the Due Process Clause.*

Mildred Jeter, a black woman, and Richard Loving, a white
man, after being married in the District of Columbia, returned to
their home in Virginia. Shortly thereafter, they were charged and
pleaded guilty to violating a Virginia law which prohibited interracial marriages. The court sentenced the Lovings to a year in jail
but suspended that sentence provided they leave the state and not
return for twenty-five years. The judge said:

> "Almighty God created the races white, black, yellow, malay and
> red, and he placed them on separate continents. And but for the in-
> terference with his arrangement there would be no cause for such
> marriages. The fact that he separated the races shows that he did not
> intend for the races to mix."[17]

The Lovings lived in the District for a while but later moved
back to Virginia where they sought a court order setting aside their
convictions on the ground that the state law violated their constitutional rights. Circuit Judge Leon M. Bazile denied the order, and the
Virginia Supreme Court of Appeals affirmed. The Lovings appealed
to the U.S. Supreme Court, which reversed in a unanimous decision. Justice Potter Stewart concurred only in the judgment.

Much of the Court's opinion in this case related to the fact that
the Virginia law singled out persons of different races who marry but
did not apply to the marriage of persons of the same race. This, the
Court held, was a racial classification forbidden by the equal protection clause of the Fourteenth Amendment. (Racial classifications
will be discussed in Chapter 3.)

Chief Justice Warren, who authored the Court's opinion, also
pointed out, however, that the law violated the due process clause.
"The freedom to marry," he wrote, "has long been recognized as one
of the vital personal rights essential to the orderly pursuit of happiness by free men."

> To deny fundamental freedom on so unsupportable a basis as the
> racial classifications embodied in these statutes, classifications so

Cleveland Bd. of Education v. LaFleur, 414 U.S. 632, 639 (1974).

directly subversive of the principle of equality at the heart of the
Fourteenth Amendment, is surely to deprive all the State's citizens
of liberty without due process of law.

For Justice Stewart, the issue was somewhat simpler. "I have
previously expressed the belief," he declared, "that 'it is simply not
possible for a state law to be valid under our Constitution which
makes the criminality of an act depend upon the race of the actor.'"
The justices had considerably more to say about the right to
marry when confronted with the question of the constitutionality of
a Wisconsin law prohibiting a person from marrying without court
permission if he had been ordered by a court to support a minor
child, even though that child is not in his custody.

That issue came before the Court in a case started by Roger G.
Redhail in the federal District Court for Wisconsin. Redhail had
been found by the county court of Milwaukee County to be the
father of a child born out of wedlock and was ordered to pay
monthly support for the child. At that time Redhail was a high
school student without means to comply with the order, and therefore the child became a public charge. Several years later, Redhail
applied to County Clerk Thomas E. Zablocki for a marriage license,
which was denied. The denial was based upon a state law which required Redhail to secure permission from the court before a license
could be issued because of the support order outstanding against
him.

Redhail sued Zablocki and argued that the law violated his constitutional right to marry and denied him equal protection of the
law. A three-judge federal district court agreed in an opinion written
by Chief Judge John W. Reynolds. Judge Reynolds took note that
although no specific provision of the Constitution protects the right
to marry, numerous Supreme Court decisions had held that such a
right exists. Although a majority of the Supreme Court voted to
affirm, not all agreed that there was a constitutional right to marry.

Justice Thurgood Marshall delivered the opinion for the majority.
The starting point for their analysis was the acknowledgment that
Redhail's constitutional right to marry was involved in this case.

Since our past decisions make clear that the right to marry is of fundamental importance, and since the [statute] at issue here significantly
interferes with the exercise of that right, we believe that "critical examination" of the state interests advanced in support of the [statute]
is required.[18]

But of course neither the right to marry nor any other constitutional right is absolute, and government can regulate and restrict our rights whenever a majority of the justices determine that governmental interests are greater.

> By reaffirming the fundamental character of the right to marry, we do not mean to suggest that every state regulation which relates in any way to the incidents of or prerequisites for marriage must be subject to rigorous scrutiny. To the contrary, reasonable regulations that do not significantly interfere with decisions to enter into the marital relationship may legitimately be imposed.

For the majority, the Wisconsin regulation was not a reasonable one. It may in some cases be an absolute bar to getting married. "Some of those in the affected class, like [Redhail], " Justice Marshall noted, "will never be able to obtain the necessary court order, because they either lack the financial means to meet their support obligations or cannot prove that their children will not become public charges." The law is therefore unconstitutional.

Justice Stewart agreed but did not believe that "there is a 'right to marry' in the constitutional sense." For him, the state law infringed upon Redhail's fundamental "freedom of personal choice in matters of marriage and family life." And he was concerned that the law would prevent some people from being able to make the choice to marry because they would be unable to meet the state's financial requirements.

Although Justice Powell concurred in the judgment, he was of the opinion that the "analysis must start from the recognition of domestic relations as 'an area that has long been regarded as a virtually exclusive province of the States.'" However, he noted, "the Due Process Clause requires a showing of justification 'when the government intrudes on choices concerning family living arrangements' in a manner which is contrary to deeply rooted traditions." He concluded that "because the State has not established a justification for this unprecedented foreclosure of marriage to many of its citizens solely because of their indigency, I concur in the judgment of the Court."

Justice Rehnquist, in dissent, based his disagreement with his brethren upon his rejection of the "conclusion that marriage is [a] 'fundamental right.'" Where no constitutional right is involved, the government may restrict the activity merely by showing that its regulations are rational. He thought the Wisconsin law met that test.

"Marriage and procreation," declared Justice Douglas, "are fundamental to the very existence and survival of the race."[19] With that as his premise, he turned to an analysis and solution of the case of Jack T. Skinner.

> [Skinner] was convicted in 1926 of the crime of stealing chickens, and was sentenced to the Oklahoma State Reformatory. In 1929 he was convicted of the crime of robbery with firearms, and was sentenced to the reformatory. In 1934 he was convicted again of robbery with firearms, and was sentenced to the penitentiary.

In 1935 the state enacted the Habitual Criminal Sterilization Act, under which a person who had been convicted two or more times for committing crimes involving moral turpitude was considered a habitual criminal and could be rendered sexually sterile. The law did not apply, however, to a person who committed crimes such as violation of revenue acts, embezzlement, or political offenses. Based upon this law, Attorney General Mac Q. Williamson commenced proceedings against Skinner to have him sterilized by a vasectomy. A jury found that Skinner came within the law and that the operation could be performed without injury to his health. The Oklahoma Supreme Court, in a 5–4 decision, affirmed. Without dissent, the U.S. Supreme Court reversed.

The majority recognized that they were "dealing here with legislation which involves one of the basic civil rights of man" – marriage and procreation – and that therefore the distinction between the kinds of crimes for which the law was applicable made it unconstitutional under the equal protection clause.

Chief Justice Harlan F. Stone and Justice Robert H. Jackson concurred, but in the words of the chief justice, "I think the real question we have to consider is not one of equal protection, but whether the wholesale condemnation of a class to such an invasion of personal liberty, without opportunity to any individual to show that his is not the type of case which would justify resort to it, satisfies the demands due process." These justices concluded that this law did not.

The *Loving, Zablocki,* and *Skinner* cases will be discussed again in Chapter 3 dealing with equal protection.

Jo Carol LaFleur, Ann Elizabeth Nelson, and Susan Cohen, all schoolteachers, found themselves faced with mandatory leave requirements when each became pregnant. LaFluer and Nelson were employed as teachers in Cleveland, Ohio, Cohen in Chesterfield

County, Virginia. Cleveland required pregnant teachers to leave their job five months before the expected birth of the child, and in Chesterfield County the time limit was four months. Although all requested permission to teach until the end of the school year, these requests were denied. Therefore, LaFleur and Nelson in Ohio and Cohen in Virginia brought suits in federal district courts challenging the constitutionality of the schools' rules. District Judge James C. Connell in Ohio upheld the leave requirements, but a divided circuit court of appeals reversed. Federal District Judge Robert R. Merhige, Jr., of Virginia held that the regulations violated the constitution, but that decision was reversed by the Court of Appeals, 4–3.

The Supreme Court, with only Chief Justice Burger and Justice Rehnquist dissenting, held that the requirements of both school districts violated the teachers' due process rights. At the outset, Justice Stewart for the majority focused upon the constitutional issue in these cases. "This Court," he declared, "has long recognized that freedom of personal choice in matters of marriage and family life is one of the liberties protected by the Due Process Clause of the Fourteenth Amendment."[20] Further: "By acting to penalize the pregnant teacher for deciding to bear a child, overly restrictive maternity leave regulations can constitute a heavy burden on the exercise of these protected freedoms."

The school boards argued that there were compelling reasons for the rules, including maintaining continuity in the classrooms and the possibility that some pregnant teachers might not be physically able to do their work. While agreeing that these were valid interests, the majority concluded that the rules were simply too restrictive of the teachers' fundamental rights. "We conclude, therefore," Justice Stewart responded, "that neither the necessity for continuity of instruction nor the state interest in keeping physically unfit teachers out of the classroom can justify the sweeping mandatory leave regulations that the Cleveland and Chesterfield County School Boards have adopted."

A concern that the principle applied by the majority in this case might require the same application to the right to pursue an occupation of one's choice caused Justice Rehnquist and Chief Justice Burger to dissent. "Since this right to pursue an occupation," Justice Rehnquist argued, "is presumably on the same lofty footing as the right of choice in matters of family life, the Court will have to strain valiantly in order to avoid having today's opinion lead to the invalidation of mandatory retirement statutes for governmental employees."

As will be discussed hereafter, the Court has held that we do have a liberty interest in choosing our lifework. However, the cases indicate that that right has not been placed "on the same lofty footing as the right of choice in matters of family life."

Mrs. Inez Moore, a sixty-three-year-old grandmother, was convicted of a criminal offense, "for refusing to expel from her home her now ten-year-old grandson who has lived with her and been brought up by her since his mother's death when he was less than a year old."[21] Mrs. Moore found herself in this predicament because of an East Cleveland ordinance defining the kind of family that could live together. Moore's family consisted of her son, Dale Moore, Sr.; his son, Dale, Jr.; and John, Jr., the son of Mrs. Moore's son, John. Under the ordinance, Dale, Sr., and his son, Dale, Jr., were allowed to reside in the home, but John, Jr., was not. He was, in effect, "an illegal occupant." When Moore refused to remove John from the home, she was charged and convicted of violating the ordinance.

Her conviction was sustained by an Ohio appellate court but reversed by the Supreme Court in an opinion joined by four justices. One justice wrote an opinion concurring only in the judgment, and four dissented. The dispute among the justices centered around the question of whether Mrs. Moore's family was entitled to constitutional protection in the same way that ordinary families were.

The four justices making up the plurality had no difficulty answering the question in the affirmative. Justice Powell, writing for these justices, first took note that this ordinance "makes a crime of a grandmother's choice to live with her grandson in circumstances like those presented here." Further, "when the government intrudes on choices concerning family living arrangements," he declared, "this Court must examine carefully the importance of the governmental interests advanced and the extent to which they are served by the challenged regulation."

The city argued that the ordinance was a means of preventing overcrowding, easing traffic and parking problems, and reducing the financial burden on the school system. These, of course, are valid governmental interests, but the justices were skeptical whether the law really solved those problems. For example, Justice Powell pointed out that "the ordinance would permit a grandmother to live with a single dependent son and children, even if his school-age children number a dozen, yet it forces Mrs. Moore to find another dwelling for her grandson John, simply because of the presence of his uncle and cousin in the same household." Such a law, he continued "has but a tenuous relation to alleviation of the conditions mentioned by the city."

The plurality then concluded:

> But unless we close our eyes to the basic reasons why certain rights associated with the family have been accorded shelter under the Fourteenth Amendment's Due Process Clause, we cannot avoid applying the force and rationale of these precedents to the family choice involved in this case.

The plurality's decision to give Inez Moore's family constitutional protection raised the question of the extent of that proctection. Are the justices "roaming at large in the constitutional field," and creating constitutional rights where none exist? Justice Powell did not think so, but acknowledged that that could happen. "Substantive due process," he acknowledged, "has at times been a treacherous field for this Court. There *are* risks when the judicial branch gives enhanced protection to certain substantive liberties without the guidance of the more specific provisions of the Bill of Rights." But that is not being done in this case because "our decisions," Justice Powell notes, "establish that the Constitution protects the sanctity of the family precisely because the institution of the family is deeply rooted in this Nation's history and tradition."

Justice White dissented, not because he did not think that Inez Moore had a liberty interest here but because that interest was not as important as other liberty interests.

> The term "liberty" is not, therefore, to be given a crabbed construction. I have no more difficulty than Mr. Justice Powell apparently does in concluding that [Mrs. Moore] in this case properly asserts a liberty interest within the meaning of the Due Process Clause.

But for him, this liberty interest did not require the same deferential treatment from the Court as, for example, the freedoms of speech, press, and religion. "I cannot believe," he argued, "that the interest in residing with more than one set of grandchildren is one that calls for any kind of heightened protection under the Due Process Clause. To say that one has a personal right to live with all, rather than some, of one's grandchildren and that this right is implicit in ordered liberty is . . . 'to extend the limited substantive contours of the Due Process Clause beyond recognition.'"

The Right to Be Let Alone

> The right to one's person may be said to be a right of complete immunity: to be let alone.*

In 1902 a Mr. Jacobson living in Cambridge, Massachusetts, found that while a constitutional right to be let alone may well exist, it by no means gives "complete immunity" from governmental interference with that right. Mr. Jacobson refused to be vaccinated for smallpox as required by a Cambridge regulation adopted at a time when smallpox was on the increase in that city. Jacobson based his refusal on rights he believed were secured by the preamble and the Fourteenth Amendment, and further "that [the regulation] was opposed to the spirit of the Constitution."[22]

After a jury trial, Jacobson was found guilty, sentenced to pay a fine of five dollars, and committed to jail until the fine was paid. The supreme court of Massachusetts affirmed. The U.S. Supreme Court agreed, two justices dissenting.

The first Justice John M. Harlan stated the question before the court: "Is the statute, so construed, therefore, inconsistent with the liberty which the Constitution of the United States secures to every person against deprivation by the State?" The answer for the majority was not difficult. "Real liberty for all," Justice Harlan declared, "could not exist under the operation of a principle which recognizes the right of each individual person to use his own, whether in respect of his person or his property, regardless of the injury that may be done to others." This led the Court to conclude that the law was constitutional and could therefore be applied to Jacobson.

The importance of *Jacobson* is the Court's recognition that an individual has a constitutionally protected liberty interest in being let alone. In this case that interest had to give way to the greater interest of protecting other people from smallpox.

This right to be let alone took on the mantle of a right to privacy in *Griswold v. Connecticut*.[23]

---

*Thomas M. Cooley, A Treatise on the Law of Torts, 2d ed. (Chicago: Callaghan, 1888), p. 29.

Estelle T. Griswold was the executive director of the Planned Parenthood League of Connecticut. She and Dr. C. Lee Buxton "gave information, instruction, and medical advice to *married persons* as to the means of preventing conception." Under Connecticut law, it was a crime to use contraceptives. And the law also punished any person who "assists, abets, counsels" in the use of contraceptives. Griswold and Buxton were found guilty and fined $100, though they argued that the law violated the Fourteenth Amendment. Two Connecticut appellate courts affirmed, and the Supreme Court agreed to hear the case.

After reviewing many due process cases and taking note that many of them dealt with rights not mentioned in the Constitution, Justice Douglas for the majority pointed out that "the foregoing cases suggest that specific guarantees in the Bill of Rights have penumbras, formed by emanations from those guarantees that help give them life and substance."

> Various guarantees create zones of privacy. The right of association contained in the penumbra of the First Amendment is one, as we have seen. The Third Amendment in its prohibition against the quartering of soldiers "in any house" in time of peace without the consent of the owner is another facet of that privacy. The Fourth Amendment explicitly affirms the "right of the people to be secure in their persons, houses, papers, and effects, against unreasonable searches and seizures." The Fifth Amendment in its Self-Incrimination Clause enables the citizen to create a zone of privacy which government may not force him to surrender to his detriment. The Ninth Amendment provides: "The enumeration in the Constitution, of certain rights, shall not be construed to deny or disparage others retained by the people."

These cases, then, clearly lead to only one conclusion: There is a right to marital privacy issue here. "Would we," Justice Douglas asks, "allow the police to search the sacred precincts of marital bedrooms for telltale signs of the use of contraceptives? The very idea is repulsive to the notions of privacy surrounding the marriage relationship." "We deal," Justice Douglas continued, "with a right of privacy older than the Bill of Rights — older than our political parties, older than our school system."

Justices Arthur Goldberg and William Brennan and Chief Justice Warren agreed but argued that the decision should not rest alone on the "penumbras" of the first eight amendments because that "is to ignore the Ninth Amendment and to give it no effect whatsoever." "The

Ninth Amendment," Justice Goldberg asserted, "expressly recognizes, there are fundamental personal rights such as this one, which are protected from abridgement by the Government though not specifically mentioned in the Constitution."

Because the dissent of justices Hugo Black and Stewart focused upon the fact that no provision of the Constitution specifically protected a right of privacy and that therefore the Court should not be reaching out to find one, the second Justice John M. Harlan (grandson of the first) felt compelled to respond. He agreed that judges should use "judicial restraint" in making constitutional decisions, but he nevertheless believed that a constitutional right of privacy did exist and was implicated in this case. "In my view," he declared, "the proper constitutional inquiry in this case is whether this Connecticut statute infringes the Due Process Clause of the Fourteenth Amendment because the enactment violates basic values 'implicit in the concept of ordered liberty.'" And he believed that it did.

Justice Black could not accept the idea than any constitutional right existed here, specifically a right of privacy. "The Court talks about a constitutional 'right of privacy,'" he argued, "as though there is some constitutional provision or provisions forbidding any law ever to be passed which might abridge the 'privacy' of individuals. But there is not." And he was particularly disturbed by the Court's creating one.

> I realize that many good and able men have eloquently spoken and written, sometimes in rhapsodical strains, about the duty of this Court to keep the Constitution in tune with the times. The idea is that the Constitution must be changed from time to time and that this Court is charged with a duty to make those changes. For myself, I must with all deference reject that philosophy. The Constitution makers knew the need for change and provided for it. Amendments suggested by the people's elected representatives can be submitted to the people or their selected agents for ratification. That method of change was good for our Fathers, and being somewhat old-fashioned I must add it is good enough for me. And so, I cannot rely on the Due Process Clause or the Ninth Amendment or any mysterious and uncertain natural law concept as a reason for striking down this state law.

Justice Stewart, who thought that "this is an uncommonly silly law," agreed.

Despite the arguments put forth by justices Black and Stewart against the "creation" of a "right of privacy," *Roe v. Wade*[24] fortified the existence of such a right as one protected by the due process clause.

Jane Roe, single, unmarried, and pregnant, wanted to terminate her pregnancy but was prevented from doing so by the Texas criminal abortion laws. She brought an action against Henry Wade, the Dallas County district attorney, seeking to have the laws declared unconstitutional. Dr. James Hubert Hallford was granted leave to intervene because he had been arrested for performing abortions. At about the same time, John and Mary Doe also sued Mr. Wade and asserted the unconstitutionality of the statutes. Mrs. Doe was suffering from a physical condition that made having children or the use of birth control pills very risky. Their lawsuit, therefore, was combined with Jane Roe's.

A three-judge federal district court declared the abortion laws unconstitutional, and this decision was affirmed by the Supreme Court, justices White and Rehnquist dissenting.

The majority opinion, written by Justice Blackmun, after reciting the facts, notes that

> The principle thrust of [the] attack on the Texas statutes is that they improperly invade a right, said to be possessed by the pregnant woman, to choose to terminate her pregnancy. [Roe] would discover this right in the concept of personal "liberty" embodied in the Fourteenth Amendment's Due Process Clause; or in personal, marital, familial, and sexual privacy said to be protected by the Bill of Rights or its penumbras, . . . or among those rights reserved to the people by the Ninth Amendment.

In response, Justice Blackmun reviews a number of cases, going back to 1891, where "the Court has recognized that a right of personal privacy, or a guarantee of certain areas or zones of privacy, does exist under the Constitution." He cites such cases as *Meyer v. Nebraska, Pierce v. Society of Sisters, Loving v. Virginia*, and *Skinner v. Oklahoma*. Justice Blackmun then states the Court's holding in this case.

> The right of privacy, whether it be founded in the Fourteenth Amendment's concept of personal liberty and restrictions upon state action, as we feel it is, or, as the District Court determined, in the Ninth Amendment's reservation of rights to the people, is broad enough to encompass a woman's decision whether or not to terminate her pregnancy.

The Court's decision focuses upon the "right of the woman to choose" whether to terminate her pregnancy but says nothing about a "right to an abortion." Even the right to choose, however, is not absolute and is subject to being weighed against asserted state interests, of which there are generally two: protecting the health of the mother and of the unborn fetus. After discussing these two state interests at great length, Justice Blackmun sums up the decision by first declaring that any criminal statute which allows for an abortion only to save the life of the mother is a violation of due process. Further:

> (a) For the stage prior to approximately the end of the first trimester, the abortion decision and its effectuation must be left to the medical judgment of the pregnant woman's attending physician.
> (b) For the stage subsequent to approximately the end of the first trimester, the State, in promoting its interest in the health of the mother, may, if it chooses, regulate the abortion procedure in ways that are reasonably related to maternal health.
> (c) For the stage subsequent to viability, the State in promoting its interest in the potentiality of human life may, if it chooses, regulate, and even proscribe, abortion except where it is necessary, in appropriate medical judgment, for the preservation of the life or health of the mother.

Justice Rehniquist acknowledged in dissent that "'liberty' . . . embraces more than rights found in the Bill of Rights. But that liberty is not guaranteed absolutely against deprivation, only against deprivation without due process of law." For him, then, the solution to this case was to ask whether the statutes were rationally related to legitimate governmental goals. He was of the opinion that they were.

For Justice White, the decision was even more troubling. "I find nothing," he argued, "in the language or history of the Constitution to support the Court's judgment. The Court simply fashions and announces a new constitutional right for pregnant mothers and, with scarcely any reason or authority for its action, invests that right with sufficient substance to override most existing state abortion statutes."

Although the Court heard and decided many abortion cases following *Roe*, a majority of the justices adhered to that case's basic holding that a pregnant woman had a constitutional right to make the choice whether to terminate her pregnancy. By 1989, however, membership on the Court had changed substantially. Justices Blackmun, Brennan, and Marshall of the *Roe* majority, remained, as did justices Rehnquist and White, who had dissented. Justice

Rehnquist had become chief justice, and justices Stevens, O'Connor, Scalia, and Kennedy had joined the Court.

The new Court heard arguments in *Webster v. Reproductive Health Serv.*[25] on April 26, 1989. That case presented the question of the constitutionality of several Missouri statutes regulating abortion. A preamble to the statutes states that "life of each human being begins at conception." The statutes then provided that (1) if a physician believes that a woman is twenty or more weeks into pregnancy, the physician must attempt to ascertain if the fetus is viable; (2) abortions not be performed by public employees or in public facilities except if necessary to save the mother's life; and (3) public funds, employees, or facilities cannot be used for "encouraging or counseling" abortions.

A majority of the justices concluded that it was not necessary to pass on the constitutionality of the preamble. They also voted to uphold the prohibitions against the use of public employees and facilities for performing abortions and the requirement that the physician determine viability in those cases where the pregnancy may be beyond twenty weeks before performing the abortion. With regard to the prohibition of using public funds for counseling, the justices unanimously agreed that that question was moot.

The significance of the *Webster* decision is that eight of the justices were unwilling to overrule *Roe*. Those remaining from the *Roe* majority did not want to do so. And Chief Justice Rehnquist and justices White, O'Connor, and Kennedy did not believe that his was the proper case for doing so. For Justice Scalia, however, the matter was very clear. *Roe v. Wade*, should be explicitly overruled.

Subsequent to *Roe v. Wade*, states enacted a variety of laws regulating abortions. Because such laws directly infringed upon the woman's liberty interest, the Court strictly scrutinized them and struck down most of them. Some laws that the Court found unduly burdened the woman's right to make that choice:

requiring the approval of two other physicians, in addition to the woman's doctor;

requiring approval of a committee of at least three hospital staff members;

prohibiting "saline amniocentesis" procedures to cause the abortion;

requiring all abortions to be performed in a full-service hospital.

States also attempted, unsuccessfully, to restrict the woman's right by requiring notice to or consent from other persons, a spouse, or parents of a minor. The requirements of parental consent and notice will be discussed hereafter when the liberty interests of minors are reviewed.

In striking down a state law requiring a woman to secure written consent from her spouse, Justice Blackmun wrote for the majority that "we recognize that the decision whether to undergo or to forgo an abortion may have profound effects on the future of any marriage, effects that are both physical and mental, and possibly deleterious.

Notwithstanding these factors, we cannot hold that the State has the consititutional authority to give the spouse unilaterally the ability to prohibit the wife from terminating her pregnancy, when the State itself lacks that right."[26]

The battle over the question of whether the Constitution protects a woman's choice to carry a child to term continued unabated into the 1991–92 term of the Court. By that time justices Brennan and Marshall, both strong supporters of the woman's right to choose, had left the Court. Justice Brennan was replaced by Justice David Souter, and Justice Marshall by Justice Clarence Thomas.

This new Court heard arguments in the case of *Planned Parenthood of S. E. Penna. v. Robert P. Casey*,[27] and rendered its decision June 29, 1992.

This case raised the following issues: (1) should *Roe v. Wade* be overruled; (2) can a state require a woman to undergo counseling and wait twenty-four hours before having an abortion; (3) must a married woman notify her husband of her desire to terminate her pregnancy; (4) must a minor seeking an abortion, first secure the consent of a parent or guardian, or a judge; and (5) can doctors be required to keep records of the abortions they perform?

Five justices voted not to overrule *Roe*, and to strike down the requirement that the woman notify her husband. A different majority upheld the counseling and twenty-four hour waiting period, record keeping by doctors, and the requirement that a minor obtain the consent of one parent, or secure permission for the abortion from a judge.

Voting to uphold *Roe* were justices O'Connor and Kennedy who had been appointed by President Ronald Reagan, and Justice Souter who had been appointed by President George Bush. These together with justices Blackmun and Stevens made up the majority.

The central theme of the majority opinion is its statement that: "It is a promise of the Constitution that there is a realm of personal liberty which the government may not enter." And further: "Neither the Bill of Rights nor the specific practices of the States at the time of the adoption of the Fourteenth Amendment marks the outer limits of the substantive sphere of liberty which the Fourteenth Amendment protects." This affirms the conclusion that the Due Process Clause protects a broad range of personal freedoms, and is clearly consistent with the Court's many decisions effecting liberty since *Meyer v. Nebraska* was decided in 1923.

The majority point out that while the Court had previously upheld some restrictions on the woman's freedom of choice, "an entire generation has come of age free to assume *Roe*'s concept of liberty in defining the capacity of women to act in society, and to make reproductive decisions; . . . ." Therefore, the majority wrote: "We conclude that the basic decision in *Roe* was based on a constitutional analysis which we cannot now repudiate."

Although a majority voted to uphold *Roe*, it is clear that the *Casey* case allows states more leeway in regulating abortions. State restrictions on abortion will hereafter be tested by asking whether the regulation is an "undue burden" upon the woman's right to choose. While only justices O'Connor, Kennedy, and Souter used this test in this case, justices White, Antonin Scalia, Clarence Thomas, and Chief Justice Rehnquist voted with them to uphold all of Pennsylvania's regulations except the spousal notification requirement.

For justices O'Connor, Kennedy, and Souter, "only where state regulation imposes an undue burden on a woman's ability to make this decision does the power of the State reach into the heart of the liberty protected by the Due Process Clause."

In using the "undue burden" test to strike down the spousal notification requirement, the majority said:

> Women do not lose their constitutionally protected liberty when they marry. The Constitution protects all individuals, male or female, married or unmarried, from the abuse of governmental power, even where that power is employed for the supposed benefit of a member of the individual's family.

For dissenters Chief Justice Rehnquist, and justices White, Scalia, and Thomas the time had come to overrule *Roe*. "We believe," the Chief Justice wrote, "that Roe was wrongly decided, and that it can and should be overruled . . . ."

After reviewing the Court's prior decisions dealing with the interpretation of the word "liberty," the dissenters concluded that these decisions "do not endorse any all-encompassing right of privacy."

> We think, therefore, both in view of this history and of our decided cases dealing with substantive liberty under the Due Process Clause, that the Court was mistaken in *Roe* when it classified a woman's decision to terminate her pregnancy as a "fundamental right" that could be abridged only in a manner which withstood "strict scrutiny."

For Justice Blackmun, who wrote the *Roe* decision, its survival by a single vote was very disappointing. He wrote: "I fear for the darkness as four justices anxiously await the single vote necessary to extinguish the light." And further: "Yet I remain steadfast in my belief that the right to reproductive choice is entitled to the full protection afforded by this Court before *Webster*." He criticizes the dissenters for what he calls their "stunted conception of individual liberty."

Justice Stevens expressed his view of freedom of choice by noting that "the woman's constitutional liberty interest also involves her freedom to decide matters of the highest privacy and the most personal nature." He pointed out that fifteen justices have participated in abortion decisions, and of those only the four dissenters in this case believe that *Roe* was not correctly decided.

Does a competent person have a right to die? That question came before the Court in December 1989. The facts of the case were as follows:

> On the night of January 11, 1983, Nancy Cruzan lost control of her car as she traveled down Elm Road in Jasper County, Missouri. The vehicle overturned, and Cruzan was discovered lying face down in a ditch without detectable respiratory or cardiac function. Paramedics were able to restore her breathing and heartbeat at the accident site, and she was transported to a hospital in an unconscious state.[28]

Subsequent medical examination found that because Cruzan had not been breathing for some period following the accident, she suffered permanent brain damage. She never regained consciousness but continued to live in a vegetative state with artificial nutrition and hydration procedures.

When hospital authorities refused to terminate the life-sustaining

treatment given to their daughter, Lester and Joyce Cruzan brought
an action in a state court seeking authority to do so. Judge Charles
E. Teel, Jr., being of the opinion "that a person in Nancy's condition
had a fundamental right . . . to refuse or direct the withdrawal of
'death prolonging procedures,'" ordered the hospital employees to
comply with the Cruzans' request. The Missouri Supreme Court reversed. The U.S. Supreme Court affirmed that decision, but it did
agree with Judge Teel that the right to die was a protected liberty
interest.

The majority, Chief Justice Rehnquist writing the opinion, held
that "the principle that a competent person has a constitutionally
protected liberty interest in refusing unwanted medical treatment
may be inferred from our prior decisions." But that is only the beginning of the analysis because "determining that a person has a 'liberty
interest' under the Due Process Clause does not end the inquiry;
'whether [Nancy's] constitutional rights have been violated must be
determined by balancing [her] liberty interests against relevant state
interests.'" Missouri argued that its interest was in the "protection
and preservation of human life," in this case, Nancy's.

Because situations such as Cruzan's involve decisions relating
to life and death, Missouri had chosen to protect its interest by requiring "clear and convincing" evidence that individuals in situations similar to Nancy's would have chosen death. Therefore, when
Curzan's parents sought permission to withhold hydration and
nutrition from their daughter, Missouri's evidentiary standard placed
the burden on them to produce "clear and convincing" evidence that
that was what Nancy would have wanted.

Given that Cruzan had a right to die, Missouri's evidentiary requirement raised the question "whether the United State Constitution forbids the establishment of this procedural requirement by the
State." To this question Chief Justice Rehnquist responded: "We
hold that it does not."

> We think a State may properly decline to make judgments about the
> "quality" of life that a particular individual may enjoy, and simply
> assert an unqualified interest in the preservation of human life to be
> weighed against the constitutionally protected interests of the
> individual.

There was very little evidence of what Nancy Cruzan would
have wanted in a situation where she could not make the life-and-
death decision herself. A housemate, however, did testify that

Cruzan had made statements some time before the accident that she would not want to live as a "vegetable."

Because the Missouri Supreme Court had found that "the testimony adduced at trial did not amount to clear and convincing proof of [Nancy's] desire to have hydration and nutrition withdrawn," its decision not to allow the Cruzans to remove life support had to be affirmed.

Justice O'Connor concurred. She agreed that a person does have a constitutionally protected liberty interest in refusing medical treatment. She expressed concern, however, that the majority did "not today decide the issue whether a State must also give effect to the decisions of a surrogate decisionmaker." "In my view," she continued, "such a duty may well be constitutionally required to protect the patient's liberty interest in refusing medical treatment." Justice O'Connor then pointed out that many states were adopting procedures whereby individuals could appoint a surrogate to make such life and death decisions for them. And "today's decision . . . ," she noted, "does not preclude a future determination that the Constitution requires the States to implement the decisions of a patient's duly appointed surrogate."

Although Justice Scalia also concurred in the decision, for him, this was a field that ought to be left to the legislative process. "The various opinions in this case," he noted, "portray quite clearly the difficult, indeed agonizing, questions that are presented by the constantly increasing power of science to keep the human body alive for longer than any reasonable person would want to inhabit it." He therefore "would have preferred that we announce, clearly and promptly, that the federal courts have no business in this field."

For dissenters Brennan, Marshall, and Blackmun, Missouri's "clear and convincing" evidentiary standard placed and impermissible burden on Cruzan's right to die. Justice Brennan expressed their views.

> Because I believe that Nancy Cruzan has a fundamental right to be free of unwanted artificial nutrition and hydration, which right is not outweighed by any interests of the State, and because I find that the improperly biased procedural obstacles imposed by the Missouri Supreme Court impermissibly burden that right, I respectfully dissent. Nancy Cruzan is entitled to choose to die with dignity.

Acknowledging that the right to be free from unwanted medical attention was not absolute, Justice Brennan could find no state interest that would outweigh Cruzan's right in this case: "Whatever a State's possible interests in mandating life-support treatment under other circumstances, there is no good to be obtained here by Missouri's insistence that Nancy Cruzan remain on life-support systems if it is indeed her wish not to do so." The dissenters believed that the evidence given by family and friends clearly indicated that she would not have wanted to be kept alive under the circumstances.

In a separate dissent, Justice Stevens stated: "Our Constitution is born of the proposition that all legitimate governments must secure the equal right of every person to 'Life, Liberty, and the pursuit of Happiness.'" "In my view," he wrote, "the Constitution requires the State to care for Nancy Cruzan's life in a way that gives appropriate respect to her own best interests." For him, Missouri had not done so in this case.

During the 1960s one of the more emotional issues in the land was that of men wearing long hair. Not only did long hair become a social issue, but it became a legal issue as well. Many lawsuits were brought by students, government employees, and servicemen seeking to overturn grooming and dress codes. The Supreme Court was eventually forced to address the question when Thomas Dwen, for himself and on behalf of the Suffold County Patrolmen's Benevolent Association, sued John L. Barry, commissioner of the county police department. Dwen sought a declaration that the grooming regulations of the police department were a violation of his and the other patrolmen's civil rights. "The regulation was directed at the style and length of hair, sideburns, and mustaches; beards and goatees were prohibited, except for medical reasons; and wigs conforming to the regulation could be worn for cosmetic reasons."[29]

After taking testimony, Judge Jacob Mishler of a federal district court in New York could find no need for the grooming code and gave judgment for Dwen. A court of appeals affirmed without opinion. The Supreme Court, however, reversed, two justices dissenting and one not participating. The issue before the Court was whether there was a liberty interest in one's personal appearance, and if there was, whether the interests of the police department outweighed that interest. For the majority, the answer to the question was just not that clear. Justice Rehnquist, who authored the Court's opinion, wrote that "whether the citizenry at large has some sort of 'liberty' interest within the Fourteenth Amendment in matters of personal appearance is a question on which this Court's cases offer little, if any, guidance."

For this case, however, the majority assumed that such a liberty interest did exist. The question remaining to be answered, therefore, was whether there were sufficient governmental interests to override that interest. The county, Justice Rehnquist noted, "has chosen a mode of organization which it undoubtedly deems the most efficient in enabling its police to carry out the duties assigned to them under state and local law." The hair-length rule is part of that organization, and as long as there is a rational connection between the rule and the organization of the police department, the rule is valid. Whether the county's goal was to "make police officers readily recognizable to the members of the public, or a desire for the esprit de corps which such similarity is felt to inculcate within the police force itself, [e]ither one is a sufficiently rational justification for regulations so as to defeat [Dwen's] claim based on the liberty guarantee of the Fourteenth Amendment."

"It seems to me manifest," wrote Justice Marshall in dissent, "that [liberty's] 'full range of conduct' must encompass one's interest in dressing according to his own taste. An individual's personal appearance may reflect, sustain, and nourish his personality and may well be used as a means of expressing his attitude and lifestyle." Having said that, he concluded that the hair-length rule was unconstitutional because he could "find no rational relationship between the challenged regulation and [the county's] goals."

Most justices who haved served on the Court since *Meyer* agree that due process "affords not only a procedural guarantee against the deprivation of 'liberty,' but likewise protects substantive aspects of liberty (such as marriage, and family relationships, etc.) against unconstitutional restrictions by the State."

Some aspects of personal freedom, however, are not protected. Michael Hardwick found that out the hard way. Hardwick was a homosexual. Together with several others, he brought an action in a federal district court challenging the validity of the Georgia sodomy statute. Under Georgia law, "A person commits the offense of sodomy when he performs or submits to any sexual act involving the sex organs of one person and the mouth or anus of another."[30]

Hardwick, arrested for committing sodomy with another male, brought the federal court action against Michael Bowers, the Georgia attorney general, while his criminal case was pending. Judge Robert H. Hall dismissed the action for failure to state a claim, and Hardwick appealed. The court of appeals, with one judge dissenting, reversed. Judge Frank M. Johnson, Jr., for himself and

Judge Elbert P. Tuttle, held that the "Georgia sodomy statute infringed upon fundamental constitutional rights of [Hardwick], a
practicing homosexual." Judge Phyllis A. Kravitch disagreed, and so
did five justices of the Supreme Court who voted to reverse the court
of appeal's decision. Four justices dissented.

The difference between the majority and the dissenters is
evidenced by their differing views about what the issue was in this
case. Justice White, for the majority, states: "The issue presented is
whether the Federal Constitution confers a fundamental right upon
homosexuals to engage in sodomy and hence invalidates the laws of
the many States that still make such conduct illegal and have done
so for a very long time."[31] But the dissenters saw the case differently.
Justice Blackmun argues, "This case is [not] about 'a fundamental
right to engage in homosexual sodomy,' as the Court purports to
declare. . . . Rather, this case is about 'the most comprehensive of
rights and the right most valued by civilized men,' namely, 'the right
to be let alone.'"

After reviewing many of the cases discussed above, Justice White
concludes that "none of the rights announced in those cases bears
any resemblance to the claimed constitutional right of homosexuals
to engage in acts of sodomy that is asserted in this case. No connection between family, marriage, or procreation on the one hand and
homosexual activity on the other has been demonstrated."

The majority agreed that a number of substantive rights have
been given protection under the umbrella of the word *liberty*. But
in doing so, the Court has been conscious of the fact that its choices
for constitutional protection must be "much more than the imposition of the Justices' own choice of values." Two criteria for identify-
ing substantive rights which are not specifically mentioned in the
Constitution are (1) the identification of "those fundamental liberties
that are 'implicit in the concept of ordered liberty,' such that 'neither
liberty nor justice would exist if [they] were sacrificed,'" and (2)
"liberties that are 'deeply rooted in the Nation's history and tradition.'" "It is obvious," Justice White declared, "that neither of these
formulations would extend a fundamental right to homosexuals to
engage in acts of consensual sodomy."

In commenting upon the majority's reluctance to discover new
fundamental rights, Justice White sounded a warning. "The Court
is most vulnerable and comes nearest to illegitimacy," he asserted,
"when it deals with judge-made constitutional law having little or no
cognizable roots in the language or design of the Constitution."

As noted, the dissenters approached the problem differently. "I believe," Justice Blackmun wrote, "we must analyze . . . Hardwick's claim in the light of the values that underlie the constitutional right of privacy. If that right means anything, it means that, before Georgia can prosecute its citizens for making choices about the most intimate aspects of their lives, it must do more than assert that the choice they have made is an 'abominable crime not fit to be named among Christians.'" While admitting that many of the liberty interests previously identified by the Court have related to family, they are protected, he argued "because they form so central a part of an individual's life."

> The fact that individuals define themselves in a significant way through their intimate sexual relationships with others suggest, in a Nation as diverse as ours, that there may be many "right" ways of conducting those relationships, and that much of the richness of a relationship will come from the freedom an individual has to *choose* the form and nature of these intensely personal bonds.

Justice Stevens found an incongruity in the majority's decision. The statute makes no distinction between hetrosexual and homosexual sodomy and provides no exemption for married persons. Further, the statute had not been applied to hetrosexuals for many years, and the Georgia attorney general conceded that the law would be unconstitutional as applied to married couples.

Minors Have Rights Too

> Minors, as well as adults, are protected by the Constitution and possess constitutional rights.*

> On Monday, June 8, 1964, at about 10 A.M., Gerald Francis Gault and a friend, Ronald Lewis, were taken into custody by the Sheriff of Gila County [Arizona]. Gerald was then still subject to a six months' probation order which had been entered on February 25, 1964, as a result of his having been in the company of another boy who had stolen a wallet from a lady's purse. The police action on June 8 was taken as the result of a verbal complaint by a neighbor of the boys, Mrs. Cook, about a telephone call made to her in which the caller or callers made lewd or indecent remarks. It will suffice for purposes of this opinion to say that the remarks or questions put to her were of the irritatingly offensive, adolescent, sex variety.[32]

Planned Parenthood of Missouri v. Danforth, 428 U.S. 52, 74 (1976).

No notice was given to Gerald's parents of his arrest, and only after making inquiries did they learn that he had been taken to the detention home. Officer Flagg, who was in charge of the home, told them why Gerald was there and that a juvenile court hearing would be held for him the next day. A petition was filed with the court the next day, but it was not served on the Gaults.

Mrs. Gault, Gerald, his brother, and officers Flagg and Henderson attended the hearing in Judge McGhee's chambers. Mrs. Cook, who had made the complaint did not attend. There was no sworn testimony or any record of the proceedings. What actually took place at that hearing was revealed in the testimony of Judge McGhee, Officer Flagg, and the Gaults two months later in other proceedings.

> From this it appears that at the June 9 hearing Gerald was questioned by the judge about the telephone call. There was conflict as to what he said. His mother recalled that Gerald said he only dialed Mrs. Cook's number and handed the telephone to his friend, Ronald. Officer Flagg recalled that Gerald had admitted making lewd remarks. Judge McGhee testified that Gerald "admitted making one of these (lewd) statements." At the conclusion of the hearing, the judge said he would "think about it." Gerald was taken back to the Detention Home.

Gerald was later released to his parents. On that same day, Mrs. Gault received a note from Officer Flagg informing her that there would be another hearing on "Gerald's delinquency" on June 15. This hearing, in substance, was very similar to the former one, with conflicting testimony about Gerald's role in the telephone call. Again Mrs. Cook was not present. A report was filed by the probation officers but was not disclosed to the Gaults. Judge McGhee then sentenced Gerald to the state industrial school "for the period of his minority (that is, until 21), unless sooner discharged by due process of law." Had Gerald served this sentence, he would have been confined to the industrial school for six years.

Although Arizona law did not provide for appellate review of juvenile court cases, the validity of Gerald's sentencing was reveiwed by the Arizona Supreme Court through habeas corpus proceedings and affirmed. The U.S. Supreme Court reversed, with only one justice voting to dismiss the appeal.

To focus properly on the issue before the Supreme Court, it is necessary to review what would have happened to Gerald had he been over the age of eighteen.

If Gerald had been over 18, he would not have been subject to Juvenile Court proceedings. For the particular offense immediately involved, the maximum punishment would have been a fine of $5 to $50, or imprisonment in jail for not more than two months. Instead, he was committed to custody for a maximum of six years. If he had been over 18 and had committed an offense to which such a sentence might apply, he would have been entitled to substantial rights under the Constitution of the United States as well as under Arizona's laws and constitution. The United States Constitution would guarantee him rights and protections with respect to arrest, search and seizure and pretrial interrogation. It would assure him of specific notice of the charges and adequate time to decide his course of action and to prepare his defense. He would be entitled to clear advice that he could be represented by counsel and, at least if a felony were involved the State would be required to provide counsel if his parents were unable to afford it. If the court acted on the basis of his confession, careful procedures would be required to assure its voluntariness. If the case went to trial, confrontation and opportunity for cross-examination would be guaranteed.

This review of the disparate treatment an adult would have received under similar circumstances raised the question whether the juvenile court proceedings in Gerald's case violated due process. Before addressing that issue, the Court examined the evolution of such proceedings.

The early reformers were appalled by adult procedures and penalities, and by the fact that children could be given long prison sentences and mixed in jails with hardened criminals. They were profoundly convinced that society's duty to the child could not be confined by the concept of justice alone. They believed that society's role was not to ascertain whether the child was "guilty" or "innocent," but "What is he, how has he become what he is, and what had best be done in his interest and in the interest of the state to save him from a downward career." The child — essentially good, as they saw it — was to be made "to feel that his is the object of (the state's) care and solicitude," not that he was under arrest or on trial. The rules of criminal procedure were therefore altogether inapplicable. The apparent rigidities, technicalities, and harshness which they observed in both substantive and procedural criminal law were therefore to be discarded. The idea of crime and punishment was to be abandoned. The child was to be "treated" and "rehabilitated" and the procedures, from apprehension through institutionalization, were to be "clinical" rather than punitive.

As exemplary as this system of justice for juveniles may have been, Justice Abe Fortas for the Court pointed out that "Juvenile

Court history has . . . demonstrated that unbridled discretion, however, benevolently motivated, is frequently a poor substitute for principle and procedure." But does that mean that it violates due process? Yes, the Court held, because "neither the Fourteenth Amendment nor the Bill of Rights is for adults alone." Further, "Under our Constitution, the condition of being a boy does not justify a kangaroo court."

Procedures that would avoid trying a juvenile in a "kangaroo court," would include timely and adequate written notice to the child and parents giving information about the questions at issue; representation by counsel and if one could not be afforded, counsel provided by the state; the right to exercise the privilege against self-incrimination; and the right to confront and cross-examine witnesses.

Although justices Black and Harlan concurred with most of what the majority decided, their concurring opinions represented widely divergent views on the issues before the Court. Justice Black was of the opinion that both the majority and Justice Harlan voted to invalidate the Arizona procedures because they thought they were "unfair." Justice Harlan, according to Black, "is here claiming for the Court a supreme power to fashion new Bill of Rights safeguards according to the Court's notions of what fits tradition and conscience." The proper approach, Black argued, was simply to recognize that certain specific provisions of the Bill of Rights were applicable to these juvenile proceedings. "I do not vote," he asserted, "to invalidate this Arizona law on the ground that it is 'unfair' but solely on the ground that it violates the Fifth and Sixth Amendments made obligatory on the States by the Fourteenth Amendment."

But Justice Harlan was unmoved. For him, the issue, simply put, was whether the Arizona proceedings violated due process. "The proper issue here is . . . not whether the State may constitutionally treat juvenile offenders through a system of specialized courts, but whether the proceedings in Arizona's juvenile courts include procedural guarantees which satisfy the requirements of the Fourteenth Amendment." And the key ingredient in due process is "fundamental fairness." He concluded that the procedure here did not comply with that standard because the Gaults were not given adequate notice of the proceedings and were not advised of their right to be represented by counsel, and no record was made of the proceedings.

Because they were subjected to many "licks with a paddle" at their school, James Ingraham and Roosevelt Andrews sued Principal

Willie J. Wright and others for damages, claiming that the corporal punishment they received violated their constitutional rights.

> Because he was slow to respond to his teacher's instructions, Ingraham was subjected to more than 20 licks with a paddle while being held over a table in the principal's office. The paddling was so severe that he suffered a hematoma requiring medical attention and keeping him out of school for several days. Andrews was paddled several times for minor infractions. On two occasions he was struck on his arms, once depriving him of the full use of his arm for a week.[33]

District Judge Joe Eaton dismissed the action because he could find no constitutional right that was violated. The court of appeals agreed, and so did five Supreme Court justices. Before focusing on the constitutional arguments, Justice Powell, writing for the Court, reviewed the history of corporal punishment.

> The use of corporal punishment in this country as a means of disciplining schoolchildren dates back to the colonial period. It has survived the transformation of primary and secondary education from the colonials' reliance on optional private arrangements to our present system of compulsory education and dependence on public schools. Despite the general abandonment of corporal punishment as a means of punishing criminal offenders, the practice continues to play a role in the public education of schoolchildren in most parts of the country. Professional and public opinion is sharply divided on the practice, and has been for more than a century. Yet we can discern no trend toward its elimination.

But that, of course, does not necessarily mean that such punishment is permitted by the Constitution. Ingraham and Andrews raised two constitutional issues: (1) that such punishment was prohibited by the cruel and unusual punishments clause of the Eighth Amendment, and (2) that it violated their liberty interest protected by the due process clause of the Fourteenth Amendment. Concluding that the Eighth Amendment was intended to protect only convicted criminals, the majority held that it did not apply in the school system. But they did agree that "corporal punishment in public schools implicates a constitutionally protected liberty interest." "Among the historic liberties so protected," Justice Powell noted, "was a right to be free from, and to obtain judicial relief for, unjustified intrusions on personal security."

Having made that determination, the Court turned its attention to the question "What process is due to Ingraham and Andrews?" Justice Powell examined recourse available under common law to those who had received corporal punishment. Common law allowed a right to recover damages against the teacher, but "to the extent that the force used was reasonable in the light of its purpose, it was not wrongful, but rather 'justifiable or lawful.'"

Still, because the child's liberty interest was involved, the Court found it necessary to examine Florida law to see whether the child's interest was fully protected.

> Under Florida law the teacher and the principal of the school decide in the first instance whether corporal punishment is reasonably necessary under the circumstances in order to discipline a child who has misbehaved. But they must exercise prudence and restraint. . . ; If the punishment inflicted is later found to have been excessive – not reasonably believed at the time to be necessary for the child's discipline or training – the school authorities inflicting it may be held liable in damages to the child and, if malice is shown, they may be subject to criminal penalties.

"In view of the low incidence of abuse, the openness of our schools, and the common-law safeguards that already exist," Justice Powell declared, "the risk of error that may result in violation of a schoolchild's substantive rights can only be regarded as minimal." Ingraham and Andrews, therefore, did not prevail on their cruel and unusual punishment or violation of liberty interest claims.

The dissenters, led by Justice White, took the majority to task for on the one hand recognizing that a paddling effected the recipients' liberty interest but on the other hand concluding that it was constitutionally permissible as long as the student could sue the teacher if the punishment was too harsh. Justice White found the right to sue the teacher "utterly inadequate," for two reasons. First, the student cannot recover damages if the teacher proceeds in good faith, but "more important, even if the student could sue for good-faith error in the infliction of punishment, the lawsuit occurs after the punishment has been finally imposed. The infliction of physical pain is final and irreparable; it cannot be undone in a subsequent proceeding."

The dissenters were of the opinion that at least "the disciplinarian [ought to] take a few minutes to give the student 'notice of the charges against him and, if he denies them, an explanation of the evidence the authorities have and an opportunity to present his side of the story.'"

Making constitutional decisions, which requires the justices to choose between the constitutional rights of individuals and legitimate interests of the state, is always a difficult task. Even more formidable for them, however, is choosing between the rights of two or more individuals when those rights are in conflict. Such was the situation when the Court was confronted with a state law requiring an unmarried woman under the age of eighteen to secure the written consent of at least one of her parents before she could obtain an abortion.

The justices recognized that "the State has somewhat broader authority to regulate the activities of children than of adults."[34] Further, the state had argued that this requirement would safeguard the "family unit and parental authority." That did not satisfy the Court's majority. "It is difficult ... to conclude," Justice Blackmun argued, "that providing a parent with asbolute power to overrule a determination, made by the physician and his minor patient, to terminate the patient's pregnancy will serve to strengthen the family unit. Neither is it likely that such veto power will enhance parental authority or control where the minor and the nonconsenting parent are so fundamentally in conflict and the very existence of the pregnancy already has fractured the family structure. Any independent interest the parent may have in the termination of the minor daughter's pregnancy is no more weighty than the right of privacy of the competent minor mature enough to have become pregnant." Justices Stewart and Powell agreed because this law gave parents an absolute veto over the abortion decision of their daughter.

For dissenting justices White and Rehnquist and Chief Justice Burger, "the parental-consent requirement is not merely to vindicate any interest of the parent or of the State. The purpose of the requirement is to vindicate the very right created in *Roe v. Wade*, ... the right of the pregnant woman to decide 'whether *or not* to terminate her pregnancy.'" "Missouri," Justice White asserted, "is entitled to protect the minor unmarried woman from making the decision in a way which is not in her own best interests, and it seeks to achieve this goal by requiring parental consultation and consent."

If giving a parent an absolute veto over the abortion decision was a violation of the daughter's right to make the choice, would the same be true if the daughter was able to bypass the parent by obtaining a court order permitting the abortion? A majority said it was not and upheld a Missouri law which required the written consent of at least one parent unless "the minor has been granted the right to self-consent to the abortion by court order . . . , and the attending physician has received the informed written consent of the minor."[35] Justice Powell, writing for himself and Chief Justice Burger, concluded that "a State's interest in protecting immature minors will sustain a requirement of a consent substitute, either parental or judicial." These justices were supported by justices O'Connor, White, and Rehnquist, who believed that parental consent with a judicial substitute imposed "no undue burden on any right that a minor may have to undergo an abortion."

As could be expected, four justices, led by Justice Blackmun, disagreed. Their principal concern was that the Missouri law permits either a parental or judicial veto of the minor's decision. Quoting from a former opinion of Justice Stevens, Justice Blackmun pointed out that "as a practical matter, I would suppose that the need to commence judicial proceedings in order to obtain a legal abortion would impose a burden at least as great as, and probably greater than, that imposed on the minor child by the need to obtain the consent of the parent."

If a state may not require parental consent to a daughter's abortion except with a judicial bypass, may the state require parents to be notified before the abortion takes place? Six justices answered that question in the affirmative in *H.L. v. Matheson*[36] The facts of this case, as set forth in the opinion, tell this story:

> In the spring of 1978, [H.L.] was an unmarried 15-year-old girl living with her parents in Utah and dependent on them for her support. She discovered she was pregnant. She consulted with a social worker and a physician. The physician advised [her] that an abortion would be in her best medical interest. However, because of Utah [law], he refused to perform the abortion without first notifying [her] parents.

H.L. believed that she should have the abortion but for her own reasons did not want to notify her parents. She therefore commenced an action in a Utah court seeking a declaration that the law was unconstitutional. With H.L. the only witness, Judge David K. Winder heard evidence concerning her pregnancy. Her attorney objected to questions about why his client did not want her parents notified. The only issue before the court, he argued, was the constitutionality of the Utah law. Judge Winder upheld the law, and the Utah Supreme Court affirmed. The U.S. Supreme Court agreed. Chief Justice Burger, for himself and four other justices, outlined the issue.

The only issue before us, then, is the facial constitutionality of a statute requiring a physician to give notice to parents "if possible," prior to performing an abortion on their minor daughter, (a) when the girl is living with and dependent upon her parents, (b) when she is not emancipated by marriage or otherwise, and (c) when she has made no claim or showing as to her maturity or as to her relations with her parents.

The chief justice, noting that the law does not give the parents an absolute veto over the abortion decision, explained that "the medical, emotional, and psychological consequences of an abortion are serious and can be lasting; this is particularly so when the patient is immature.... Parents can provide medical and psychological data, refer the physician to other sources of medical history, such as family physicians, and authorize family physicians to give relevant data." This led these justices to conclude that the law was constitutional, a decision in which Justice Stevens concurred.

In dissent, Justice Marshall first reviewed what prior cases held with regard to the right to make the abortion decision. "Our cases have established," he pointed out, "that a pregnant woman has a fundamental right to choose whether to obtain an abortion or carry the pregnancy to term.... Her choice like the deeply intimate decisions to marry, to procreate, and to use contraceptives, is guarded from unwarranted state intervention by the right to privacy." Further: "It is also settled that the right to privacy, like many constitutional rights, extends to minors." He acknowledged, however, that the Court has also long recognized the constitutional protection given to the family as a unit. "Parental authority," however, Justice Marshall pointed out, "is never absolute, and has been denied legal protection when its exercise threatens the health or safety of the minor children." And in this case "I am persuaded that the Utah notice requirement in not necessary to assure parents this traditional child-rearing role, and that it burdens the minor's fundamental right to choose with her physician whether to terminate her pregnancy." He was joined in this opinion by justices Brennan and Blackmun.

In balancing parental control with the minor's liberty interest in making the abortion decision, it is clear that a majority of the Court have given great weight to parental interests. As noted above, however, the Court approved a procedure whereby a minor could bypass *parental consent* by securing court approval for an abortion. After the Court approved a Utah law requiring *parental notice* in H.L.'s case, it was eventually faced with the question of whether that notice could also be dispensed with by the minor securing court approval for the abortion. That question was presented when federal District Judge Ann Aldrich struck down an Ohio law which required parental notice but also provided that such notice could be dispensed with if a juvenile court authorized the minor to consent to the abortion. A court of appeals affirmed, but a majority of the Supreme Court reversed and upheld the statute. Justice Kennedy delivered the opinion for the majority.

> It is both rational and fair for the State to conclude that, in most instances, the family will strive to give a lonely or even terrified minor advice that is both compassionate and mature. The statute in issue here is a rational way to further those ends. It would deny all dignity to the family to say that the State cannot take this reasonable step in regulating its health professions to ensure that, in most cases, a young woman will receive guidance and understanding from a parent.[37]

Justice Scalia agreed but wanted it understood that he continued to believe "that the Constitution contains no right to abortion."

The decision disturbed dissenters justices Blackmun, Brennan, and Marshall. "I conclude," Justice Blackmun argued, "that, because of the minor's emotional vulnerability and financial dependency on her parents, and because the 'unique nature of the abortion decision' . . . and its consequences, a parental-notice statute is tantamount to a parental-consent statute."

The dissenters also believed that the procedure for securing permission from the juvenile court to consent to the abortion was fatally defective. "The pleading requirements," Justice Blackmun insisted, "the so-called and fragile guarantee of anonymity, the insufficiency of the expedited procedures, the constructive-authorization provision, and the 'clear and convincing evidence' requirement singly and collectively cross the limit of constitutional acceptance."

When J.L's and J.R.'s case reached the Supreme Court, Chief Justice Burger, who delivered the majority opinion, accepted the fact that "it is not disputed that a child, in common with adults, has a substantial liberty interest in not being confined unnecessarily for medical treatment."[38] J.L. and J.R., who were being treated in a Georgia mental hospital, had brought an action in the federal district court seeking a declaration that the laws which permitted parents to commit minor children for treatment voluntarily violated their constitutional right to liberty. The district court agreed, but a majority of the Supreme Court did not and reversed.

Among the questions raised by the minors in this case was whether the parental control of minor children, previously recognized by the Court as a constitutional liberty interest, included the power of parents to commit their children to a mental institution. They argued that previous Court decisions denying parents an absolute veto over their minor daughter's decision to have an abortion required a negative answer to the question. The majority disagreed and pointed out that because there were procedures to be followed at the time of commitment, the parents had no *absolute* right to commit their children to an institution. The chief justice stressed that "in defining the respective rights and prerogatives of the child and parent in the voluntary commitment setting, we conclude that our precedents permit the parents to retain a substantial, if not the dominant, role in the decision, absent a finding of neglect or abuse, and that the traditional presumption that the parents act in the best interests of their child should apply. We also conclude, however, that the child's rights and the nature of the commitment decision are such that parents cannot always have absolute and unreviewable discretion to decide whether to have a child institutionalized."

Justice Stewart's response was even more emphatic. "For centuries," he insisted, "it has been a canon of the common law that parents speak for their minor children. So deeply imbedded in our traditions is this principle of law that the Constitution itself may compel a State to respect it." Because "parents constantly make decisions for their children that deprive the children of liberty," he could see "no basic constitutional differences between commitment to a mental hospital and other parental decisions that result in a child's loss of liberty." The other kinds of decisions affecting the child's liberty would include, for example, the decision of the parent to consent to major surgery for a child.

Although the dissenting justices agreed with much of the majority's decision, they believed that some of the state's procedures in the commitment process were constitutionally deficient.

Liberty for the Mentally Ill

> A finding of "mental illness" alone cannot justify a State's locking a person up against his will and keeping him indefinitely in simple custodial confinement.*

*O'Connor v. Donaldson, 422 U.S. 563, 575 (1975).

Recognition that the mentally ill are persons who have substantive and procedural constitutional rights was long in coming. No doubt the blame lies primarily with society's views on mental illness. As recently as 1979, Chief Justice Burger, in discussing the treatment of the mentally ill, stated that "until recently, most of the states did little more than provide custodial institutions for the confinement of persons who were considered dangerous."[39] The chief justice went on to point out, however, that times were changing and courts were increasingly being called upon to examine state procedures for treatment and incarceration of those with mental illness.

The Supreme Court itself may have contributed to the lateness of judicial involvement by its decision in *Buck v. Bell*[40] in 1927. The Court's opinion gives the facts of this case.

> Carrie Buck is a feeble minded white woman who was committed to the State Colony [for Epileptics and Feeble Minded] in due form. She is the daughter of a feeble minded mother in the same institution, and the mother of an illegitimate feeble minded child. She was eighteen years old at the time of the trial of her case in the Circuit Court, in the latter part of 1924. An Act of Virginia . . . recites that the health of the patient and the welfare of society may be promoted in certain cases by the sterilization of mental defectives, under careful safeguard.

Carrie Buck's trial resulted in a court order permitting the superintendent of the State Colony to proceed with medical procedures to sterilize her. That order was affirmed by the Virginia Supreme Court of Appeal and by the U.S. Supreme Court. Only Justice Pierce Butler dissented.

Buck's attorney had argued that the law was "illegal in that it violates her constitutional right of bodily integrity and is therefore repugnant to the due process of law clause of the Fourteenth Amendment." While Justice Holmes, for the majority, recognized the argument, he did no more than that. For him, the welfare of the public was at issue here, and that was sufficient to affirm the order for sterilization.

> We have seen more that once that the public welfare may call upon the best citizens for their lives. It would be strange if it could not call upon those already sap the strength of the State for these lesser sacrifices, often not felt to be such by those concerned, in order to prevent our being swamped with incompetence. It is better for all the world, if instead of waiting to execute degenerate offspring for

crime, or to let them starve for their imbecility, society can prevent those who are manifestly unfit from continuing their kind. The principle that sustains compulsory vaccination is broad enough to cover cutting the Fallopian tubes.... Three generation of imbeciles are enough.

Although there certainly is a difference between a requirement of vaccination to prevent the spread of disease and sterilization to prevent birth, Carrie Buck's case has never been overruled by the Court.

When cases involving the mentally ill began to appear in the judicial system, the issues generally dealt with the validity of the process by which the commitment to the institution was made. The examination of those procedures brought an acknowledgment that the individual involved had a liberty interest protected by the due process clauses.

The case of Theon Jackson illustrates the acceptance by the Court of a liberty interest of a mentally ill person which requires procedures consistent with due process. "Theon Jackson," Justice Blackmun wrote, "is a mentally defective deaf mute with a mental level of a pre-school child. He cannot read, write, or otherwise communicate except through limited sign language. In May 1968, at age 27, he was charged ... with separate robberies of two women.... The first involved property (a purse and its contents) of the value of four dollars. The second concerned five dollars in money."[41] Jackson's plea of not guilty set in motion state procedures for determining whether he was competent to stand trial. A report by court-appointed psychiatrists concluded that "Jackson's almost nonexistent communication skill, together with his lack of hearing and his mental deficiency, left him unable to understand the nature of the charges against him or to participate in his defense."

Judge John T. Davis conducted a hearing but was unable to communicate with Jackson. On the basis of the psychiatric report, Judge Davis then ordered Jackson "committed to the Indiana Department of Mental Health until such time as that Department should certify to the court that 'the defendant is sane.'" Counsel for Jackson requested a new trial, arguing that there was no evidence that his client was insane or that he would ever become "sane" in the sense used by the court in its commitment. "Counsel argued that Jackson's commitment under these circumstances amounted to a 'life sentence' without his ever having been convicted of a crime, and that the commitment therefore deprived Jackson of his Fourteenth

Amendment rights to due process and equal protection, and constituted cruel and unusual punishment under the Eighth Amendment made applicable to the States through the Fourteenth." Judge Davis denied the request, and the Indiana Supreme Court affirmed. All justices of the U.S. Supreme Court voted to reverse, justices Powell and Rehnquist not participating. The Court's opinion was delivered by Justice Blackmun, who stated, "We . . . hold that Indiana's indefinite commitment of a criminal defendant solely on account of his incompetency to stand trial does not square with the Fourteenth Amendment's guarantee of due process."

> We hold, consequently, that a person charged by a State with a criminal offense who is committed solely on account of his incapacity to proceed to trial cannot be held more than the reasonable period of time necessary to determine whether there is substantial probability that he will attain that capacity in the foreseeable future. If it is determined that this is not the case, then the State must either institute the customary civil commitment proceeding that would be required to commit indefinitely any other citizen, or release the defendant.

In requiring civil commitment procedures in cases such as Jackson's, the Court is recognizing that his liberty is at issue, and that cannot be taken without due process. Civil commitment procedures for the mentally ill will be discussed in Chapter 2.

Even when a person has been civilly committed under proper due process procedures, that person still retains his or her right to liberty, and the state must justify its continued confinement. This message was brought home to Dr. J. B. O'Connor, and other mental institution directors in the case of Kenneth Donaldson. Donaldson was confined as a mental patient in the Florida State Hospital. He had been there for fifteen years despite his continuing efforts to be released. He eventually brought an action seeking damages from Dr. O'Connor, the hosptial superintendent, for violating his constitutional right to liberty.

Donaldson had originally been committed by his father, "who thought that his son was suffering from 'delusions.'"[42] Under Florida law, Donaldson could have been released by the hospital staff if they believed he was "not dangerous to himself or others, even if he remained mentally ill and had been lawfully committed. Despite many requests, O'Connor refused to allow that power to be exercised in Donaldson's case."

The testimony at the trial demonstrated, without contradiction, that Donaldson had posed no danger to others during his long confinement, or indeed at any point in his life. O'Connor himself conceded that he had no personal or secondhand knowledge that Donaldson had ever committed a dangerous act. There was no evidence that Donaldson had ever been suicidal or been thought likely to inflict injury upon himself. One of O'Connor codefendants acknowledged that Donaldson could have earned his own living outside the hospital.

The evidence also revealed that an organization called Helping Hands, Inc., which operated a halfway house for the mentally ill, had agreed to accept Donaldson. O'Connor rejected this offer, concluding that Donaldson should be released only to his parents, even though they were elderly and not able to care for him. It appeared also that "Donaldson's confinement was a simple regime of enforced custodial care, not a program designed to alleviate or cure his supposed illness."

Dr. O'Connor's response to this evidence was that he acted in good faith and therefore was immune from liability. The jury disagreed and gave Donaldson $38,500 in damages and another $10,000 in punitive damages. The court of appeals affirmed. A unanimous Supreme Court agreed that Donaldson's liberty interest had been violated by Dr. O'Connor. The Court, however, vacated the judgment and remanded the case for determination whether Judge David L. Middlebrooks, Jr., had improperly instructed the jury on the possibility that Dr. O'Connor may have been immune from liability under state law.

While Donaldson may not have won this war, he did for himself and for other mental patients win a significant victory. Before the trial commenced, O'Connor had retired, and with the help of the hospital staff, Donaldson had been released. But just as important was the fact that his case gave the Court an opportunity to make significant rulings relating to the rights of mental patients. As the Court stated, "This case raises a single, relatively simple, but nonetheless important question concerning every man's constitutional right to liberty." Justice Stewart, writing for all the justices, declared that "a finding of 'mental illness' alone cannot justify a State's locking a person up against his will and keeping him indefinitely in simple custodial confinement. Assuming that that term can be given a reasonably precise content and that the 'mentally ill' can be identified with reasonable accuracy, there is still no constitutional basis for confining such persons involuntarily if they are dangerous to no one and can live safely in freedom."

Justice Stewart then asked and answered several questions: May the State confine the mentally ill merely to ensure them a living standard superior to that they enjoy in the private community? His response was: "The mere presence of mental illness does not disqualify a person from preferring his home to the comforts of an institution." May the State fence in the harmless mentally ill solely to save its citizens from exposure to those ways are different? To this question the justice responded: "Mere public intolerance or animosity cannot constitutionally justify the deprivation of a person's physical liberty."

The above cases clearly hold that committing a mentally ill person to an institution affects that person's liberty interest protected by the due process clause. However, it was in the case of *Youngberg v. Romeo*[43] that the Court first addressed the extent of the protection to which the committed person is entitled.

> Nicholas Romeo is profoundly retarded. Although 33 years old, he has the mental capacity of an 18-month-old child, with an I. Q. between 8 and 10. He cannot talk and lacks the most basic self-care skills. Until he was 26, [he] lived with his parents in Philadelphia. But after the death of his father in May 1974, his mother was unable to care for him. Within two weeks of the father's death, [Nicholas's] mother sought his temporary admission to a nearby Pennsylvania hospital.

Eventually Mrs. Romeo petitioned the court to confine Nicholas permanently because she could not care for him or handle his violence. The court granted the petition. Some time thereafter Mrs. Romeo brought an action for damages against the hospital's director and two of its supervisors for injuries Nicholas had received while at the institution. She alleged that he had been injured at least sixty-three times and that the hospital staff had failed to take measures to prevent such injuries.

After eight days of trial, the jury exonerated the defendants, and Judge Joseph L. McGlynn, Jr., entered judgment for them. The court of appeals remanded the case for a new trial, being of the opinion that Judge McGlynn had not properly presented the case to the jury. But even that court could not agree on the rules of law that should govern cases such as this. The case was appealed to the Supreme Court, which acknowledged that it was considering "for the first time the substantive rights of involuntarily committed mentally retarded persons under the Fourteenth Amendment to the Constitution."

The attorneys for Nicholas argued he had "a constitutionally protected liberty interest in safety, freedom of movement, and training within the institution; and that [the hospital staff] infringed these rights by failing to provide constitutionally required conditions of confinement." The attorneys representing the state (the hospital staff, in this case) agreed that Romeo had "a right to adequate food, shelter, clothing, and medical care" and that those were being provided to him. But was he entitled to more than that? That was the question facing the justices. "We must decide," wrote Justice Powell for the majority, "whether liberty interests also exist in safety, freedom of movement, and training."

The justices had little difficulty with the safety and freedom of movement questions. "If it is cruel and unusual punishment to hold convicted criminals in unsafe conditions, it must be unconstitutional to confine the involuntarily committed — who may not be punished at all — in unsafe conditions." Further, the Court recognized that "liberty from bodily restraint always has been recognized as the core of the liberty protected by the Due Process Clause from arbitrary government action." And because that "interest survives criminal conviction and incarceration, . . . it must also survive involuntary commitment."

This brought the justices to Romeo's claim for some "training within the institution," which Justice Powell found "more troubling." Romeo's attorney argued that he had a "constitutional right to minimally adequate habilitation," training and development. The parties all agreed, however, that even with training Romeo would never be able to leave the institution. Nevertheless, the majority agreed with his position and concluded that his "liberty interests require the State to provide minimally adequate or reasonable training to ensure safety and freedom from undue restraint." But like all our constitutional rights, none are absolute, and neither are the rights of the confined mentally ill. "In operating an institution such as Pennhurst," Justice Powell noted, "there are occasions in which it is necessary for the State to restrain the movement of residents — for example, to protect them as well as others from violence. Similar restraints may also be appropriate in a training program. And an institution cannot protect its residents from all danger of violence if it is to permit them to have any freedom of movement."

How best, then, can the rights of the individuals be protected and the interests of the state accommodated? The necessary accommodation would be reached by requiring such training as is "reasonable in light of [the person's] liberty interests in safety and freedom from unreasonable restraints. In determining what is 'reasonable' — in this and in any case presenting a claim for training by a State . . . courts must show deference to the judgment exercised by a qualified professional. By so limiting judicial review of challenges to conditions in state institutions, interference by the federal judiciary with the internal operations of these institutions should be minimized. Moreover, there certainly is no reason to think judges or juries are better qualified than appropriate professionals in making such decisions." Chief Justice Burger concurred in the judgment but stated: "I would hold flatly that [Romeo] has no constitutional right to training, or 'habilitation,' *per se*."

Prisoners and Their Liberty

> There is no iron curtain drawn between the Constitution and the prisons of the country.*

Robert O. McDonnell, an inmate in a Nebraska prison, brought an action for himself and other inmates against Charles Wolff, Jr., the warden. He claimed that the disciplinary proceedings at the prison violated due process. Of particular concern to McDonnell and the other inmates was that "in cases of flagrant or serious misconduct, the [warden] may order that a person's reduction in term [good-time credit] be forfeited or withheld."[44] The state responded to the lawsuit by arguing "that whatever may be true of the Due Process Clause in general or of other rights protected by that Clause against state infringement, the interest of prisoners in disciplinary proceedings is not included in that 'liberty' protected by the Fourteenth Amendment."

District Judge Robert V. Denny, concluding that he was bound by prior case law, agreed with the state and rejected the due process argument made by the inmates. The court of appeals reversed, holding that disciplinary proceedings were subject to the requirements of due process, and the Supreme Court agreed.

*Wolff v. McDonnell, 418 U.S. 539, 555-556 (1974).

Good-time credits are earned for "good behavior and faithful performance of duties" and for donating blood to the American Red Cross. These good-time credits create a "liberty" interest, the Court held. "But the State having created the right to good time," Justice White asserted for the Court, "and itself recognizing that its deprivation is a sanction authorized for major misconduct, the prisoner's interest has real substance and is sufficiently embraced within Fourteenth Amendment 'liberty' to entitle him to those minimum procedures appropriate under the circumstances and required by the Due Process Clause to insure that the state-created right is nor arbitrarily abrogated."

Justice Marshall, writing for himself and Justice Brennan, agreed. "I have previously stated my view," he contended, "that a prisoner does not shed his basic constitutional rights at the prison gate, and I fully support the Court's holding that the interest of the inmates in freedom from imposition of serious discipline is a 'liberty' entitled to due process protection."

Because of a number of serious fires at the Massachusetts Correctional Institution, Norfolk, Arthur Fano and five other prisoners were transferred to more secure prisons in the state. They brought an action in the federal district court against Larry Meachum, the superintendent, alleging that the transfers infringed their liberty interests and therefore violated due process. Judge Walter J. Skinner agreed, and the court of appeals, with one judge dissenting, affirmed.

Meachum appealed to the Supreme Court, which reversed in a 6–3 decision, with Justice White delivering the opinion for the majority. The question before the Court, Justice White wrote, was "whether the Due Process Clause of the Fourteenth Amendment entitles a state prisoner to a hearing when he is transferred to a prison the conditions of which are substantially less favorable to the prisoner." The majority responded that "it does not."[45]

> Our cases hold that the convicted felon does not forfeit all constitutional protections by reason of his conviction and confinement in prison. He retains a variety of important rights that the courts must be alert to protect. . . . But none of [our] cases reaches this one; and to hold as we are urged to do that *any* substantial deprivation imposed by prison authorities triggers the procedural protections of the Due Process Clause would subject to judicial review a wide spectrum of discretionary actions that traditionally have been the business of prison administrators rather than of the federal courts.

The dissenters took issue with majority's conclusion. These inmates did have a liberty interest in not being transferred without procedural due process. And it was one of those "important rights that the courts must be alert to protect." "I think it clear," Justice Stevens insisted, "that even the inmate retains an unalienable interest in liberty—at the very minimum the right to be treated with dignity—which the Constitution may never ignore." "The transfer involved in this case," he emphasized, "was sufficiently serious to invoke the protection of the Constitution."

If the transfer from one prison to another does not infringe any liberty interest, would the same hold true if the inmate was transferred from a correctional institution to a mental hospital? That was the question put to the district court by Larry D. Jones and a number of other inmates at a Nebraska state prison.

> On May 31, 1974, Jones was convicted of robbery and sentenced to a term of three to nine years in state prison. He was transferred to the penitentiary hospital in January 1975. Two days later he was placed in solitary confinement, where he set his mattress on fire, burning himself severely. He was treated in the burn unit of a private hospital. Upon his release and based on findings required by [law] that he was suffering from a mental illness or defect and could not receive proper treatment in the penal complex, he was transferred to the security unit of Lincoln Regional Center, a state mental hospital under the jurisdiction of the Department of Public Institutions.[46]

Jones' transfer to the mental hospital was in accordance with state law, which required only that "when a designated physician or psychologist finds that a prisoner 'suffers from a mental disease or defect' and 'cannot be given proper treatment in [the prison]' the director may transfer him for examination, study, and treatment to another institution within or without the Department of Correctional Services." A three-judge district court, acting through judges Warren K. Urbom, Robert V. Denny, and Donald P. Lay, held that the Nebraska law allowing for transfer of prisoners to the mental institution deprived the inmates of their liberty without due process of law.

The district court was of the opinion that an inmate's liberty interest arose from two distinct sources. One was the inmate's expectation that under state law "he would not be transferred to a mental hospital without a finding that he was suffering from a mental illness for which he could not secure adequate treatment in the correctional facility." Second, the court "was convinced that characterizing Jones as a mentally ill patient and transferring him to the [mental hospital] had 'some stigmatizing' consequences which, together with the mandatory behavior modification treatment to which Jones would be subject at the [hospital,] constituted a major change in the conditions of confinement amounting to a 'grievous loss' that should not be imposed without the opportunity for notice and an adequate hearing."

A majority of the Supreme Court agreed with both positions. "We have repeatedly held," Justice White and the majority maintained, "that statutes may create liberty interests that are entitled to procedural protections of the Due Process Clause of the Fourteenth Amendment."

With regard to district court's holding that "Jones retained a residuum of liberty that would be infringed by a transfer to a mental hospital," Justice White noted that "we have recognized that for the ordinary citizen, commitment to a mental hospital produces 'a massive curtailment of liberty' . . . and in consequence 'requires due process protection.'"

> The loss of liberty produced by an involuntary commitment is more than a loss of freedom from confinement. It is indisputable that commitment to a mental hospital "can engender adverse social consequences to the individual" and that "[w]hether we label this phenomena 'stigma' or choose to call it something else . . . we recognize that it can occur and that it can have a very significant impact on the individual." . . . Also, "[a]mong the historic liberties" protected by the Due Process Clause is "the right to be free from, and to obtain judicial relief for, unjustified intrusions on personal security."

The majority then held that even though Jones was an inmate, he was nevertheless still entitled to full protection of due process before being transferred to a mental institution.

Four justices dissented. They thought that this case was moot because in the meantime Jones had been transferred back to the prison and paroled but had violated his parole and been returned to the prison. On this issue the majority held that the case was not moot because once the legal proceedings were terminated, the state still retained the power to transfer Jones back to the mental hospital.

> John T. Morrissey was convicted of false drawing or uttering of checks in 1967 pursuant to his guilty plea, and was sentenced to not more than seven years' confinement. He was paroled from the Iowa

State Penitentiary in June of 1968. Seven months later, at the direction of his parole officer, he was arrested in his home town as a parole violator and incarcerated in the county jail. One week later, after review of the parole officer's written report, the Iowa Board of Parole revoked Morrissey's parole, and he was returned to the penitentiary located about 100 miles from his home.[47]

Not until after he had been returned to the prison was Morrissey given any type of hearing concerning the revocation of his parole, and as a result of that hearing, the revocation was upheld.

Morrissey sought release by way of a writ of habeas corpus from federal District Judge Roy L. Stephenson, which was denied. The court of appeals, in a 4–3 decision, affirmed. The Supreme Court unanimously disagreed and reversed. The justices accepted the fact that Morrissey had a liberty interest in being on parole which required due process protection, but they did not all agree on the procedure to which a parolee was entitled.

Chief Justice Burger, for the majority, first discussed the historical background of parole.

> Rather than being an *ad hoc* exercise of clemency, parole is an established variation on imprisonment of convicted criminals. Its purpose is to help individuals reintegrate into society as constructive individuals as soon as they are able, without being confined for the full term of the sentence imposed. It also serves to alleviate the costs to society of keeping an individual in prison. The essence of parole is release from prison, before the completion of sentence, on the condition that the prisoner abide by certain rules during the balance of the sentence. Under some systems, parole is granted automatically after the service of a certain portion of a prison term. Under others, parole is granted by the discretionary action of a board, which evaluates an array of information about a prisoner and makes a prediction whether he is ready to reintegrate into society.

Revocation of parole involves not only a determination of whether the parolee has violated the terms of the parole but also "the ability of the individual to live in society without committing anti-social acts." The answers to these questions will determine whether the inmate will be able to continue his liberty, or returned to confinement. "Revocation," Chief Justice Burger noted, "deprives an individual, not of the absolute liberty to which every citizen is entitled, but only of the conditional liberty properly dependent on observance of special parole restrictions."

Because of this conditional liberty, the parolee may have been free for a number of years, gotten a job, and enjoyed friends and family. "We see, therefore," the chief justice wrote, "that the liberty of a parolee, although indeterminate, includes many of the core values of unqualified liberty and its termination inflicts a 'grievous loss' on the parolee and often on others. It is hardly useful any longer to try to deal with this problem in terms of whether the parolee's liberty is a 'right' or a 'privilege.' By whatever name, the liberty is valuable and must be seen as within the protection of the Fourteenth Amendment. Its termination calls for some orderly process, however informal."

The question whether a prison inmate had a constitutional liberty interest that would prevent the administration to him of anti-psychotic drugs against his will, came before the courts in the case of *Washington v. Harper*.[48] Walter Harper had been involved with the Washington penal system since 1976. During that time, whether in prison or on parole, he had received psychiatric treatment, which included taking preventive medicine. When not taking the drugs, he sometimes became violent. He was placed in the Special Offender Center where "he was diagnosed as suffering from a manic-depressive disorder [and] required to take antipsychotic drugs against his will pursuant to an SOC policy."

Harper brought suit against the state claiming that "the failure to provide a judicial hearing before the involuntary administration of antipsychotic medication violated the Due Process Clause of the Fourteenth Amendment." The trial court rejected the claim, but the Washington Supreme Court "reversed . . . concluding that, under the Clause, the State could administer such medication to a competent, nonconsenting inmate only if, in a judicial hearing at which the inmate had the full panoply of adversarial procedural protections, the State proved by 'clear, cogent, and convincing' evidence that the medication was both necessary and effective for furthering a compelling state interest." Underlying this decision was the acknowledgment that Harper had a liberty interest in being free from forced administration of drugs without a judicial determination that "the medication was both necessary and effective."

A unanimous Supreme Court agreed that Harper was protected by the due process clause. A majority of the justices, however, held that a judicial proceeding was not necessary prior to the administration of the drugs because the state's procedures were constitutionally sufficient. The justices found that a liberty interest was created by the state's policy and also an inherent part of Harper's person, which was protected by due process. Justice Kennedy discussed the liberty question for the majority, noting that "we have no doubt that, in addition to the liberty interest created by the State's Policy, [Harper] possesses a significant liberty interest in avoiding the unwanted administration of antipsychotic drugs under the Due Process Clause of the Fourteenth Amendment."

Harper had argued that the state "may not override his choice to refuse antipsychotic drugs unless he has been found to be incompetent, and then only if the factfinder makes a substituted judgment that he, if competent, would consent to drug treatment." The majority disagreed. "The extent of a prisoner's right under the Clause to avoid the unwanted administration of antipsychotic drugs must be defined in the context of the inmate's confinement." In other words, were there governmental interests of sufficient importance to outweigh Harper's liberty rights? The answer was that the government's interest in security of the prison was indeed of greater weight. "The legitimacy, and the necessity, of considering the State's interests in prison safety and security are well established by our cases," wrote Justice Kennedy. And regulations which are "reasonably related to legitimate penological interests" will be upheld. In this case, before drugs could be forcefully administered to an inmate, the decision had to be approved by a "special committee consisting of a psychiatrist, a psychologist, and a Center official, none of whom may be currently involved in the inmate's diagnosis or treatment, [and] the psychiatrist [must be] in the majority."

> In sum, we hold that the regulation before us is permissible under the Constitution. It is an accommodation between an inmate's liberty interest in avoiding the forced administration of antipsychotic drugs and the State's interests in providing appropriate medical treatment to reduce the danger that an inmate suffering from a serious mental disorder represents to himself or others.

Justice Blackmun concurred but suggested that the problem could have been avoided had the state followed the same procedure used in committing other mentally ill persons to institutions. Three justices, although concurring in the decision that Harper had a constitutional liberty interest, argued that the "Court has undervalued [Harper's] liberty interest; has misread the Washington involuntary medication Policy and misapplied [a recent decision of the Court]; and has concluded that a mock trial before an institutionally biased tribunal constitutes 'due process of law.'" Writing for himself and justices Brennan and Marshall, Justice Stevens stated that for them, "a competent individual's right to refuse psychotropic medication is an aspect of liberty requiring the highest order of protection under the Fourteenth Amendment."

In *Harper*, the justices found the Harper's liberty interest came from two sources. One was the state's written policy governing the administration of antipsychotic drugs to inmates. The other was Harper's personal liberty under the due process clause. George Allen and Dale Jacobsen, prisoners in the Montana State Prison, asked the courts to find that they had similar liberty interests in being paroled. The sources for their liberty, they argued, was Montana's policy concerning paroles as well as their personal liberty protected by due process.

Whether a liberty interest is created by law requires an examination of the Montana statute relating to parole release. That statute reads as follows:

> Prisoners eligible for parole. (1) Subject to the following restrictions, the board *shall* release on parole . . . any person confined in the Montana state prison or the women's correction center . . . when in its opinion there is reasonable probability that the prisoner can be released without detriment to the prisoner or to the community. . . .

> (2) A parole shall be ordered only for the best interests of society and not as an award of clemency or a reduction of sentence or pardon. A prisoner shall be placed on parole only when the board believes that he is able and willing to fulfill the obligations of a law-abiding citizen.[49]

Federal District Judge William D. Murray dismissed Allen and Jacobsen's lawsuit. He "concluded that, because the Board [of Pardons] is required to make determinations with respect to the best interest of the community and the prisoner, its discretion is too broad to provide a prisoner with a liberty interest in parole release." The court of appeals reversed and remanded the case to the district court, being of the opinion that because the statute used the word *shall*, the board does not have uncontrolled discretion in granting or denying parole release. The statute, therefore, created an interest in the prisoner in the parole process.

Six justices of the Supreme Court agreed and affirmed. "Significantly, the Montana statute," declared Justice Brennan for the majority, "uses mandatory language ('shall') to 'creat[e] a presumption that parole release will be granted' when the designated findings are made." Taking note of the fact that the legislative history of the statute buttresses the conclusion that the board's discretion is limited, Justice Brennan ended the opinion by stating, "We find in the Montana statute, . . . a liberty interest protected by the Due Process Clause." Justices O'Connor and Scalia and Chief Justice Rehnquist emphatically disagreed. "Relying on semantics and ignoring altogether the sweeping discretion granted to the Board of Pardons by Montana law," Justice O'Connor insisted, "the Court today concludes that [Allen and Jacobsen] had a legitimate expectation of parole sufficient to give rise to [a liberty] interest protected by procedural due process. Because I conclude that the discretion accorded the Board of Pardons belies any reasonable claim of *entitlement* to parole, I respectfully dissent."

While this case basically deals with the question whether the state by its actions, regulations, or laws has created some kind of "entitlement" in people, Justice Brennan pointed out in a footnote that "there is far more to liberty than interests conferred by language in state statutes. . . . Four members of this Court are of the view that the existence of a liberty interest in parole release is not solely a function of the wording of the governing statute." The four justices he referred to were justices Powell, Stevens, Marshall, and himself. In the same footnote, Justice Brennan quotes Justice Marshall: "At stake in the parole-release decision is a return to freedom, albeit conditional freedom; liberty from bodily restraint is at the heart of the liberty protected by the Due Process Clause."

The Right to Work, Contract, and Do Business

> The liberty mentioned in [the Fourteenth] amendment . . . is deemed to embrace the right of the citizen to be free in the enjoyment of all his faculties; to be free to use them in all lawful ways; to live and work where he will; to earn his livelihood by any lawful calling; to pursue any livelihood or avocation, and for that purpose to enter into all contracts which may be proper, necessary and essential to his carrying out to a successful conclusion the puposes above mentioned.*

This declaration that the Fourteenth Amendment includes a constitutional liberty interest in working, contracting, and doing

Allgeyer v. Louisiana, 165 U.S. 578, 589 (1897).

business has been affirmed again and again by the justices. However, it has rarely been relied upon as a basis for nullifying federal or state government regulation of those activities.

Justice Stephen J. Field, who had been appointed to the Court by President Lincoln, expressed the opinion that such a liberty interest existed when he dissented in an 1873 case. That case involved the validity of a Louisana statute that gave the Cresent City Live-Stock Landing and Slaughter-House Company a monopoly for landing and slaughtering cattle in several parishes in and around New Orleans. While the law did not prevent others from butchering, anyone wishing to do so had to use the facilities of the company. A majority of the justices voted to uphold the law against arguments that it violated the Thirteenth and Fourteenth amendments. Specifically, they held that the law did not violate any privileges and immunities of citizens or deny them due process of law.[50]

Justice Field, in a dissenting opinion in which Chief Justice Salmon P. Chase and justices Joseph P. Bradley and Noah H. Swayne joined, expressed the view that "to [citizens] everywhere, all pursuits, all professions, all avocations are open without other restrictions than such as are imposed equally upon all others of the same age, sex, and condition."

Subsequent to the *Crescent City* case the Court upheld government regulation of grain elevators, a prohibition on operating a laundry from 10 P.M. until 6 A.M., a prohibition on the manufacture of intoxicating liquor within a state, prohibiting the manufacture of oleomargarine or imitation butter, licensing of doctors, and limiting attorney's fees in certain cases.[51]

Justice Field acquiesced in some of these cases, but he did so after first recognizing that the individuals involved had a liberty interest. Thereafter, for him, the question was whether the government's regulation was reasonable. For example, he wrote an opinion upholding West Virginia's law requiring a license to practice medicine, finding that law to be a reasonable regulation of the right to work. "The law of West Virginia," he emphasized, "was intended to secure such skill and learning in the profession of medicine that the community might trust with confidence those receiving a license under authority of the State."[52]

State laws regulating the hours that people could work were also upheld by the Court, and the same reasoning applied: Such regulations were reasonable and not arbitrary.

On June 20, 1896, complaint was made to a justice of the peace of
Salt Lake City that [Mr.] Holden had unlawfully employed "one
John Anderson to work and labor as a miner in the underground
workings of the Old Jordan mine in Bingham [canyon] . . . for the
period of ten hours each day; and said [Mr. Holden] continuously
since said time, has unlawfully required said John Anderson . . . to
work and labor in the underground workings of the mine aforesaid,
for the period of ten hours each day."[53]

The employment of John Anderson for ten hours a day was in
violation of a Utah statute which limited the "employment of work-
ingmen in all underground mines or workings [to] eight hours per
day, except in cases of emergency where life or property is in immi-
nent danger." Holden admitted the violation but defended his actions by asserting that the Utah statute was "repugnant to the Constitution of the United States in these respects: 'It deprives . . . all
employers and employees of the right to make contracts in a lawful
way . . .; [and] It deprives . . . him of his property and liberty
without due process of law.'" Holden was found guilty as charged,
fined $50, and sent to the county jail for fifty-seven days. He sought
release by a writ of habeas corpus from the Utah Supreme Court,
which was denied.

The U.S. Supreme Court affirmed, with justices David J. Brewer
and Rufus W. Peckham dissenting. In determining that the Utah law
was reasonable, the majority was aware of the statement from the
Allgeyer case, set forth above, which accepts a right of contract as
part of the liberty interest of working people. "The right of contract,
however," Justice Henry B. Brown stated for the Court, "is itself subject to certain limitations which the State may lawfully impose in the
exercise of its police powers." The opinion then cites a long litany
of the kinds of regulations that affect businesses which courts have
upheld. Such regulations are valid as long as they are reasonable and
not arbitrary. "The question in each case," Justice Brown maintained,
"is whether the legislature has adopted the statute in exercise of a
reasonable discretion, or whether its action be a mere excuse for an
unjust discrimination, or the oppression, or spoliation of a particular class."

Bakers fared better — or worse, depending upon one's point of
view — at the hands of the Court than the miners. Joseph Lochner
was indicted in New York because he had "wrongfully and unlawfully required and permitted an employee working for him in his
biscuit, bread and cake bakery and confectionery establishment,

at the city of Utica, ... to work more than sixty hours in one week."⁵⁴ This was in violation of a state law which limited the hours of bakers to no more than sixty hours a week or ten hours a day. Lochner was found guilty, and because this was his second offense, sentenced to a fine of $50 and sent to jail until the fine was paid. Lochner's conviction was upheld by two New York appellate courts but reversed by the Supreme Court.

Writing for the majority, Justice Peckham accepted the fact that "the right to purchase or to sell labor is part of the liberty protected by [the Fourteenth] amendment, unless there are circumstances which exclude the right." The government, however, has certain powers, called the *police power*. "Those powers, broadly stated," he declared, "relate to the safety, health, morals, and general welfare of the public. Both property and liberty are held on such reasonable conditions as may be imposed by the governing power of the state in the exercise of those powers, and with such conditions the 14th Amendment was not designed to interfere." But of course there must be a limit to the police power; "otherwise the 14th Amendment would have no efficacy and the legislatures of the states would have unbounded power." But in this case, Justice Peckham argued, "the question whether this act is valid as a labor law, pure and simple, may be dismissed in a few words. There is no reasonable ground for interfering with the liberty of person or the right of free contract, by determining the hours of labor, in the occupation of a baker."

The Court then took note of the fact that working in a bakery may not be as healthy as some occupations, but it could not be considered unhealthy. The majority also saw a real threat to working people if legislatures were allowed to interfere with working conditions just because they might be somewhat unhealthy.

> No trade, no occupation, no mode of earning one's living, could escape this all-pervading power, and the acts of the legislature in limiting the hours of labor in all employments would be valid, although such limitation might seriously cripple the ability of the laborer to support himself and his family.

The decision to strike down the New York Law did not go unchallenged. The first Justice Harlan, in dissent, quoted from a prior case:

> We are reminded by counsel that it is the solemn duty of the courts in cases before them to guard the constitutional rights of the citizens

against merely arbitrary power. That is unquestionably true. But it is equally true — indeed, the public interests imperatively demand — that legislative enactments should be recognized and enforced by the courts as embodying the will of the people, unless they are plainly and palpably, beyond all question, in violation of the fundamental law of the Constitution.

Justice Holmes also dissented. "I think," he wrote, "that the word liberty in the Fourteenth Amendment is perverted when it is held to prevent the natural outcome of a dominant opinion, unless it can be said that a rational and fair man necessarily would admit that the statute proposed would infringe fundamental principles as they have been understood by the traditions of our people and our law." He was of the opinion that reasonable men would find the law a proper health measure.

Following the *Lochner* decision, the views of the dissenters became the voice of the Court. It upheld an Oregon law setting the hours that women could work "in any mechanical establishment, or factory, or laundry in this State [at] ten hours during any one day."[55] The Court also upheld a New York law which prohibited women from working in restaurants in large cities between the hours of 10 P.M. and 6 A.M.[56] These laws were upheld with the understanding that they did infringe upon the right to work. That infringement was justified, however, because these regulations protected the health and welfare of the workers and were reasonable.

The same kind of debate took place among the justices when they were confronted with a law fixing the minimum wage for women in the District of Columbia.

> [Willie A. Lyons,] twenty-one years of age, was employed by the Congress Hall Hotel Company as an elevator operator, at a salary of $35 per month and two meals a day. She alleges that the work was light and healthful, the hours short, with surroundings clean and moral, and that she was anxious to continue it for the compensation she was receiving and that she did not earn more. Her services were satisfactory to the Hotel Company and it would have been glad to retain her but was obliged to dispense with her services by reason of the order of the board and on account of the penalties prescribed by the act.[57]

The board referred to was the Minimum Wage Board of the District of Columbia, which had ordered the employer to pay certain wages to the employee. The court of appeals upheld permanent injunctions against the Wage Board, prohibiting it from enforcing the minimum wage law, being of the opinion that the wage law was unconstitutional.

An appeal was taken to the Supreme Court, which affirmed, Chief Justice William H. Taft and justices Edward T. Sanford and Holmes dissenting. In seeking a solution to the question of the validity of the law, Justice Sutherland took notice that "the judicial duty of passing upon the constitutionality of an act of Congress is one of great gravity and delicacy." But "to hold [a law] invalid (if it be invalid) is a plain exercise of the judicial power—that power vested in courts to enable them to administer justice according to law."

In seeking the injunction against enforcement of the law, the company argued that the right to contract, which is part of liberty, was being violated in this case. Justice Sutherland, examining that argument, noted that "within this liberty are contracts of employment of labor. In making such contracts, generally speaking, the parties have an equal right to obtain from each other the best terms they can as the result of private bargaining." On that basis, the majority agreed that the law was unconstitutional.

Chief Justice Taft agreed that "the boundary of the police power beyond which its exercise becomes an invasion of the guaranty of liberty under the Fifth and Fourteenth Amendments to the Constitution is not easy to mark." "But," he emphasized, "it is not the function of this Court to hold congressional acts invalid simply because they are passed to carry out economic views which the Court believes to be unwise or unsound." Justice Holmes agreed. If the government could limit the hours workers, as the Court had approved in the case of the miners, it also ought to be able to set their wages. Almost fourteen years later, the views of the dissenters became the position of the majority when the Court overruled the *Willie A. Lyons* case and upheld a Washington law which set minimum wages for women.[58]

But the overruling did not come easily. Four of the justices who voted to strike down the District of Columbia minimum wage law were still on the Court when it considered the Washington case. These justices vigorously dissented to overruling *Lyons*. Justice Brandeis, who was on the Court at the time of the *Lyons* decision but did not participate in it, joined four new justices to overrule that case. Their philosophy was substantially the same as that expressed many times by Justice Holmes. "Liberty under the Constitution," wrote Chief Justice Charles Evans Hughes, "is thus necessarily

subject to the restraints of due process, and regulation which is
reasonable in relation to its subject and is adopted in the interests
of the community is due process."

The dissenters here were not moved by the majority's analysis.
Justice Sutherland expressed their views that the judiciary "must
have the power to say the final work as to the validity of a statute
assailed as unconstitutional." Further, "while there was no such
thing as absolute freedom of contract, . . . [and] that it was subject
to a great variety of restraints, nevertheless, freedom of contract
was the general rule and restraint the exception; and that the power
to abridge that freedom could only be justified by the existence of
exceptional circumstances."

The opinions of Chief Justice Hughes and the majority in the
Washington case are those that prevail today. Those views were expressed by Justice Douglas in a case in which the Court unanimously
upheld an Oklahoma law which made it "unlawful for any person
not a licensed optometrist or ophthalmologist to fit lenses to a
face."⁵⁹ Justice Douglas wrote, "The day is gone when this Court uses
the Due Process Clause of the Fourteenth Amendment to strike
down state laws, regulatory of business and industrial conditions,
because they may be unwise, improvident, or out of harmony with
a particular school of thought." And when the Court had before it
a Kansas law "making it a misdemeanor for any person to engage
'in the business of debt adjusting' except as an incident to 'the lawful
practice of law in this state,'" it unanimously upheld that law.⁶⁰ The
philosophy of cases such as *Lochner* and *Lyons* has "long since been
discarded," Justice Black asserted in the Kansas case, and "we have
returned to the original constitutional proposition that courts do not
substitute their social and economic beliefs for the judgment of
legislative bodies, who are elected to pass laws."

Does this mean that the justices no longer recognize a liberty interest in working, contracting, or engaging in business? No, but it
does mean that anyone asserting such a right as against government
regulation thereof has to establish that the regulation is arbitrary
and unreasonable. And that is a difficult task, for the Court has said:
"The due process clause is [not] to be so broadly construed that the
Congress and state legislatures are put in a straitjacket when they attempt to suppress business and industrial conditions which they
regard as offensive to the public welfare."⁶¹

But the right to work is still alive in some situations. Recently,
Herman Louis Di Martini brought civil rights actions against Lynn

Jay Ferrin, special agent of the FBI, claiming that Ferrin was responsible for Di Martini's begin discharged when he refused to cooperate with the FBI. Among the conclusions reached by a court of appeals was that "Di Martini has a clearly established constitutional right to be free from unreasonable government interference with his private employment."[62]

Liberty and the Bill of Rights

> On the other hand, the due process clause of the Fourteenth Amendment may make it unlawful for a state to abridge by its statutes the freedom of speech which the First Amendment safeguards against encroachment by the Congress, . . . or the like freedom of the press, . . . or the free exercise of religion, . . . or the right of peaceable assembly, . . . or the right of one accused of crime to the benefit of counsel. . . . In these and other situations immunities that are valid as against the federal government by force of the specific pledges of particular amendments have been found to be implicit in the concept of ordered liberty, and thus through the Fourteenth Amendment, become valid as against the states.*

In 1833 the Supreme Court was challenged, for the first time, to decide whether the guarantees embodied in the Bill of Rights gave protection to people from actions of *state governments* as well as from the federal government. The case concerned a wharf owned by John Barron and John Craig in Baltimore Harbor which had been rendered useless after the city had made street improvements that diverted runoff water into the bay near the wharf. Barron and Craig brought suit claiming that the runoff caused sediment to accumulate near the wharf, making it impossible for cargo vessels to tie up there. Having thus been put out of business, they argued that their property had been taken and that they were therefore entitled to just compensation. They relied on that part of the Fifth Amendment which states, "Nor shall private property be taken for public use, without just compensation." "This amendment," they asserted, "being in favour of the liberty of the citizen, ought to be so construed as to restrain the legislative power of a state, as well as that of the United States."[63]

In a comprehensive analysis of the history surrounding the adoption of the Constitution and the Bill of Rights, the Supreme Court concluded that the Bill of Rights applied only to the federal

Palko v. Connecticut, 302 U.S. 319, 324–325 (1937).

government, and therefore Barron and Craig were not entitled to compensation from the city. Chief Justice John Marshall delivered the opinion for the Court.

> We are of the opinion, that the provision in the fifth amendment to the constitution declaring that private property shall not be taken for public use, without just compensation, is intended solely as a limitation on the exercise of power by the government of the United States, and is not applicable to the legislation of the states.

For almost one hundred years, the decision in *Barron's* case was the law of the land. However, following the adoption of the Fourteenth Amendment in 1868, lawyers began to argue that some of the provisions of the Bill of Rights became applicable to the states by virtue of that amendment. They were unsuccessful. In 1925, however, Benjamin Gitlow's case came to the Court.[64] Gitlow was charged with having "advocated, advised and taught the duty, necessity and propriety of overthrowing and overturning organized government by force, violence and unlawful means, by certain writings . . . entitled 'The Left Wing Manifesto.'" This was alleged to be in violation of a New York law punishing "advocacy of criminal anarchy." Gitlow did not deny publishing the *Manifesto* but argued that his actions were protected by the free speech and press clauses of the First Amendment. Although a majority of the justices recognized the First Amendment claim, they nevertheless upheld the conviction, being of the opinion that "the statute is not in itself unconstitutional, and that it [had] not been applied in the present case in derogation of any constitutional right." In referring to the First Amendment, however, Justice Edward T. Sanford wrote:

> For present purposes we may and do assume that freedom of speech and of the press — which are protected by the First Amendment from abridgment by Congress — are among the fundamental personal rights and "liberties" protected by the due process clause of the Fourteenth Amendment from impairment by the States.

Justices Holmes and Brandeis dissented from the affirmance of the conviction because they did not believe that there was any clear and present danger to the government from Gitlow's *Manifesto*. They did, however, agree with the majority that the First Amendment was applicable in this case. "The general principle of free speech, it seems to me," Justice Holmes insisted, "must be taken to be included in the Fourteenth Amendment, in view of the scope that has been given the word 'liberty' as there used."

As noted in the quotation from *Palko*, above, by 1937 the Court had held that most of the covenants contained in the First Amendment were applicable to state action "because they [had] been found to be implicit in the concept of ordered liberty." However, in *Palko*, the Court held that the double jeopardy clause of the Fifth Amendment was not part of the "concept of ordered liberty" and therefore not applicable to the states. In an opinion by Justice Benjamin N. Cardozo, the Court answered the question whether the prohibition of double jeopardy should be applied in state cases.

> Is that kind of double jeopardy to which the statute has subjected [Frank Palko] a hardship so acute and shocking that our polity will not endure it? Does it violate those "fundamental principles of liberty and justice which lie at the base of all our civil and political institutions?" . . . The answer surely is "no."

But almost thirty-two years later the Court overruled the *Palko* decision. At that time Justice Thurgood Marshall pointed out that "our recent cases have thoroughly rejected the *Palko* notion that basic constitutional rights can be denied by the States so long as the totality of the circumstances does not disclose a denial of 'fundamental fairness.' Once it is decided that a particular Bill of Rights guarantee is 'fundamental to the American scheme of justice,' . . . the same constitutional standards apply against both the State and Federal Governments. *Palko's* roots had thus been cut away years ago."[65]

Justice Marshall was certainly correct. By a case-by-case process during those thirty-two years, the Court eventually required states to abide by almost all clauses of the Bill of Rights. Early in this period Justice Black took the position that it was the intention of the writers of the Fourteenth Amendment to require states to comply with *all* provisions of the Bill of Rights thereafter. He expressed his understanding of events leading up to the adoption of the Fourteenth Amendment:

> My study of the historical events that culminated in the Fourteenth Amendment, and the expressions of those who sponsored and favored, as well as those who opposed its submission and passage, persuades me that one of the chief objects that the provisions of the Amendment's first section, separately, and as a whole, were intended to accomplish was to make the Bill of Rights, applicable to the states.[66]

In discussing Roth's position on the faculty, Justice Stewart explained that "as a matter of statutory law, a tenured teacher cannot be 'discharged except for cause upon written charges' and pursuant to certain procedures. A nontenured teacher, similarly, is protected to some extent *during* his one-year term. . . . But the Rules provide no real protection for a nontenured teacher who simply is not re-employed for the next year."[1] The question to be decided, then, was whether these rules gave Roth any kind of liberty or property interest that due process protected. "The requirements of procedural due process," Justice Stewart noted, "apply only to the deprivation of interests encompassed by the Fourteenth Amendment's protection of liberty and property. When protected interests are implicated, the right to some kind of prior hearing is paramount."

In an attempt to find a meaning for the term *liberty* the Court adopted the quotation from the *Meyer* case set forth at the beginning of Chapter 1. And although acknowledging "that the meaning of 'liberty' must be broad indeed," the majority concluded that the decision not to rehire a person such as Roth was not included within that definition. "It stretches the concept too far," Justice Stewart declared, "to suggest that a person is deprived of 'liberty' when he simply is not rehired in one job but remains as free as before to seek another."

Had the school made "any charge against him that might seriously damage his standing and associations in his community," his reputation would have been at stake, and a liberty interest in his good name would have been implicated. Not to have given him a hearing under such circumstances would have been a violation of due process.

Even if no liberty interest of Roth's had been affected by the nonrenewal of his contract, did he have a property interest that could not be taken away without due process of law? Justice Stewart next turned to that question.

> To have a property interest in a benefit, a person clearly must have more than an abstract need or desire for it. He must have more than a unilateral expectation of it. He must, instead, have a legitimate claim of entitlement to it. It is a purpose of the ancient institution of property to protect those claims upon which people rely in their daily lives, reliance that must not be arbitrarily undermined. It is a purpose of the constitutional right to a hearing to provide an opportunity for a person to vindicate those claims.

However:

> Property interests, of course, are not created by the Constitution. Rather, they are created and their dimensions are defined by existing rules or understandings that stem from an independent source such as state law — rules or understandings that secure certain benefits and that support claims of entitlement to those benefits.

In examining the arrangement under which Roth had been hired, the majority noted that his one-year contract gave him no "interest" in future employment. Further, there was no state law or school rule that he could rely upon as evidence of a right to continue his present position. "In these circumstances," Justice Stewart asserted for the majority, "[Roth] surely had an abstract concern in being rehired, but he did not have a *property* interest sufficient to require the University authorities to give him a hearing when they declined to renew his contract of employment."

What he deemed a denial of Roth's free speech rights, caused Justice Douglas to dissent. Taking note that Roth had been very critical of the university's administration, Justice Douglas believed that the decision not to renew the contract was in retaliation for that criticism. Justice Marshall, referring to the constitutional right to work, advanced the idea that "every citizen who applies for a government job is entitled to it unless the government can establish some reason for denying the employment. This is the 'property' right that I believe is protected by the Fourteenth Amendment and that cannot be denied 'without due process of law.' And it is also liberty — liberty to work — which is the 'very essence of the personal freedom and opportunity' secured by the Fourteenth Amendment." This concept of government employment has never been accepted by a majority of justices.

When Is Due Process Due?

> An essential principle of due process is that a deprivation of life, liberty, or property "be preceded by notice and opportunity for hearing appropriate to the nature of the case."*

In the spring of 1968, several New York residents receiving welfare benefits petitioned the federal district court seeking a

Cleveland Board of Education v. Loudermill, 470 U.S. 532, 542 (1985).

declaration that New York's procedure for termination of such benefits was inconsistent with due process standards. New York did provide notice to the beneficiary, a limited discussion with a social worker, and a review of the social worker's decision by a different welfare official. There was no opportunity, however, for the recipient to appear personally before the official and give oral evidence, nor was confrontation and cross-examination of adverse witnesses allowed.

The district court, in an opinion written by Circuit Judge Wilfred Feinberg, held that due process required a pre termination hearing before benefits could be terminated. "The stakes are simply too high," Judge Feinberg maintained, "for the welfare recipient, and the possibility for honest error or irritable misjudgment too great, to allow termination of aid without giving the recipient a chance, if he so desires, to be fully informed of the case against him so that he may contest its basis and produce evidence in rebuttal."[2]

The Supreme Court agreed, three justices dissenting, in *Goldberg v. Kelly*.[3] "The constitutional issue to be decided," the Court's opinion states, "is the narrow one whether the Due Process Clause requires that the recipient be afforded an evidentiary hearing *before* the termination of benefits." By focusing on this issue, the majority assumed and New York agreed, that welfare recipients had a property interest in their benefits which required some procedure consistent with due process. New York argued, however, that its interest in conserving funds available for welfare and the need to save the time and energy of its employees justified its summary proceedings and delay in a formal hearing. Justice Brennan, for the majority, disagreed. "But we agree with the District Court," he wrote, "that when welfare is discontinued, only a pre-termination evidentiary hearing provides the recipient with procedural due process. . . . For qualified recipients, welfare provides the means to obtain essential food, clothing, housing, and medical care." And there are other "important governmental interests [that] are promoted by affording recipients a pre-termination evidentiary hearing. From its founding the Nation's basic commitment has been to foster the dignity and well-being of all persons within its borders. We have come to recognize that forces not within the control of the poor contribute to their poverty. . . . Welfare, by meeting the basic demands of subsistence, can help bring within the reach of the poor the same opportunities that are available to others to participate meaningfully in the life of the community. . . . Public assistance, then, is not mere charity, but a means to 'promote the general Welfare, and secure the Blessings of Liberty to ourselves and our Posterity.'"

Any process which requires the weighing of competing interests, such as those of welfare recipients versus the needs of government, will certainly result in disagreement as to whose interests are of greater value. This case was no exception. In Justice Black's weighing process, the government's interests weighed more. His concern was the impact pre-termination hearings would have on the administrative process. "Although some recipients might be on the lists for payment wholly because of deliberate fraud on their part," he argued, "the Court holds that the government is helpless and must continue, until after an evidentiary hearing, to pay money that it does not owe, never has owed, and never could owe. I do not believe there is any provision in our Constitution that should thus paralyze the government's efforts to protect itself against making payments to people who are not entitled to them."

When George H. Eldridge's claim for continued Social Security disability benefits went through this balancing process, Judge James C. Turk found his interest substantial and held in his favor. Six Supreme Court justices thought that the balance should be in the government's favor and voted to reverse.

Eldridge's request for disability benefits had been granted in 1968 and reviewed periodically thereafter. On the basis of medical reports, the state agency notified him that in their opinion he was able to work and that his benefits would be terminated. He was given an opportunity to submit additional medical information but did not do so, believing that the agency already had enough. The agency's decision was then reviewed by the Social Security Administration, which agreed that the benefits should be terminated. Eldridge then brought an action against Caspar Weinberger, secretary of health, education and welfare, asserting that the process by which the benefits were terminated did not comply with due process. Judge Turk agreed and wrote that Eldridge's "contention that an evidentiary hearing is a constitutional prerequisite to the termination of disability benefits finds support in [*Goldberg v. Kelly*].[4]

In the opinion reversing Judge Turk, Justice Powell stated that "the issue in this case is whether the Due Process Clause of the Fifth Amendment requires that prior to the termination of Social Security disability benefit payments the recipient be afforded an opportunity for an evidentiary hearing."[5] The Fifth Amendment was at issue here because it was that amendment's due process clause that applied to the federal government. Although Justice Powell acknowledged that the Court "consistently [has] held that some form of hearing is required before an individual is finally deprived of a property interest," that hearing did not necessarily have to be *before* the deprivation took place.

The justices then balanced Eldridge's interest in continuation of the benefits against "the administrative burden and other societal costs that would be associated with requiring . . . an evidentiary hearing upon demand in all cases prior to the termination of disability benefits." Disability benefits, the Court believed, were not the same as welfare benefits, because they do not relate to the financial need of the recipient. They are "wholly unrelated to the worker's income or support from many other sources, such as earnings of other family members, workmen's compensation awards, tort claims awards, savings, private insurance, public or private pensions, veterans' benefits, food stamps, public assistance, . . . or the 'many other important programs.'" This weighing of interests led the majority to conclude that no prior evidentiary hearing was necessary because the administrative procedures for a subsequent hearing fully complied with due process.

What Process Is Due?

"The fundamental requisite of due process of law is the opportunity to be heard." . . . The hearing must be "at a meaningful time and in a meaningful manner."*

Once the majority determined in *Goldberg* that welfare recipients had a property interest which required a pre-termination hearing, they were left with the question "What process is due?"

The justices responded to that question: "The extent to which procedural due process must be afforded the recipient is influenced by the extent to which he may be 'condemned to suffer grievous loss' . . . and depends upon whether the recipient's interest in avoiding that loss outweighs the governmental interest in summary adjudication."[6] After examining these elements, the majority's response was that at a minimum the individuals were entitled to a notice setting

---

*Goldberg v. Kelly, 397 U.S. 254, 267 (1970).

forth the reasons for termination, an opportunity to challenge those presenting evidence against them, and time to present their arguments and evidence.

The Court found that under New York's procedure the recipient was given timely and adequate notice. It found fault, however, with the hearing procedures because the beneficiary was not permitted to appear personally or with counsel. This foreclosed the opportunity to confront adverse witnesses and present evidence supporting the continuation of benefits. "The opportunity to be heard must be tailored," Justice Brennan emphasized, "to the capacities and circumstances of those who are to be heard. It is not enough that a welfare recipient may present his position to the decision maker in writing or secondhand through his caseworker. Written submissions are an unrealistic option for most recipients, who lack the educational attainment necessary to write effectively and who cannot obtain professional assistance. Moreover, written submissions do not afford the flexibility of oral presentations; they do not permit the recipient to mold his argument to the issues the decision maker appears to regard as important."[7]

Counsel need not be appointed for the recipient, but if he or she desires to have assistance at the hearing, counsel must be allowed. "Counsel can help delineate the issues, present the factual contentions in an orderly manner, conduct cross-examination, and generally safeguard the interests of the recipient."

Procedures That Protect Liberty

Parents and the Process That's Due

> A parent's interest in the accuracy and justice of the decision to terminate his or her parental status is . . . a commanding one.*

When Wright and Alice Armstrong were divorced in 1959, Mrs. Armstrong was given custody of their daughter, Molly Page Armstrong. The divorce decree required Mr. Armstrong to pay $50 per month for Molly's support. Shortly thereafter, Alice Armstrong married Salvatore E. Manzo, and two years later the Manzos started legal proceedings for Salvatore to adopt Molly.

*Lassiter v. Department of Social Services, 452, U.S. 18, 27 (1981).

At that time, Texas law required written consent from the natural father before an adoption could take place, unless the father had not contributed to the support of the child for at least two years. In the adoption proceedings, the Manzos alleged that Armstrong had not supported Molly for more than two years and asked Judge H. E. Brockmoller of the juvenile court to consent to the adoption without notice to Armstrong, which he did.

When Armstrong learned of the adoption, he immediately filed an action to have the decree set aside, alleging that he had not been notified of the proceedings and therefore had not consented to the adoption. A hearing was granted in which Armstrong introduced evidence that he had not failed to support Molly, but the court affirmed the adoption decree, as did a Texas appellate court.

The Supreme Court reversed, unanimously concluding that by not receiving notice of the pending adoption proceedings, Armstrong had been denied due process of law. This was not a difficult case. Justice Stewart, who delivered the opinion for the Court, wrote that "in disposing of the first issue [lack of notice to Armstrong], there is no occasion to linger long. It is clear that failure to give petitioner notice of the pending adoption proceedings violated the most rudimentary demands of due process of law."[8] Furthermore, Justice Stewart declared, "as to the basic requirement of notice itself there can be no doubt, where, as here, the result of the judicial proceeding was permanently to deprive a legitimate parent of all that parenthood implies."

The Manzos argued that even if notice had not been given, Armstrong had had an opportunity to present evidence in the hearing held after the adoption and that that should fulfill all due process requirements. The Court disagreed. "Had [Armstrong] been given the timely notice which the Constitution requires," Justice Stewart insisted, "the Manzos, as the moving parties [in the adoption proceedings], would have had the burden of proving their case as against whatever defenses the [father] might have interposed."

It would have been incumbent upon them to show not only that Salvatore Manzo met all the requisites of an adoptive parent under Texas law, but also to prove why [Armstrong's] consent to the adoption was not required. Had neither side offered any evidence, those who initiated the adoption proceedings could not have prevailed.

The Court sent the case back to the Texas courts so that Armstrong could be heard on his assertions that he had supported Molly to the best of his ability. Not much guidance was given to the Texas courts, however, as to what would be the essential elements of a due process hearing. Left unanswered, for example, was how great a burden the Manzos had to establish that Armstrong had not contributed to Molly's support for two years and whether Armstrong was entitled to a court-appointed attorney if he could not afford to pay for one himself.

The Court gave a clue to the answer to the first question in a case involving a slightly different setting. John and Annie Santosky were the natural parents of Tina, John III, and Jed. Believing that the children were being neglected, the county, represented by Bernhardt S. Kramer, the commissioner of the Department of Social Services, removed the children and placed them in foster homes. Subsequently the Santoskys had two other children, James and Jeremy. The county petitioned the court to terminate the parental rights to Tina, John III, and Jed.

After conducting a hearing, Judge Hugh R. Elwyn "concluded that the Santoskys were incapable, even with public assistance, of planning for the future of their children . . . and ruled that the best interests of the three children required permanent termination of the Santoskys' custody."[9] Under New York law, a court could find that a child is permanently neglected and take the child away from its parents if a "fair preponderance of the evidence" supported that conclusion. Under this standard, "the factual certainty required to extinguish the parent-child relationship is no greater than that necessary to award money damages in an ordinary civil action." Judge Elwyn's decision to terminate the parental rights of the Santoskys was affirmed by an appellate court, and an appeal to the New York Court of Appeals was dismissed without a hearing.

The Santoskys then sought review in the Supreme Court, which reversed in a 5–4 decision. Justice Harry A. Blackmun, writing for the majority, noted that "the question here is whether New York's 'fair preponderance of the evidence' standard is constitutionally sufficient." The answer that he provided to that question was straightforward.

> Today we hold that the Due Process Clause of the Fourteenth Amendment demands more than this. Before a State may sever completely and irrevocably the rights of parents in their natural child, due process

requires that the State support its allegations by at least clear and convincing evidence.

The beginning for discussion of the question was found in the Supreme Court's "historical recognition that freedom of personal choice in matters of family life is a fundamental liberty interest protected by the Fourteenth Amendment." "In parental rights termination proceedings," therefore, wrote Justice Blackmun, "the private interest affected is commanding; the risk of error from using a preponderance standard is substantial; and the countervailing governmental interest favoring that standard is comparatively slight."

The justices recognized that the state had an interest in the welfare of children and in reducing the cost and burden of termination proceedings. But in balancing these interests against the liberty interest of the parents, the majority concluded that the Santoskys were entitled to another hearing where the question of their unfitness to retain custody of their children would have to be proved by "clear and convincing evidence." It must be kept in mind, Justice Blackmun stressed, that "the fundamental liberty interest of natural parents in the care, custody, and management of their child does not evaporate simply because they have not been model parents or have lost temporary custody of their child to the State."

The dissenters saw the case in an entirely different light. Justice Rehnquist, for the minority, wrote that "the Fourteenth Amendment guarantees that a State will treat individuals with 'fundamental fairness' whenever its actions infringe their protected liberty or property interests." He recognized that "on one side is the interest of parents in a continuation of the family unit and the raising of their own children. The importance of this interest cannot easily be overstated."

"On the other side of the termination proceeding," Rehnquist noted, "are the often countervailing interests of the child. A stable, loving homelife is essential to a child's physical, emotional, and spiritual well-being." Because New York's termination procedures have as their "central purpose" the reuniting of families, Justice Rehnquist argued, the "preponderance of the evidence" standard is an acceptable balance between the conflicting interests of parents and the state.

It may be true that one does not have to be a model parent to be entitled to some due process protection. But one's behavior, or lack of it, may be the determining factor in a court's decision whether to appoint counsel for a parent in a parental termination proceeding. In Abby Gail Lassiter's case, it was the alleged lack of attention to her son, William, that resulted in her losing her parental rights. William was taken from his mother in the spring of 1975 and placed in custody of the Durham (N.C.) County Department of Social Services. In 1976, Abby Lassiter was convicted of second-degree murder and sentenced to twenty-five to forty years in prison. Two years later, the county started proceedings to terminate her parental rights, asserting that "she 'has not had any contact with the child since December of 1975.'"[10]

Lassiter was notified of the hearing and brought from the prison to the court, where a discussion was had concerning "whether Ms. Lassiter should have more time in which to find legal assistance." Judge Samuel F. Gantt concluded that she had had ample time to obtain counsel, and because she did not say that she did not have funds to pay an attorney, he did not appoint one for her. Evidence presented by the department indicated that before the county had taken custody of William, Lassiter had been lax in caring for him and had made little effort to see him. Ms. Lassiter attempted to the best of her ability to cross-examine the social worker who gave this testimony. "Lassiter herself then testified, under the judge's questioning, that she had properly cared for William."

Judge Gantt "found that Ms. Lassiter 'has not contacted the Department of Social Services about her child since December 1975, has not expressed any concern for his care and welfare, and has made no efforts to plan for his future.'" He then terminated her parental rights to William. The appellate courts of North Carolina affirmed.

Five justices of the Supreme Court reached the same conclusion. Four dissented. The question before the Court was whether Lassiter had been denied due process because counsel was not appointed to assist her at the termination hearing. In delivering the opinion for the majority, Justice Stewart took note that due process "expresses the requirement of 'fundamental fairness,' a requirement whose meaning can be as opaque as its importance is lofty. Applying the Due Process Clause is therefore an uncertain enterprise which must discover what 'fundamental fairness' consists of in a particular situation by first considering any relevant precedents and then assessing the several interests that are at stake."

Recognizing that "a parent's interest in the accuracy and justice of the decision to terminate his or her parental status is . . . a commanding one," Justice Stewart then discussed at length the part counsel can play in such proceedings.

> Since the State has an urgent interest in welfare of the child, it shares the parent's interest in an accurate and just decision. For this reason, the State may share the indigent parent's interest in the availability of appointed counsel. If, as our adversary system presupposes, accurate and just results are most likely to be obtained through the equal contest of opposed interests, the State's interest in the child's welfare may perhaps best be served by a hearing in which both the parent and the State acting for the child are represented by counsel, without whom the contest of interests may become unwholesomely unequal.

Furthermore, Justice Stewart emphasized, "the ultimate issues with which a termination hearing deals are not always simple, however commonplace they may be. Expert medical and psychiatric testimony, which few parents are equipped to understand and fewer still to confute, is sometimes presented. The parents are likely to be people with little education, who have had uncommon difficulty in dealing with life, and who are, at the hearing, thrust into a distressing and disorienting situation. That these factors may combine to overwhelm an uncounseled parent is evident from the findings some courts have made." Therefore, "informed opinion has clearly come to hold that an indigent parent is entitled to the assistance of appointed counsel not only in parental termination proceedings, but in dependency and neglect proceedings as well."

In spite of the admission that counsel for the parent and the state would probably result in more fairness and better justice for all, the majority was unwilling to hold that due process required appointment of counsel for all parents who could not afford to hire one, holding that "the decision whether due process calls for the appointment of counsel for indigent parents in termination proceedings [should] be answered in the first instance by the trial court, subject, of course, to appellate review."

Did that approach provide due process to Ms. Lassiter? The majority thought it did. Counsel would not have changed the result. "While hearsay evidence was no doubt admitted, and while Ms. Lassiter no doubt left incomplete her defense that the Department had not adequately assisted her in rekindling her interest in her son, the weight of the evidence that she had few sparks of such an interest was sufficiently great that the presence of counsel for Ms. Lassiter could not have made a determinative difference."

Believing that the majority was not giving sufficient weight to the parental interests at stake, Justice Blackmun authored a dissenting opinion in which justices Brennan and Marshall joined. First he pointed out that even though the Constitution says nothing about family matters, the Court has given them constitutional protection for many years. "The Court," he noted, "has accorded a high degree of constitutional respect to a natural parent's interest in both controlling the details of the child's upbringing . . . and in retaining the custody and companionship of the child."

Justice Blackmun reminded the majority that "the State's aim is not simply to influence the parent-child relationship but to *extinguish* it. A termination of parental rights is both total and irrevocable. Unlike other custody proceedings, it leaves the parent with no right to visit or communicate with the child, to participate in, or even to know about, any important decision affecting the child's religious, educational, emotional, or physical development." Turning to the case before the Court, the justice acknowledged that Lassiter "plainly has not led the life of the exemplary citizen or model parent." "But the issue before the Court," he insisted, "is not [Lassiter's] character; it is whether she was given a meaningful opportunity to be heard when the State moved to terminate absolutely her parental rights." His conclusion was that she had not been given such an opportunity. "I find virtually incredible," he declared, "the Court's conclusion today that her termination proceeding was fundamentally fair."

Justice Stevens, in dissent, chided the majority for putting administrative costs ahead of the rights of parents. "Even if the costs to the State were not relatively insignificant but rather were just as great as the costs of providing prosecutors, judges, and defense counsel to ensure the fairness of criminal proceedings, I would reach the same result in this category of cases. For the value of protecting our liberty from deprivation by the State without due process of law is priceless."

Due Process in Paternity Cases

This Court frequently has stressed the importance of familial bonds, whether or not legitimized by marriage, and accorded them constitu-

tional protection. . . . Just as the termination of such bonds demands
procedural fairness, . . . so too does their imposition.*

"On May 21, 1975, . . . Gloria Streater, while unmarried, gave
birth to a female child, Kenyatta Chantel Streater. As a requirement
stemming from her child's receipt of public assistance, [Streater]
identified . . . Walter Little as the child's father to the Connecticut
Department of Social Services. . . . The Department then provided
an attorney for . . . [her] to bring a paternity suit against . . . [Little]
to establish his liability for the child's support."[11]
    Little, who was in prison at the time, petitioned the court to
have blood-grouping tests made. At that time, Connecticut law required that the person requesting such tests must pay for them, but
Little had no money; therefore, no tests were performed. Without
that evidence, the court heard other testimony and concluded that
Little was the father of Kenyatta. The court entered judgment
against him for support of the child in excess of $6,000 plus continu-
ing support of $163.58 per month. He was to pay $1.00 per month
toward payment of the arrearage and another $1.00 for current sup-
port from his prison income. Connecticut appellate courts affirmed
finding no violation of due process.
    A unanimous Supreme Court reversed, Chief Justice Warren
Burger delivering the opinion for the Court. The chief justice reviewed
the due process standards the Courts had previously established
and announced that "these standards govern [Little's] due process
claim, which is premised on the unique quality of blood grouping
tests as a source of exculpatory evidence, the State's prominent role
in the litigation, and the character of paternity actions under Connecticut law." The chief justice discussed the scientific development
of blood tests and noted that in negating paternity, they are 91
percent accurate for black men and 93 percent accurate for white
men.
    In examining Connecticut's paternity proceedings, the chief
justice found that although they are considered "civil," they "have
'quasi-crinimal' overtones." "If a putative father 'is found *guilty*,'" he
noted, "'the court shall order him to stand charged with the support
and maintenance of such child;' . . . and his subsequent failure to
comply with the court's order is punishable by imprisonment."

*Little v. Streater, 452 U.S. 1, 13 (1981).

Of further concern to the justices was the fact that under Connecticut law, if a mother was "'constant' in her accusation" that a certain person was the father, that was enough to make out a prima facie case of paternity, and the alleged father had the burden of introducing evidence to the contrary, but his testimony alone was not enough. This brought the Court to the conclusion that without blood-test evidence, a person "who must overcome the evidentiary burden Connecticut imposes, lacks 'a meaningful opportunity to be heard.' . . . Therefore, 'the requirement of 'fundamental fairness' expressed by the Due Process Clause was not satisfied here."

In *Santosky*, discussed above, the Court held that in proceedings to terminate parental rights, fundamental fairness required that the state prove by "clear and convincing evidence" that the children were permanently neglected. The case of *Rivera v. Minnich*[12] brought to the Court the question whether the "clear and convincing" standard was also applicable in *paternity* proceedings. Eight justices held that due process did not require such a strict standard and that paternity could be established by a "preponderance of the evidence."

Rivera began when Jean Marie Minnich gave birth to Cory Michael Minnich and commenced an action against Gregory Rivera for support claiming he was Cory's father. Before the case came to trial, Gregory requested the trial judge to instruct the jury that his paternity must be established by "clear and convincing evidence." The judge refused to do so, and the jury subsequently found that the preponderance of the evidence proved Gregory the father. The state supreme court affirmed, with Chief Justice Robert N. C. Nix, Jr., dissenting. He thought that the same rule which applies to termination of parental rights should be used when the state attempts to prove parentage. The Supreme Court disagreed, with only Justice Brennan dissenting, and upheld the lower court's decision that Gregory was Cory's father.

In approving the use of the "preponderance of the evidence" standard in paternity cases, Justice Stevens for the majority discussed two reasons why that standard would not violate due process. First, paternity cases are civil in nature, and the preponderance standard is the one used in such cases. "More specifically," he stated, "it is the same standard that is applied in paternity litigation in the majority of American jurisdictions that regard such proceedings as civil in nature." Second, he emphasized that there was a great difference between termination of the parent-child relationship and the establishment of paternity. "Resolving the question whether there is a casual connection between an alleged physical act of a putative father," Justice Stevens insisted, "and the subsequent birth of [a child] sufficient to impose financial liability on the father will not trammel any pre-existing rights; the putative father has no legitimate right and certainly no liberty interest in avoiding financial obligations to his natural child that are validly imposed by state law." On the other hand, "the parent's desire for, and right to, the companionship, care, and custody of his children [is] 'an interest far more precious than any property right.'" That interest, therefore, should be protected by requiring "clear and convincing evidence" of neglect before it is ended.

Justice Brennan did not accept the majority's position that there was a great difference between termination of parental relationships and finding paternity. "The establishment of a parental relationship," he claimed, "may at the outset have fewer emotional consequences than the termination of one. It has, however, the potential to set in motion a process of engagement that is powerful and cumulative, and whose duration spans a lifetime." He was also concerned about the "social stigma" resulting from the finding of paternity. A putative father "is seen as a parent apparently impervious to the moral demand of that role, who must instead be coerced by law to fulfill his obligation." This brought Justice Brennan to the conclusion that "a paternity proceeding thus implicates significant property and liberty interests of [Rivera]."

The majority did not believe that a paternity action affected any liberty interest of Rivera's in his attempt to avoid being found Cory's father.

Would it then follow that a man who seeks to establish his parentage but is prevented from doing so by state law would also not have a liberty interest? This unusual question came to the Court in the case of *Michael H. v. Gerald D.*[13]

In May 1981, . . . Victoria D. was born to Carole D., who was married to and resided with . . . Gerald D. in California. Although Gerald was listed as father on the birth certificate and has always claimed Victoria as his daughter, blood tests showed a 98.07 % probability that . . . Michael H., with whom Carole had had an adulterous affair, was Victoria's father. During Victoria's first three years, she and her mother resided at times with Michael, who held her out as his own, at times with another man, and at times with Gerald, with whom they have lived since June 1984.

Michael H. brought an action against Gerald, Carole, and Victoria to establish that he was Victoria's father and for visitation rights. Judge Stephen M. Lachs granted judgment against Michael, relying upon a state law which provided "that a child born to a married woman living with her husband, who is either impotent nor sterile, is presumed to be a child of the marriage, and that this presumption may be rebutted only by the husband or wife." A court of appeal affirmed, concluding that Michael's due process claim of a parental liberty interest in Victoria was outweighed by the state's interest in preservation of the existing family relationship as well as the welfare of Victoria.

When the case reached the Supreme Court, it spawned five opinions, none of which commanded a majority of the justices. Five justices, however, did agree that "Michael H. has a liberty interest in his relationship with Victoria." One of these, Justice Stevens, agreed with Judge Lachs that the best interests of Victoria outweighed Michael's liberty interest. "The record . . . shows," he pointed out, "that after its rather shaky start, the marriage between Carole and Gerald developed a stability that now provides Victoria with a loving and harmonious family home."

For dissenting justices Brennan, Marshall, and Blackmun, the fault with the law's presumption that makes the husband the father of the child is that it denies the real father the opportunity to be heard with regard to any rights he may have. "We must first understand the nature of the challenged statute," Justice Brennan wrote. "It is a law that stubbornly insists that Gerald is Victoria's father, in the face of evidence showing a 98 percent probability that her father is Michael. What Michael wants is a chance to show that he is Victoria's father. By depriving him of this opportunity, California prevents Michael from taking advantage of the best-interest standard embodied in [the law], which directs that *parents* be given visitation rights unless 'the visitation would be detrimental to the best interest of the child.'"

Justice White also thought that Michael had a liberty interest in a relationship with Victoria and that the statutory presumption denies him due process protection for that interest. "California plainly denies Michael this protection, by refusing him the opportunity to rebut the State's presumption that the mother's husband is the father of the child."

Four justices — Scalia, O'Connor, Kennedy, and Chief Justice Rehnquist — concluded that Michael had no due process rights that the statute infringed upon. Quoting from a previous case, these justices pointed out that "the Due Process Clause affords only those protections 'so rooted in the traditions and conscience of our people as to be ranked fundamental.'" "Thus, the legal issue in the present case," Justice Scalia maintained, "reduces to whether the relationship between persons in the situation of Michael and Victoria has been treated as a protected family unit under the historic practices of our society, or whether on any other basis it has been accorded special protection. We think it impossible to find that it has. In fact, quite to the contrary, our traditions have protected the marital family (Gerald, Carole, and the child they acknowledge to be theirs) against the sort of claim Michael asserts."

Juveniles and the Due Process Clause

> The same considerations that demand extreme caution in factfinding to protect the innocent adult apply as well to the innocent child.*

Winship's case was not a complicated one. He was a twelve-year-old boy who stole $112 from a woman's pocketbook. When he was brought into New York Family Court, he was charged with doing an act that "if done by an adult, would constitute the crime or crimes of Larceny."[14]

When Judge Joseph C. Di Carlo heard the case, he "acknowledged that the proof might not establish guilt beyond a reasonable doubt, but rejected [Winship's] contention that such proof was required by the Fourteenth Amendment." State law required that Judge Di Carlo's finding that Winship had committed the acts "must be based on a preponderance of the evidence." Using that standard, the judge found that Winship had committed the acts, and he therefore sentenced him to a training school for eighteen months, such sentence to be reviewed annually with the possibility that Winship could be incarcerated for as many as six years.

An appellate court affirmed, as did the New York Court of Appeals in a 4–3 decision. The Supreme Court reversed, with three justices dissenting. The majority opinion, written by Justice Brennan, states the question before the Court:

*In re Winship, 397 U.S. 358, 365 (1970).

This case presents the single, narrow question whether proof beyond a reasonable doubt is among the "essentials of due process and fair treatment" required during the adjudicatory stage when a juvenile is charged with an act which would constitute a crime if committed by an adult.

Beginning its analysis of the question, the majority noted that "the requirement that guilt of a criminal charge be established by proof beyond a reasonable doubt dates at least from our early years as a Nation." And "lest there remain any doubt about the constitutional stature of reasonable-doubt standard, we explicitly hold that the Due Process Clause protects the accused against conviction except upon proof beyond a reasonable doubt of every fact necessary to constitute the crime with which he is charged."

Does that mean that juveniles are also protected by the reasonable-doubt standard when they are charged with violation of a criminal law in juvenile delinquency proceedings? New York argued that they should not be because those proceedings were not really criminal; there was no real conviction; and the proceedings "are designed 'not to punish, but to save the child.'" These arguments fell on deaf ears. Justice Brennan responded by referring to the *Gault* case in which the Court had rejected similar arguments. Having thus disposed of the state's contentions, the majority said that they agreed with Chief Judge Stanley H. Fuld, of the New York Court of Appeals, who wrote in dissent when the case was in that court that "where a 12-year-old child is charged with an act of stealing which renders him liable to confinement for as long as six years, then, as a matter of due process . . . the case against him must be proved beyond a reasonable doubt."

In concurring, Justice Harlan expressed one of the basic principles underlying our American system of justice. "I view," he proclaimed, "the requirement of proof beyond a reasonable doubt in a criminal case as bottomed on a fundamental value determination of our society that it is far worse to convict an innocent man than to let a guilty man go free." Furthermore, Justice Harlan did not believe that imposing the reasonable-doubt standard on juvenile courts would in any way jeopardize the state's purpose of treating juveniles differently than adults. "I think it worth emphasizing that the requirement of proof beyond a reasonable doubt that a juvenile committed a criminal act before he is found to be a delinquent does not (1) interfere with the worthy goal of rehabilitating the juvenile,

(2) make any significant difference in the extent to which a youth is stigmatized as a 'criminal' because he has been found to be a delinquent, or (3) burden the juvenile courts with a procedural requirement that will make juvenile adjudications significantly more time consuming, or rigid."

This decision, however, greatly disturbed Chief Justice Burger and Justice Stewart. Their concern was with the effect it would have upon the juvenile justice system. The chief justice expressed these concerns. "Since I see no constitutional requirement of due process sufficient to overcome the legislative judgment of the States in this area, I dissent from further strait-jacketing of an already overly restricted system. What the juvenile court system needs is not more but less of the trappings of legal procedure and judicial formalism; the juvenile court system requires breathing room and flexibility in order to survive, if it can survive the repeated assaults from this Court."

Justice Black restated his long-held view that the only restrictions on the state's conduct of criminal proceedings are those found in the Bill of Rights. "In two places the Constitution," he insisted, "provides for trial by jury, but nowhere in that document is there any statement that conviction of crime requires proof of guilt beyond a reasonable doubt. The Constitution thus goes into some detail to spell out what kind of a trial a defendant charged with crime should have, and I believe the Court has no power to add to or subtract from the procedures set forth by the Founders."

The debate over what procedures were necessary in juvenile court to provide the minor with due process did not end with *Winship*. A little over two years later, the cases of Joseph McKeiver and Edward Terry came to the Court from Pennsylvania and Barbara Burrus's case from North Carolina.

> It suffices to say that McKeiver's offense was his participating with 20 or 30 youths who pursued three young teenagers and took 25 cents from them; that McKeiver never before had been arrested and had a record of gainful employment; that the testimony of two of the victims was described by the court as somewhat inconsistent and as "weak"; and that Terry's offense consisted of hitting a police officer with his fists and with a stick when the officer broke up a boys' fight Terry and others were watching.[15]

Barbara Burrus was one of "approximately 45 other black children, ranging in age from 11 to 15 years," who were involved in some demonstrations protesting school assignments and consolidation. They were charged "with willfully impeding traffic."

When Joseph McKeiver's attorney requested a jury trial for him, Judge Theodore S. Gutowicz denied the request and after hearing the evidence, adjudged Joseph a delinquent. Judge Gutowicz placed him on probation.

Edward Terry's counsel also requested that he be tried before a jury, but Judge Joseph C. Bruno refused to grant the request. He held that Edward was a delinquent and committed him to the Youth Development Center. The supreme court of Pennsylvania reviewed both cases and affirmed each, deciding that due process did not require a jury trial in juvenile proceedings. The same process was repeated in the case of Burrus and her friends in North Carolina. In addition, the general public was excluded from those proceedings.

Six justices of the U.S. Supreme Court agreed with the result reached in Pennsylvania and North Carolina, but two of them, justices Brennan and Harlan, did so for reasons that differed from those of the other four. In an opinion authored by Justice Blackmun, the plurality agreed with prior cases in which the Court had held that "some of the constitutional requirements attendant upon the state criminal trial have equal application to that part of the state juvenile proceeding that is adjudicative in nature." And that was required to provide "fundamental fairness" to juvenile court proceedings. The plurality acknowledged that the goals of the juvenile court system had not been realized. Nevertheless, they held that "the imposition of the jury trial on the juvenile court system would not strengthen greatly, if at all, the factfinding function, and would, contrarily, provide an attrition of the juvenile court's assumed ability to function in a unique manner. It would not remedy the defects in the system."

Justice Brennan concurred in the judgment in McKeiver's and Terry's cases, even though they were tried without a jury, because the public's attendance at their attendance at their trials provided sufficient safeguards to comply with due process. "The availability of trial by jury," he declared, "allows an accused to protect himself against possible oppression by what is in essence an appeal to the community conscience, as embodied in the jury that hears his case. To some extent, however, a similar protection may be obtained when an accused may in essence appeal to the community at large, by focusing public attention upon the facts of his trial, exposing improper judicial behavior to public view, and obtaining,

if necessary, executive redress through the medium of public in-
dignation."

Dissenting justices Douglas, Black, and Marshall would have
required the states to abide by the Sixth Amendment and provide
jury trials for minors as for adults. Among their concerns was the
fact that McKeiver and Terry could have been incarcerated for as
long as five years, and Burrus and her friends in North Carolina
could have faced imprisonment from six to ten years. "By reason of
the Sixth and Fourteenth Amendments," Justice Douglas argued,
"the juvenile is entitled to a jury trial 'as a matter of right where the
delinquency charged is an offense that, if the person were an adult,
would be a crime triable by jury.'"

Civil Commitment of the Mentally Ill

> This Court repeatedly has recognized that civil commitment for any
> purpose constitutes a significant deprivation of liberty that requires
> due process protection.*

The Court has not had the opportunity to articulate all the procedures that due process requires in the commitment of a mentally
ill person to an institution. When such cases have come to the Court,
the justices have been concerned with the fundamental fairness of
the commitment process, thus giving recognition to the fact that
such process involves a "significant deprivation of liberty."

The justices had no difficulty in finding that Edward McNeil's
confinement in a Maryland institution was unfair. McNeil had been
convicted of assault and sentenced to five years' imprisonment. Instead of being sent to a prison, however, the trial judge sent him to
an institution for the mentally ill "to determine whether he should
be committed to that institution for an indeterminate time under
Maryland's Defective Delinquency Law."[16]

Before the state could make a decision that McNeil was a defective delinquent, his sentence had expired. Because he allegedly refused
to cooperate with psychiatrists during his confinement, the state
kept him at the institution indefinitely. He sought to obtain release
from Maryland courts, but that was denied. He then petitioned the
Supreme Court, arguing that "when his sentence expired, the State
lost its power to hold him, and that his continued detention violates

---

*Addington v. Texas, 441 U.S. 418, 425 (1979).

his rights under the Fourteenth Amendment." The justices unanimously agreed.

The state argued that it had the power to retain McNeil indefinitely without judicial permission "merely for observation." Justice Marshall responded for the Court that McNeil has "been committed 'for observation' for six years, and on [the state's] theory of his confinement there is no reason to believe it likely that he will ever be released." The state then argued that because of McNeil's refusal to talk to the psychiatrist, examining him was very difficult. And his confinement was therefore similar to civil contempt, which he could change at any time simply by cooperating with medical personnel. But Justice Marshall pointed out that "the contempt analogy cannot justify the State's failure to provide a hearing of any kind." The Court then ordered that McNeil be released.

Releasing McNeil, however, did not foreclose the state from starting civil commitment procedures against him which would have given him a hearing before a judicial officer with authority to determine whether there were sufficient grounds to institutionalize him.

Civil commitment of the mentally ill, like detention of a juvenile, is not considered a criminal proceeding. However, as the Court held in *Winship*, confinement of a juvenile can occur only after a judicial finding, "beyond a reasonable doubt," that the juvenile committed the acts with which he or she is charged. In cases involving other important interests, such as termination of parental rights and deportation, a decision can be made only upon a finding of "clear and convincing" evidence. And juries are required to use the "preponderance of the evidence" standard in ordinary civil cases. Should there be a different standard for the confinement of one who is mentally ill?

Frank O'Neal Addington's case presented the Court with the question "What standard of proof is required by the Fourteenth Amendment to the Constitution in a civil proceeding brought under state law to commit an individual involuntarily for an indefinite period to a state mental hospital."[17] After Addington threatened to harm his mother, she filed a petition to have him committed to an institution.

> The State offered evidence that [Addington] suffered from
> serious delusions, that he often had threatened to injure both of his

The trial . . . extended over six days.

parents and others, that he had been involved in several assaultive
episodes while hospitalized and that he had caused substantial property damage both at his own apartment and at his parents' home.
From these undisputed facts, two psychiatrists, who qualified as ex-
perts, expressed opinions that [Addington] suffered from psychotic
schizophrenia and that he had paranoid tendencies. They also expressed medical opinions that [he] was probably dangerous both to
himself and to others.

Addington, through his counsel, agreed that he had a mental
illness but argued that there was no evidence to show that he was
dangerous. Judge Jerome Jones, who presided at the trial, submitted
two questions to the jury:

> 1. Based on clear, unequivocal and convincing evidence, is
> Frank O'Neal Addington mentally ill?
> 2. Based on clear, unequivocal and convincing evidence, does
> Frank O'Neal Addington require hospitalization in a mental hospital
> for his own welfare and protection or the protection of others?

Addington's counsel objected to these questions, arguing that the
jury should have been instructed that their answers to the questions
must be based upon "proof beyond a reasonable doubt."

The jury responded with affirmative answers to both questions:
Addington was mentally ill and should be hospitalized. The trial of
this case through the appellate process was somewhat unusual. The
Texas Court of Appeals agreed with Addington that Judge Jones had
erred and that he should have instructed the jury that their answers
to the questions must be based upon findings beyond a reasonable
doubt. It reversed and sent the case back to Judge Jones. The Texas
Supreme Court thought differently. Because it had previously held
"that a 'preponderance of the evidence' standard of proof in a civil
commitment proceeding satisfied due process,' the supreme court
reversed.

In an opinion written by Chief Justice Burger in which seven
justices joined, the U.S. Supreme Court reversed and sent the case
back to the Texas Supreme Court "for further proceedings not inconsistent with this opinion." Justice Lewis F. Powell did not participate.

To put the analysis in proper perspective, the chief justice
discussed the role that the standard of proof plays in fact-finding.

"The function of a standard of proof," he said, "as that concept is embodied in the Due Process Clause and in the realm of factfinding, is to 'instruct the factfinder concerning the degree of confidence our society thinks he should have in the correctness of factual conclusions for a particular type of adjudication.'"

> At one end of the spectrum is the typical civil case involving a monetary dispute between parties. Since society has a minimal concern with the outcome of such private suits, plaintiff's burdened of proof is a mere preponderance of the evidence....
>
> In a criminal case, on the other hand, the interests of the defendant are of such magnitude that historically and without any explicit constitutional requirement they have been protected by standards of proof designed to exclude as nearly as possible the likelihood of an erroneous judgment. In the administration of criminal justice, our society imposes almost the entire risk of error upon itself. This is accomplished by requiring under the Due Process Clause that the state prove the guilt of an accused beyond a reasonable doubt....
>
> The intermediate standard, which usually employs some combination of the words, 'clear,' 'cogent,' 'unequivocal' and 'convincing,' is less commonly used, but nonetheless is no stranger to the civil law.

The chief justice then admitted that jurors may find it difficult to distinguish one standard from another. "Candor suggests," he acknowledged, "that, to a degree, efforts to analyze what lay jurors understand concerning the differences among these three tests or the nuances of a judge's instructions on the law may well be largely an academic exercise; there are no directly relevant empirical studies. Indeed, the ultimate truth as to how the standards of proof affect decisionmaking may well be unknowable, given that factfinding is a process shared by countless thousands of individuals throughout the country." Nevertheless, the problem needs a solution, one which will accommodate both the interests of the state in providing for the care of persons with mental disorders as well as the right of those persons to be free from unnecessary confinement.

The justices were concerned that the "preponderance" standard might result in some people being incarcerated for nothing more than different or unusual behavior. "At one time or another," the chief justice suggested, "every person exhibits some abnormal behavior which might be perceived by some as symptomatic of a mental or emotional disorder, but which is in fact within a range of

conduct that is generally acceptable. Obviously such behavior is
no basis for compelled treatment and surely none for confinement."
On the other hand, "given the lack of certainty and the fallibility
of psychiatric diagnosis, there is a serious question as to whether
a state could ever prove beyond a reasonable doubt that an individual is both mentally ill and likely to be dangerous." The Court's decision, then, was to conclude that the proper standard was at the
middle level — "clear and convincing," but not necessarily "clear,
unequivocal and convincing," as Judge Jones had instructed the
jury.

At the time the Court upheld the right of parents to commit
their children to a mental hospital, in J.L.'s *and* J.R.'s case, it also
spelled out the procedural requirements necessary to comply with
due process.

> We now turn to consideration of what process protects adequately
> the child's constitutional rights by reducing risks of error without un-
> duly trenching on traditional parental authority and without under-
> cutting "efforts to further the legitimate interests of both the state and
> the patient that are served by" voluntary commitments.[18]

The justices thought that protection of the child's interests would
best be served by a "neutral factfinder," who could see that all of the
state's commitment requirements had been met. "That inquiry,"
Chief Justice Burger explained, "must carefully probe the child's
background using all available sources, including, but not limited
to, parents, schools, and other social agencies. Of course, the review
must also include an interview with the child. It is necessary that the
decisionmaker have the authority to refuse to admit any child who
does not satisfy the medical standards for admission. Finally, it is
necessary that the child's continuing need for commitment be
reviewed periodically by a similarly independent procedure." The
Court then examined the procedures under which J.L. and J.R. were
committed and found them "consistent with constitutional guarantees."

Justices Brennan, Marshall, and Stevens, however, thought
that the Court was not giving sufficient consideration to the interests
of the minors in approving the state's commitment procedures. "Notions of parental authority and family autonomy," Justice Brennan
declared, "cannot stand as absolute and invariable barriers to the

assertion of constitutional rights by children." Furthermore, "children incarcerated in public mental institutions are constitutionally entitled to a fair opportunity to contest the legitimacy of their confinement. They are entitled to some champion who can speak on their behalf and who stands ready to oppose a wrongful commitment."

Prisoners, Parolees, and Probationers

> Our cases hold that the convicted felon does not forfeit all constitutional protections by reason of his conviction and confinement in prison.*

A federal district court in Nebraska from which Larry Jones sought protection when the state transferred him from a prison to a mental hospital held that such transfer affected his liberty interests and that therefore procedures consistent with due process were necessary. The Court spelled out precisely the due process requirements.

A. Written notice to the prisoner that a transfer to a mental hospital is being considered:
B. A hearing, sufficiently after the notice to permit the prisoner to prepare, at which disclosure to the prisoner is made of the evidence being relied upon for the transfer and at which an opportunity to be heard in person and to present documentary evidence is given;
C. An opportunity at the hearing to present testimony of witnesses by the defense and to confront and cross-examine witnesses called by the state, except upon a finding, not arbitrarily made, of good cause for not permitting such presentation, confrontation, or cross-examination;
D. An independent decisionmaker;
E. A written statement by the factfinder as to the evidence relied on and the reasons for transferring the inmate;
F. Availability of legal counsel, furnished by the state, if the inmate is financially unable to furnish his own; and
G. Effective and timely notice of all foregoing rights.[19]

A majority of the Supreme Court, in an opinion authored by Justice White, approved all of the above requirements except

---

Meachum v. Fano, 427 U.S. 215, 225 (1976).

paragraph F, relating to the appointment of counsel if the inmate could not afford one. "Because prisoners facing involuntary transfer to a mental hospital are threatened with immediate deprivation of liberty interests they are currently enjoying," Justice White argued, "and because of the inherent risk of a mistaken transfer, the District Court properly determined that procedures similar to those required by the court [in the *Morrissey* case] were appropriate in the circumstances present here."

Only four justices, however, agreed that the district court was right in also requiring the appointment of counsel for indigent inmates being transferred to the hospital. Justice Powell, who approved all except paragraph F, did not believe that "the fairness of an informal hearing designed to determine a medical issue requires participation by lawyers, . . . so long as an inmate facing involuntary transfer to a mental hospital is provided qualified and independent assistance."

When the Court heard this case, Jones was back in prison and was scheduled to be released in about two years. Four justices, therefore, thought the case was moot and would have ordered it dismissed.

When the Court determined in *Morrissey* that parolees had a liberty interest in retaining their freedom, it turned its attention to the question, What process is due? The justices found "two important stages in the typical process of parole revocation."[20] The first stage is when the parolee is arrested. Because he or she may have been arrested some distance from the prison and some time would probably elapse before the formal parole-board hearing, some minimal inquiry should be made at the time of arrest. Such a preliminary hearing should determine whether there was "probable cause" that the individual had committed the acts with which he is charged. "In our view," Chief Justice Burger declared, "due process requires that after the arrest, the determination that reasonable ground exists for revocation of parole should be made by someone not directly involved in the case." The justices did not want to say that the parole officer might or might not be biased. "We need make no assumptions one way or the other to conclude that there should be an uninvolved person to make this preliminary evaluation of the basis for believing the conditions of parole have been violated. The officer directly involved in making recommendations cannot always have complete objectivity in evaluating them."

The parolee is entitled to notice of the hearing and to be informed of his alleged violations. He should be able to appear and speak on his own behalf and present relevant evidence. Unless there is some personal risk to those testifying adversely to the parolee, he should have the opportunity to question them. The person conducting the hearing should make a summary of the evidence, and based upon this report, the parolee may be detained until a decision is made by the parole board whether to revoke the parole.

The chief justice pointed out that insofar as the revocation hearing is concerned, the Court's "task is limited to deciding the minimum requirement of due process" for that hearing. Those requirements

> include (a) written notice of the claimed violations of parole; (b) disclosure to the parolee of evidence against him; (c) opportunity to be heard in person and to present witnesses and documentary evidence; (d) the right to confront and cross-examine adverse witnesses (unless the hearing officer specifically finds good cause for not allowing confrontation); (e) a "neutral and detached" hearing body such as a traditional parole board, members of which need not be judicial officers or lawyers; and (f) a written statement by the fact-finders as to the evidence relied on and reasons for revoking parole. We emphasize there is no thought to equate this second stage or parole revocation to a criminal prosecution in any sense. It is a narrow inquiry; the process should be flexible enough to consider evidence including letters, affidavits, and other material that would not be admissible in an adversary criminal trial.

The justices then decided not to decide whether the parolee was entitled to have counsel represent him at the hearing.

Justice Douglas dissented in part. He would have required that the parolee remain free until the revocation hearing is held unless the violation in a new criminal offense. And he should be "entitled to counsel."

About a year after *Morrissey*, the question of the right to counsel came to the Court again in *Gagnon v. Scarpelli*.[21] Gerald Scarpelli, who had pleaded guilty to armed robbery, was out on probation when he was surprised by the police in the midst of burglarizing a home. He was returned to prison and his probation revoked without a hearing. He brought an action in federal district court seeking release. Judge John W. Reynolds held that the revocation of probation without a hearing violated due process, and the court of appeals affirmed, as did the Supreme Court.

The Court first held that "a probationer, like a parolee, is entitled to a preliminary and a final revocation hearing, under the conditions specified in *Morrissey v. Brewer.*" But the more difficult question, Justice Powell wrote for the majority, was "whether an indigent probationer or parolee has a due process right to be represented by appointed counsel at these hearings." All justices except Justice Douglas held that the decision to appoint counsel should be decided by the body conducting the hearing on a case-by-case basis. Recognizing that both the individual and the state had an interest in the hearing, the majority was concerned that the presence of counsel might change the proceeding and make it "less attuned to the rehabilitative needs of the individual probationer or parolee." In addition, Justice Powell asserted, "the decisionmaking process will be prolonged, and the financial cost to the State—for appointed counsel, counsel for the State, a longer record, and the possibility of judicial review—will not be insubstantial." For these reasons, the majority believed that appointment of counsel on a case-by-case basis would satisfy due process. Justice Douglas disagreed.

Morrissey and *Gagnon* dealt with revocation of parole and probation, situations in which the individual faced the possibility of losing his or her freedom and being returned to prison. This differs, of course, from the situation where the grant of probation or parole will free the prisoner. In those cases, such as the *Allen/Jacobsen* case, where the Court held that Montana law created a liberty interest in parole, the Court has not required the same kind of procedural due process. A more informal proceeding is permissible.

Citizenship and Due Process

> To take away a man's citizenship deprives him of a right no less precious than life or liberty, indeed of one which today comprehends those rights and almost all others.*

When Gin Sang Get and Gin Sang Mo arrived in the United States, they claimed American citizenship. Before allowing them to enter, the Immigration and Naturalization Service conducted a hearing and "ordered them admitted as citizens."[22] Some months later, both were arrested in Arizona, where they had been living, and ordered deported. They sought a writ of habeas corpus from

---

*Justice Rutledge, concurring in Klapprott v. United States, 335 U.S. 601, 616 (1949).

Judge Frank H. Rudkin, of a federal district court in California, which was denied. The court of appeals affirmed, but all justices of the Supreme Court disagreed.

"The constitutional question presented as to [Get and Mo]," Justice Brandeis wrote, "is: May a resident of the United States who claims to be a citizen be arrested and deported on executive order?" In answering the question in the negative, the justices held that "jurisdication in the executive [president] to order deportation exists only if the person arrested is an alien." When a person claims to be a citizen, however, jurisdiction no longer resides in the president.

> To deport one who so claims to be a citizen, obviously deprives him of liberty. . . . It may result also in loss of both property and life; or of all that makes life worth living. Against the danger of such deprivation without the sanction by judicial proceedings, the Fifth Amendment affords protection in its guarantee of due process of law.

"It [therefore] follows," Justice Brandeis asserted, "that Gin Sang Get and Gin Sang Mo are entitled to a judicial determination of their claims that they are citizens of the United States; but it does not follow that they should be [immediately] discharged."

In Get and Mo's case, the Court held that some due process is necessary when the government attempts to deport someone who claims to be a U.S. citizen. Closely akin to this case is one where the government attempts to revoke citizenship previously granted. Revocation can occur when a person has obtained citizenship by giving false information at the time of application. The Court has held that "in view of the grave consequences to the citizen, naturalization decrees are not lightly to be set aside — the evidence must indeed by 'clear, unequivocal, and convincing' and not leave 'the issue . . . in doubt.'"[23]

While revocation is concerned with the validity of the original grant of citizenship, expatriation generally deals with taking away citizenship because the person has done some act inconsistent with allegiance to his or her country. In *Afroyim v. Rusk*,[24] however, the Court held that "Congress has no power under the Constitution to divest a person of his United States citizenship absent his voluntary renunciation thereof."

> [Beys Afroyim], born in Poland in 1893, immigrated to this country in 1912 and became a naturalized American citizen in 1926. He went

to Israel in 1950, and in 1951 he voluntarily voted in an election for
the Israeli Knesset, the legislative body of Israel. In 1960, when he
applied for renewal of his United States passport, the Department of
State refused to grant it on the sole ground that he had lost his
American citizenship by virtue of . . . the Nationality Act of 1940
which provides that a United States citizen shall "lose" his citizenship
if he votes "in a political election in a foreign state."

Afroyim sought a declaration from District Judge Frederick van
Pelt Bryan that the law was unconstitutional, which was denied.
Five justices of the Supreme Court voted to reverse, relying upon the
Fourteenth Amendment, which reads in part: "All persons born or
naturalized in the United States, and subject to the jurisdiction
thereof, are citizens of the United States and of the state wherein
which they reside."

Justice Black, writing for the majority, acknowledged that the
clause was intended to protect the citizenship of blacks but insisted
that the goal "would be frustrated by holding that the Government
can rob a citizen of his citizenship without his consent."

In some instances, loss of citizen can mean that a man is left without
the protection of citizenship in any country in the world — as a man
without a country. Citizenship in this Nation is a part of a cooperative affair. Its citizenry is the country and the country is its citizenry.
The very nature of our free government makes it completely in-
congruous to have a rule of law under which a group of citizens tem-
porarily in office can deprive another group of citizens of their citizenship. We hold that the Fourteenth Amendment was designed to,
and does, protect every citizen of this Nation against a congressional
forcible destruction of his citizenship, whatever his creed, color, or
race. Our holding does no more than give to this citizen that which
is his own, a constitutional right to remain a citizen in a free country
unless he voluntarily relinquishes that citizenship.

The dissenters, led by Justice Harlan, did not believe that the
citizenship clause created "an additional and entirely unwarranted,
restriction upon legislative authority" over citizenship. Despite the
majority's holding that government cannot take away citizenship, a
person can lose it if he or she voluntarily commits an act of expatriation. And a finding of voluntariness may be established on a mere
preponderance of the evidence. That was a decision of a majority

of the justices in Lawrence J. Terrazas's case. Terrazas became a citizen of Mexico and the United States at birth. Later in life he applied for a certificate of Mexican citizenship and in the process "swore allegiance to Mexico and expressly renounced his United States citizenship."[25]

A certificate of loss of nationality was issued by the State Department when it learned of Terrazas's actions. He then sued the secretary of state seeking an order that he was still a U.S. citizen. Judge Abraham J. Marovitz, using the preponderance of the evidence test, held that the Terrazas had "knowingly and voluntarily taken an oath of allegiance to Mexico and renounced allegiance to the United States, thus voluntarily relinquishing United States citizenship." The court of appeals reversed, the judges holding that "the Constitution required that proof be not merely be a preponderance of the evidence, but by 'clear, convincing and unequivocal evidence.'"

Six members of the Supreme Court thought otherwise and reversed. "We are unable to conclude," Justice White stated, "that the specific evidentiary standard [of preponderance of the evidence] is invalid under either the Citizenship Clause or the Due Process Clause of the Fifth Amendment." Furthermore, "the preponderance standard of proof provides sufficient protection for the interest of the individual in retaining his citizenship."

The result displeased justices Brennan, Stewart, and Stevens. "Because I would hold," Justice Brennan argued, "that one who acquires United States citizenship by virtue of being born in the United States, U.S. Const., Amdt. 14, Sec. 1, can lose that citizenship only by formally renouncing it, and because I would hold that the act of which [Terrazas] is accused in this case cannot be an expatriating act, I dissent."

Justice and the Alien

It is well established that if an alien is a lawful permanent resident of the United States and remains physically present there, he is a person within the protection of the Fifth Amendment. He may not be deprived of his life, liberty or property without due process of law.*

The power to admit and exclude aliens is part of the sovereignty of a nation. In the United States that power is exercised by Congress and the executive branch of the government and is almost absolute.[26]

*Kwong Hai Chew v. Colding, 344 U.S. 590, 596, (1953).

> The power to exclude or to expel aliens . . . is vested in the political departments of the government, and is to be regulated by treaty or by an act of Congress, and to be executed by the executive authority according to the regulations so established, except so far as the judicial department has been authorized by treaty or by statute, or is required by the paramount law of the Constitution, to intervene.[27]

The Court has largely adopted a hands-off policy with regard to immigration and naturalization matters, with some strong dissents. This was evidenced in an 1893 case in which a majority of the justices upheld the deportation of three Chinese laborers who did not have a certificate of residence to remain in the country. Two of these individuals, Fong Yue Ting and Wong Quan, had come to the United States some years before Congress passed a law requiring all Chinese laborers to obtain a certificate from the collector of internal revenue permitting them to remain in this country. The third, Lee Joe, also a laborer, had applied for a certificate, but "the collector refused to give him a certificate, on the ground that the witnesses whom he produced to prove that he was entitled to the certificate were persons of the Chinese race and not credible witnesses."[28] He was unable to produce any "person other than one of the Chinese race who knew and could truthfully swear that he was lawfully within the United States"; thus no certificate was issued to him. Each of the laborers, upon being arrested, sought his release by a writ of habeas corpus, which was denied. Upon appeal to the Supreme Court, the decisions were affirmed, with justices Brewer, Field, and Melville W. Fuller dissenting.

For the majority, the issue was simply whether Congress had the authority under the Constitution to adopt the certificate requirement. Based upon their view that the power of Congress was extensive in immigration cases, they held that "Congress, having the right, as it may see fit, to expel aliens of a particular class, or to permit them to remain, has undoubtedly the right to provide a system of registration and identification of the members of that class within the country, and to take all proper means to carry out the system which it provides."

Justice Brewer's quarrel with the majority was not over Congress's authority to enact the certificate requirement but with its implementation. For him, deportation was punishment, and before one can be punished, he or she is entitled to due process. "Due process requires that a man be heard before he is condemned," he insisted, "and both heard and condemned in the due and orderly procedure of a trial as recognized by the common law from time im-memorial." He was also greatly disturbed that only the Chinese were required to obtain a certificate. "It is true this statute is directed only against the . . . Chinese; but if the power exist," he maintained, "who shall say it will not be exercised to-morrow against other classes and other people? If the guarantees of these amendments can be thus ignored in order to get rid of this . . . class, what security have others that a like disregard of its provisions may not be resorted to?"

"The decision of the court," wrote Justice Field, "and the sanction it would give to legislation depriving resident aliens of the guaranties of the Constitution fills me with apprehensions. Those guaranties are of priceless value to every one resident in the country, whether citizen or alien. I cannot but regard the decision as a blow against constitutional liberty, when it declares that Congress has the right to disregard the guaranties of the Constitution intended for the protection of all men, domiciled in the country with the consent of the government, in their rights of person and property."

Some sixty years later, Chinese seaman Kwong Hai Chew found a far more receptive Supreme Court in his attempt to remain in this country upon his return from a voyage abroad.

> It appears that [Kwong Hai Chew] is of the Chinese race, having originally arrived here in 1941 as a seaman. Following his occupation, he made entries as a seaman until January 10, 1945, [having served with credit in the U.S. Merchant Marine during World War II]. On June 22, 1946, he married a native born citizen of the United States. . . . In November 1950 he signed articles for service as a seaman on the S.S. *Sir John Franklin*, and at that time he was screened by the Coast Guard and passed by them. On the return of the vessel, on the voyage which began in November 1950, he was detained on the vessel when it docked at Pier 7, Bush Terminal, Brooklyn, New York on March 29, 1951, and was held upon the instructions of the Immigration and Naturalization Service without bail.[29]

Chew brought a habeas corpus proceeding claiming that his detention was a violation of the due process clause of the Fifth Amendment. The government responded that in detaining Chew it was acting under a federal law which gave the Department of Justice authority to exclude "those defined 'to be prejudicial to the public interest.'"[30] A person would fall under that designation if he or she was a member of a "'political organization associated with or carrying out policies of any foreign government opposed to the measures adopted by the Government of the United States in the public interest . . .' or being 'engaged in organizing, teaching, advocating, or directing any rebellion, insurrection, or violent uprising against the United States.'"

Judge Clarence G. Galston upheld the government's actions and dismissed Chew's petition. The court of appeals affirmed, but with only Justice Sherman Minton dissenting, The Supreme Court reversed. The justices, to avoid declaring the law unconstitutional, concluded that it applied only to those being "excluded," not to those being "expelled," as the government was trying to do to Chew.

To put the case in proper perspective, Justice Harold H. Burton pointed out, a person who continuously resides in the United States and is physically present there, is entitled to due process protection before expulsion. "Although it later may be established," Justice Burton noted, "as [the government contends], that [Chew] can be expelled and deported, yet before his expulsion, he is entitled to notice of the nature of the charge and a hearing at least before an executive or administrative tribunal. Although Congress may prescribe conditions for his expulsion and deportation, not even Congress may expel him without allowing him a fair opportunity to be heard."

The Court has not spelled out in detail the kind of a hearing required by due process in an exclusion hearing. But that some due process protection must be given to one whom the government seeks to exclude was affirmed in *Landon v. Plasencia*.[31] Maria Antonieta Plasencia, a citizen of El Salvador, became a permanent resident alien in March 1970. She married a U.S. citizen, established a home, and raised a family.

> On June 2, 1975, she and her husband traveled to Tijuana, Mexico. During their brief stay in Mexico, they met with several Mexican and Salvadoran nationals and made arrangements to assist their illegal entry into the United States. She agreed to transport the aliens to Los Angeles and furnished some of the aliens with alien registration receipt cards that belonged to her children. When she and her husband attempted to cross the international border at 9:27 on the evening of June 29, 1975, and INS officer at the port of entry found six nonresident aliens in the Plasencias' car.

The INS began proceedings to have Mrs. Plasencia excluded under a law that allows for such exclusion for one who assists another alien to enter the country illegally. An exclusion hearing was held by an immigration law judge, who after hearing the facts of the case, "ordered her 'excluded and deported.'" The matter then came before a federal magistrate, who held that Mrs. Plasencia was entitled to a "deportation" hearing. A district court and the court of appeals agreed: The Supreme Court did not and reversed. The Court, however, was careful to point out that while deportation proceedings must provide the alien with substantial due process protection, fundamental fairness demands that some due process protection must be given to the person whose continued residence here will be terminated by exclusion.

An alien's status regarding entitlement to protection of the Constitution generally falls into three classes. Those attempting to enter the country for the first time are not entitled to constitutional protection, "for the power to admit or exclude aliens is a sovereign prerogative." Many aliens, however, live in our country with permission of the government. Such an alien who has been "continuously present [in the United States] is entitled to a fair hearing when threatened with deportation." Those aliens who at one time lived in the United States with government permission (such as Maria Antonieta Plasencia) who leave the country may find themselves subject to exclusion. It is clear from the *Kwong Hai Chew* case that these individuals are entitled to some constitutional guarantees because exclusion can result in serious consequences, as Justice O'Connor pointed out.

> Plasencia's interest here is, without question, a weighty one. She stands to lose the right "to stay and live and work in this land of freedom." . . . Further, she may lose the right to rejoin her immediate family, a right that ranks high among the interests of the individual. . . . The Government's interest in efficient administration of the immigration laws at the border also is weighty.

Justice O'Connor then reasoned that "the role of the judiciary is limited to determining whether the procedures meet the essential standard of fairness under the Due Process Clause and does not extend to imposing procedures that merely displace congressional choices of policy."

Justice Marshall was not satisfied with this solution. He did not believe that Plasencia had been given adequate notice of the exclusion hearing or that she had ample opportunity to obtain counsel. "The Immigration Judge's decision to exclude [Plasencia]," he noted, "was handed down less than 24 hours after she was detained at the border on the night of June 29, 1975. By notice in English dated June 30, 1975, she was informed that a hearing would be conducted at 11 o'clock

on the morning of the same day." Further, "it was not until the com-
mencement of the hearing that she was given notice in her native
language of the charges against her and of her right to retain counsel
and to present evidence."

Procedures That Protect Property

> Property interests, of course, are not created by the Constitution.
> Rather, they are created and their dimensions are defined by existing
> rules or understandings that stem from an independent source such
> as state law – rules or understandings that secure certain benefits and
> that support claims of entitlement to those benefits.*

The Right to a Public Education

> Having chosen to extend the right to an education, . . . Ohio may
> not withdraw that right on grounds of misconduct, absent fun-
> damentally fair procedures to determine whether the misconduct has
> occurred.†

In the spring of 1971, Dwight Lopez was suspended from Central High School, Columbus, Ohio. At a hearing in a U.S. district
court regarding his suspension,

> Dwight Lopez testified that in late February, 1971, there was tension
> at Central High School over Black History Week. On the morning
> of February 26, 1971, he had a free study period in the lunch room.
> While he was in the lunch room, black students came in and started
> overturning tables. Dwight Lopez testified that he and several of his
> friends walked out of the lunch room. He testified that he took no
> part in the unlawful activity, and that he did not violate any school
> rule or any other rule.[32]

After the disturbance, the school was closed and Lopez returned
to his home. Shortly thereafter, Principal Calvin Parks called and
informed him that he was suspended. No reasons were given. The
Lopezes received two letters from the school, one from Parks telling
them of the problem at the school and instructing them to keep
Dwight at home, the other requesting them to appear before the
board of education. When they went to that meeting, the entrance
to the building was blocked by protesters, and they were unable

---

*Board of Regents v. Roth, 408 U.S. 564, 577 (1972).
†Goss v. Lopez, 419 U.S. 565, 574 (1975).

to get in. Because Dwight was nineteen years old, he was transferred from the high school to the adult day school.

Lopez and students from other schools in Columbus who had also been suspended brought suit in the federal district court against various school administrators of the Columbus school system. The students claimed that their suspensions violated due process because they were not given a hearing before the punishment was inflicted. The district court agreed, and the Supreme Court affirmed in a 5–4 decision. At issue was whether the students had any right protected by due process. The school administrators contended that "because there is no constitutional right to an education at public expense, the Due Process Clause does not protect against expulsions from the public school system."[33] Justice White, for the majority, responded: "This position misconceives the nature of the issue and is refuted by prior decisions. The Fourteenth Amendment forbids the State to deprive any person of life, liberty, or property without due process of law. Protected interests in property are normally 'not created by the Constitution. Rather, they are created and their dimensions are defined' by an independent source such as state statutes or rules entitling the citizen to certain benefits." In this case, because the state law provides for "free education to all children between the ages of six and 21," the students "plainly had legitimate claims of entitlement to a public education."

"Once it is determined," Justice White declared, "that due process applies, the question remains what process is due." In searching for an answer to the question, the majority acknowledged that "our schools are vast and complex. Some modicum of discipline and order is essential if the educational function is to be performed. Events calling for discipline are frequent occurrences and sometimes require immediate, effective action. Suspension is considered not only to be a necessary tool to maintain order but a valuable educational device." Nevertheless, because "students facing temporary suspension have interests qualifying for protection of the Due Process Clause, and due process requires, in connection with a suspension of 10 days or less, that the student be given oral or written notice of the charges against him and, if he denies them, an explanation of the evidence the authorities have and an opportunity to present his side of the story. The Clause requires at least these rudimentary precautions against unfair or mistaken findings of misconduct and arbitrary exclusion from school."

The Court pointed out that it was specifically limiting its decision to suspensions of ten days or less and therefore was not requiring that the student have "the opportunity to secure counsel, to confront and cross-examine witnesses supporting the charge, or to call his own witnesses to verify his version of the incident."

This decision bothered the four dissenters. "The decision," Justice Powell argued, "unnecessarily opens avenues for judicial intervention in the operation of our public schools that may affect adversely the quality of education." Further, "in assessing in constitutional terms the need to protect pupils from unfair minor discipline by school authorities, the Court ignores the commonality of interest of the State and pupils in the public school system. Rather, it thinks in traditional judicial terms of an adversary situation. To be sure, there will be the occasional pupil innocent of any rule infringement who is mistakenly suspended or whose infraction is too minor to justify suspension. But, while there is no evidence indicating the frequency of unjust suspensions, common sense suggests that they will not be numerous in relation to the total number, and that mistakes or injustices will usually be righted by informal means."

If a student must be given some due process before being suspended for disciplinary reasons, does due process provide protection from suspension or dismissal for academic reasons? Five justices answered that it did not. Two justices disagreed with that conclusion, and two others took the position that the question should not have been decided in the case before them. The case was brought to the Court by Charlotte Horowitz, who was dropped from the Medical School at the University of Missouri–Kansas City for unsatisfactory clinical performance. Prior to this action against Horowitz she was given several evaluations by faculty members as well as an opportunity to take an examination under the supervision of seven practicing physicians. Her case against the university was heard by Judge William G. Juergens, who held that she had been given all of the due process to which she was entitled. The court of appeals reversed, but six justices of the Supreme Court found that Judge Juergens was correct and reversed the court of appeals.

The majority, in an opinion by Justice Rehnquist, held that no due process protections were required in academic dismissals. "Since the issue first arose 50 years ago," Justice Rehnquist maintained, "state and lower federal courts have recognized that there are distinct differences between decisions to suspend or dismiss a student for disciplinary purposes and similar actions taken for academic reasons which may call for hearings in connection with the former but not the latter."[34] "Reason, furthermore," he continued, "clearly supports the perception of these decisions. A school is an academic institution, not a courtroom or administrative hearing room." Justice White thought differently and concurred only in the judgment. He believed that Ms. Horowitz was entitled to some due process but that the opportunity to discuss her failures with members of the faculty and the practicing physicians was sufficient. Justice Marshall also thought that Horowitz had had all the due process to which she was entitled but parted company with the majority in their assumption that there was a difference between "academic" and "disciplinary" dismissals. He assumed that dismissals for either reason required some notice and opportunity to be heard.

The Public Employee and Due Process

> A property interest in employment can, of course, be created by ordinance or by an implied contract.*

Teachers who have been granted tenure have a property interest in their continued employment which requires procedures that comport with due process before they can be discharged. Robert P. Sindermann, however, was employed as a government and social science professor at Odessa Texas Junior College, which had no tenure system. The *Faculty Guide* did provide, however, that "the Administration of the College wishes the faculty member to feel that he has permanent tenure as long as his teaching services are satisfactory and as long as he displays a cooperative attitude toward his coworkers and his superiors, and as long as he is happy in his work."[35]

Sindermann's problems with the college began when he "was elected president of the Texas Junior College Teachers Association. In this capacity, he left his teaching duties on several occasions to testify before committees of the Texas Legislature, and he became involved in public disagreements with the policies of the college's Board of Regents. In particular, he aligned himself with a group advocating the elevation of the college to four-year status — a change opposed by the Regents. And, on one occasion, a newspaper advertisement appeared over his name that was highly critical of the Regents."

Bishop v. Wood, 426 U.S. 341, 344 (1976).

In May 1969 the board issued an eleven-page press release de-
tailing his time with the college. Reference was made to the time he
was away from the college on Teachers Association business as well
as the fact that he opposed the board's position on whether the college should become a four-year institution. The board then voted
not to renew his contract for the coming academic year. In bringing
an action against the board, Sindermann alleged (1) that the nonrenewal of his contract was in retaliation for speaking out on the
issue of a four-year versus a two-year institution and (2) that he was
denied due process of law because he had not been given a hearing
of any kind.

Judge Ernest Guinn granted judgment for the board and dismissed the action. The court of appeals reversed, for two reasons.
First, the First Amendment precluded Sindermann's discharge for
speaking out against the board, and the court concluded that a hearing should be held to ascertain if that was the reason for nonrenewal.
Second, if he had a reasonable "expectancy" of continued employment, similar to tenure, he was entitled to a due process hearing
before termination. The board appealed to the Supreme Court,
which affirmed the decision of the court of appeals.

Justice Stewart opened the discussion of the legal issues:

> The first question presented is whether [Sindermann's] lack of con-
> tractual or tenure right to re-employment, taken alone, defeats his
> claim that the nonrenewal of his contract violated the First and Four-
> teenth Amendments. We hold that it does not.

On the free speech issue, Justice Stewart noted that the "Court
has specifically held that the nonrenewal of a nontenured public
school teacher's one-year contract may not be predicated on his exercise of First and Fourteenth Amendment rights. . . . We affirm
those holdings here." Thus, the district court must conduct a hearing
to determine whether Sindermann's First Amendment rights were
violated.

Somewhat more troublesome was Sindermann's due process
claim because it was clear that there was no tenure system at the college. "He alleged, [however], that [a property] interest, though not
secured by a formal contractual tenure provision, was secured by a
no less binding understanding fostered by the college administration. In particular, [he] alleged that the college had a *de facto* tenure
program, and that he had tenure under that program." The justices

agreed. This, of course, did not entitle Sindermann to immediate reinstatement, but if after a hearing the district court agreed that he did have *de facto* tenure, he was entitled to notice of the charges against him and an opportunity to challenge them at a hearing conducted by the college.

In the *Eldridge* case, the Court wrote: "This Court consistently has held that some form of hearing is required before an individual is finally deprived of a property interest."[36] The Court held that due process was complied with even though the hearing was held after the decision was made to terminate Eldridge's disability benefits.

The question of the validity of holding a hearing after the discharge of a public employee reached the Court in the case of *Cleveland Board of Education v. Loudermill*.[37] James Loudermill, who was employed by a private firm, worked as a security guard for the Cleveland School Board. When his company went bankrupt, he applied for a position with the school system. In responding to a question on an application, "Have you ever been convicted of a crime (felony)?" he answered no.[38] His application was accepted, and he went to work in September 1979 as a classified employee, subject to being discharged only for cause. If he was to be discharged, the law entitled him to a hearing before a board within thirty days.

About a year later, during a check of employee records, it was learned that in 1968 Loudermill had been convicted of a felony. The business manager of the board immediately wrote him a letter informing him that he was being discharged because of "his dishonesty in filling out the employment application." Loudermill filed an appeal with the Cleveland Civil Service Commission, which was heard by a referee who recommended that he be reinstated. The commission thought otherwise and upheld the dismissal. Loudermill's lawsuit against the board of education followed.

District Judge John M. Manos dismissed the action, being of the opinion that "because the very statute that created the property right in continued employment also specified the procedures for discharge, and because those procedures were followed, Loudermill was, by definition afforded all the process due."[39]

The court of appeals reversed, holding that Loudermill "had been deprived of due process and that the compelling private interest in retaining employment, combined with the value of presenting evidence prior to dismissal, outweighed the added administrative burden of a pretermination hearing." The Supreme Court affirmed, with only Justice Rehnquist dissenting.

The majority examined Judge Manos's ruling to the effect that because the law under which Loudermill was employed specified the procedure to be followed in dismissal, that was all the process due him. This ruling in effect says that one who takes a job (the sweet) is bound by the rules for discharge (the bitter). Justice White and the majority did not accept that as sound constitutional doctrine. "It is settled," he insisted, "that the 'bitter with the sweet' approach misconceives the constitutional guarantee. If a clearer holding is needed, we provide it today. The point is straightforward: the Due Process Clause provides that certain substantive rights — life, liberty, and property — cannot be deprived except pursuant to constitutionally adequate procedures. . . . The right to due process 'is conferred, not by legislative grace, but by constitutional guarantee. While the legislature may elect not to confer a property interest in [public] employment, it may not constitutionally authorize the deprivation of such an interest, once conferred, without appropriate procedural safeguards.'"

The majority then held that due process required some type of hearing before termination of the employee's property right in his or her job. "The tenured public employee," Justice White stated, "is entitled to oral or written notice of the charges against him, an explanation of the employer's evidence, and an opportunity to present his side of the story. . . . To require more than this prior to termination would intrude to an unwarranted extent on the government's interest in quickly removing an unsatisfactory employee." If the employee was terminated at this point, he or she would thereafter be entitled to an administrative hearing which would include timely notice and information concerning the reasons for the termination. The employee should have the opportunity to confront adverse witnesses and to present evidence.

The decision of the majority did not completely satisfy Justice Marshall. He concurred with the result but was concerned with the effect the discharge would have upon the employee and therefore thought that the minimum due process given before termination was too little. "To my mind," he maintained, "the disruption caused by a loss of wages may be so devastating to an employee, that whenever there are substantial disputes about the evidence, additional predeprivation procedures are necessary to minimize the risk of an erroneous termination. That is, I place significantly greater weight than does the Court on the public employee's substantial interest in the accuracy of the pretermination proceeding."

Justice Rehnquist adhered to a position he had previously taken, that the government at the time of the creation of a property interest could spell out the due process to which the employee was entitled upon termination. He chided the majority for using "tortured reasoning" to create a property right for Loudermill and suggested that the "balancing process" used to determine how much of a hearing due process required did not produce consistent results. "The balance is simply an ad hoc weighing," he argued, "which depends to a great extent upon how the Court subjectively views the underlying interests at stake. The results in previous cases and in [this case have] been quite unpredictable."

Licenses Are Property

Once licenses are issued, . . . their continued possession may become essential in the pursuit of a livelihood. Suspension of issued licenses thus involves state action that adjudicates important interests of the licensees. In such cases the licenses are not to be taken away without the procedural due process required by the Fourteenth Amendment.*

"[Paul J. Bell, Jr.,] is a clergyman whose ministry requires him to travel by car to cover three rural Georgia communities. On Sunday afternoon, Novermber 24, 1968, [Bell] was involved in an accident when five-year-old Sherry Capes rode her bicycle into the side of his automobile. The child's parents filed an accident report with the director of the Georgia Department of Public Safety indicating that their daughter had suffered substantial injuries for which they claimed damages of $5,000."[40]

Bell was informed by the department's director that the law required him to show proof that he was covered by liability insurance or to post a bond or deposit cash in the amount of $5,000. If he did neither, his driver's license and car registration would be suspended. Bell asked for a hearing, and one was scheduled. However, he was told that "the only evidence that the Department can accept and consider is: (a) was [he] or his vehicle involved in the accident; (b) has [he] complied with the provisions of the Law as provided; or (c) does [he] come within any of the exceptions of the Law.'"

At the hearing, Bell offered evidence relating to whether the accident was his fault, which was rejected. He was ordered to submit proof of liability insurance or deposit the cash within thirty days.

*Bell v. Burson, 402 U.S. 535, 539 (1971).

On appeal to the Georgia Superior Court, Judge H. W. Lott found Bell free of negligence and ordered that he need not surrender his license. The Georgia Supreme Court disagreed and reversed. All justices of the U.S. Supreme Court were of the opinion that Bell had been denied due process of law, and they reversed.

Having concluded that possession of a license creates a property interest that prevents that state from taking it away without due process, the justices turned to the question, What process is due? Justice Brennan, who wrote the Court's opinion, first acknowledged that not all claims demand the same kind of procedures. "A procedural rule that may satisfy due process in one context may not necessarily satisfy procedural due process in every case. Thus, procedures adequate to determine a welfare claim may not suffice to try a felony charge." In this case, the purpose of the law was to assure that persons injured in accidents would be compensated. "We hold," Justice Brennan declared, "that procedural due process will be satisfied by an inquiry limited to the determination whether there is a reasonable possibility of judgments in the amounts claimed being rendered against the licensee."

The Court rejected Georgia's argument that its desire to protect those injured outweighed the licensee's interest in the license, pointing out that if the licensee is not at fault, no judgment can be rendered against him in any event. The justices rejected the argument that it should not be necessary to hold the hearing before suspension of the license. "While '[m]any controversies have raged about . . . the Due Process Clause,'" Justice Brennan noted," it is fundamental that except in emergency situations (and this is not one) due process requires that when a State seeks to terminate an interest such as that here involved, it must afford 'notice and opportunity for hearing appropriate to the nature of the case' *before* the termination becomes effective." The Court left it to Georgia to take whatever action it deemed desirable, provided, of course, that that action comports with due process.

One of those emergency situations wherein the government is permitted to act first and ask questions afterwards is the suspension of a driver's license for refusal to take a breath-analysis test.

> While driving a vehicle in Acton, Mass., . . . Donald Montrym was involved in a collision about 8:15 P.M. on May 15, 1976. Upon arrival at the scene of the accident an Acton police officer observed . . . that Montrym was "glassy eyed," unsteady on his feet, slurring his speech, and emitting a strong alcoholic odor from his person. The officer ar-

rested Montrym at 8:30 p.m. for operating his vehicle while under the influence of intoxicating liquor, driving to endanger, and failing to produce his motor vehicle registration upon request. Montrym was then taken to the Acton police station. There, Montrym was asked to take a breath-analysis examination at 8:45 p.m. He refused to do so."[41]

After Montrym had consulted an attorney, he said that he would take the test, but the police refused to let him do so because state law provided that when a person refused to take the test, "the police officer before whom such refusal was made *shall immediately* prepare a written report of such refusal."

When Montrym was brought into court, the judge dismissed the driving under the influence charge, apparently deciding that the police should have allowed him to take the test when he asked to do so. Although Montrym's attorney wrote the registrar of motor vehicles telling him of the dismissal of the DUI charge, the registrar, who had no authority to do otherwise, suspended Montrym's license for ninety days and informed him of a right to appeal.

Montrym surrendered his license, and his counsel attempted to have it returned. Not successful and without taking advantage of his client's right to appeal, counsel brought suit in the federal district court, arguing that his client had been denied due process of law in not being given a hearing before the license was suspended. The case was heard by a three-judge court which, with one judge dissenting, agreed that Montrym was entitled to a presuspension hearing, and because the state law did not allow for one, it was unconstitutional as inconsistent with the due process clause.

In a 5–4 decision, the Supreme Court held that no presuspension hearing was necessary and reversed. Chief Justice Burger wrote the Court's opinion. For the majority, the starting point was the restatement of the balancing approach it had established in *Eldridge*. This approach called for the evaluation of several interests.

> First, the private interest that will be affected by the official action; second, the risk of an erroneous deprivation of such interest through procedures used, and the probable value, if any, of additional or substitute procedural safeguards; and finally, the Government's interest, including the function involved and the fiscal and administrative burdens that the additional or substitute procedural requirements would entail.

The majority agreed that Montrym's interest in the continued possession of a driver's license was valuable. "That interest is a substantial one," the chief justice conceded, "for the Commonwealth will not be able to make a driver whole for any personal inconvenience and economic hardship suffered by reason of any delay in redressing an erroneous suspension through postsuspension review procedures." But what most impressed the justices was that the length of the suspension could have been reduced simply by Montrym's asking for a hearing before the registrar immediately after the suspension was ordered. Thus, when weighing the licensee's interest against the government's need for the information sought from the test, the balance went to the government.

The second inquiry to be made focused upon the possibiliy of an erroneous decision that might be made without a prior hearing. But in these kinds of cases, such a decision is unlikely, given the factual conditions under which the request to take the test is made. "The facts of the arrest," the chief justice pointed out, "and the driver's refusal will inevitably be within the personal knowledge of the reporting officer; indeed, Massachusetts requires that the driver's refusal be witnessed by two officers. At the very least, the arresting officer ordinarily will have provided the driver with an informal opportunity to tell his side of the story and, as here, will have had the opportunity to observe the driver's condition and behavior before effecting any arrest." This led the majority to conclude that there was little risk of an erroneous decision at the time the driver was requested to take the test.

Turning then to an evaluation of the state's interest in taking action and asking questions afterward, the justices believed that the issue was simply one of public safety.

> The Commonwealth's interest in public safety is substantially served in several ways by the summary suspension of those who refuse to take a breath-analysis test upon arrest. First, the very existence of the summary sanction of the statute serves as a deterrant to drunken driving. Second, it provides strong inducement to take the breath-analysis test and thus effectuates the Commonwealth's interest in obtaining reliable and relevant evidence for use in subsequent criminal proceedings. Third, in promptly removing such drivers from the road, the summary sanction of the statute contributes to the safety of public highways.

The majority's decision was met with a forceful dissent, written by Justice Stewart and joined by justices Brennan, Marshall, and Stevens. They were concerned with the effect that the summary suspension would have upon the driver's right to drive. They disputed that the refusal to take the test was related to a solution to the drunk driving problem and argued that there was no real effective appellate process because the registrar had little authority to reinstate the license.

With regard to the effect of even a temporary loss of license, Justice Stewart stressed, "we should, in my opinion, be even less enchanted by the proposition that due process is satisfied by delay when the wrong cannot be undone at all, but at most can be limited in duration. Even a day's loss of a driver's license can inflict grave injury upon a person who depends upon an automobile for continued employment in his job."

In support of their position that the suspension for refusal to take the test did not really relate to getting the driver off the road, the dissenters maintained that

> the breath-analysis test is plainly not designed to remove an irresponsible driver from the road as swiftly as possible. For if a motorist *submits* to the test and fails it, he keeps his driver's license – a result wholly at odds with any notion that summary suspension upon refusal to take the test serves an emergency protective purpose. A suspension for refusal to take the test is obviously premised not on intoxication, but on noncooperation with the police.

Although the law provided for a "walk-in" hearing by the registrar after suspension, Justice Stewart and the dissenters did not think it was very meaningful. "The Registrar – according to the Court's own description of the Massachusetts scheme – quite possibly does not have authority to resolve even the most basic questions that might be raised about the validity of a breath-analysis suspension."

On the same day that the Court decided *Montrym*, it upheld the summary suspension of the license of a horse trainer whose horse tested positive for drugs after a race. The trainer, John Barchi, insisting that he had not drugged the horse, passed two lie-detector tests, but to no avail. Barchi was suspended for fifteen days. Under New York law, "When a postrace test, which must be administered to horses finishing first, second, or third, reveals the presence of drugs, it is to be presumed – subject to rebuttal – that the drug 'was either administered by the trainer or resulted from his negligence in failing to adequately protect against such occurrence.'"[42] The suspension remains in effect until a hearing is held to determine whether the trainer was responsible for administering drugs to the horse.

As against a claim that New York's procedures violated the due process clause the court responded:

> Unquestionably, the magnitude of a trainer's interest in avoiding suspension is substantial; but the State also has an important interest in assuring the integrity of the racing carried on under its auspices. In these circumstances, it seems to us that the State is entitled to impose an interim suspension, pending a prompt judicial or administrative hearing that would definitely determine the issue, whenever it has satisfactorily established probable cause to believe that a horse has been drugged and that a trainer has been at least negligent in connection with the drugging.

The Court in *In re Ruffalo*[43] said: "Disbarment, designed to protect the public, is a punishment or penalty imposed on the lawyer. ... He is accordingly entitled to procedural due process, which includes fair notice of the charge."[44] If a lawyer is entitled to due process before being disciplined by a bar association, does it follow that an applicant for admission to the bar must also be accorded notice and an opportunity to be heard before the application can be denied? When called upon to answer that question, the justices responded affirmatively.

Nathan Willner passed the New York State bar exam in 1936. Before being admitted to practice, however, Willner needed to be certified by a committee as to character and fitness. After conducting several hearings at which Willner was not given an opportunity to confront his accusers, the New York Bar Character and Fitness Committee recommended that he not be admitted. Between 1936 and 1960 Willner tried several times to have his case reviewed, but to no avail. In his last attempt to reverse the committee's decision, Willner alleged that he had been shown a letter by a New York attorney containing certain accusations against him but had never had an opportunity to confront that attorney, although he had been promised such a confrontation. Further, he "alleged that the had been involved in litigation with another lawyer who had as his purpose 'to destroy me'; that the secretary of the Committee was taking orders from that lawyer and that two members of the committee were 'in cahoots' with that lawyer."

The New York courts refused to recognize the constitutional claim that he had been denied due process in the hearings before the bar's committee. Willner appealed to the Supreme Court, which agreed with him. Quoting from one of its prior cases, the Court declared: "A State cannot exclude a person from the practice of law or from any other occupation in a manner or for reasons that contravene the Due Process or Equal Protection Clause of the Fourteenth Amendment."⁴⁵ The justices were concerned with the fact that Willner had never had an opportunity to face his accusers. "It does not appear from the record," Justice Douglas noted, "that either the Committee or the Appellate Division, at any stage in these proceedings, ever apprised [Willner] of its reasons for failing to be convinced of his good character. [He] was clearly entitled to notice of and a hearing on the grounds of his rejection either before the Committee or before the Appellate Division." This required reversal of the New York court's decision.

Debtors and the Right to Be Heard

The leverage of the creditor on the wage earner is enormous.*

Christine Sniadach was indebted to Family Finance Corp. in the amount of $420 on a promissory note. In an effort to secure payment, Family Finance commenced a garnishment proceeding against her. The complaint and garnishment notice were served upon her and her employer, Miller Harris Instrument Co., on the same day. Miller Harris was required by law to withhold one-half of Sniadach's wages for the benefit of Family Finance until the lawsuit had been determined but could release the remainder to her. The wages due totaled $63.18.

> What happens in Wisconsin is that the clerk of the court issues the summons at the request of the creditor's lawyer; and it is the latter who by serving the garnishee [the employer] sets in motion the machinery whereby the wages are frozen. They may, it is true, be unfrozen if the trial of the main suit is ever had and the wage earner wins on the merits. But in the interim the wage earner is deprived of his enjoyment of earned wages without any opportunity to be heard and to tender any defense he may have, whether it by fraud or otherwise.⁴⁶

Sniadach moved that the proceedings be dismissed, asserting that she had been denied due process because she did not have notice and an opportunity to be heard before half her wages was withheld.

*Sniadach v. Family Finance Corp., 395 U.S. 337, 341 (1969).

The motion was denied by Judge Thaddeus J. Pruss, and his decision was upheld by the Wisconsin Supreme Court. With only Justice Black dissenting, the Supreme Court reversed.

To put the case in proper perspective, Justice Douglas for the majority declared, "the question is not whether the Wisconsin law is a wise law or unwise law. Our concern is not what philosophy Wisconsin should or should not embrace.... We do not sit as a super-legislative body. In this case the sole question is whether there has been a taking of property without that procedural due process that is required by the Fourteenth Amendment." The answer was that the Wisconsin procedure did indeed take property from debtors without any preseizure notice and opportunity to be heard. "The result," Justice Douglas stressed, "is that a prejudgment garnishment of the Wisconsin type may as a practical matter drive a wage-earning family to the wall. Where the taking of one's property is so obvious, it needs no extended argument to conclude that absent notice and a prior hearing . . . this prejudgment garnishment procedure violates the fundamental principles of due process."

The fact that the law allowed Sniadach to present defenses at the trial on the merits was sufficient due process, according to Justice Black. He thought the majority was striking down the Wisconsin procedure because they thought it was just bad policy.

Debtors whose interest in property is shared by their creditors may be required to surrender that property to the creditor upon default in payment, without notice or an opportunity to be heard. Lawrence Mitchell's refrigerator, range, stereo, and washing machine were taken from him when his creditor, W. T. Grant Co., filed an action for the overdue balance of the purchase price of these items. This all happened because under Louisiana law an unpaid creditor, without notice to the debtor, could secure a court order permitting seizure and sequestration of property sold under an installment sales contract.

W. T. Grant petitioned the court for an order of sequestration, which was granted by Judge Arthur J. O'Keefe. Mitchell had no notice of the procedure and probably did not learn that the order had been issued until the constable came to get the property.

Mitchell filed a motion to dissolve the writ of sequestration issued on February 2. The motion asserted that the personal property at issue had been seized under the writ on February 7, 1972, and claimed, first, that the goods were exempt from seizure under state law and,

second that the seizure violated the Due Process Clauses of the State
and Federal Constitutions in that it had occurred without prior
notice and opportunity to defend [his] right to possession of the
property.[47]

The motion was denied. The trial judge specifically held that the
property was not exempt under state law and that there was no
denial of due process in the Louisiana procedures. The Louisiana appellate courts came to the same conclusion, as did five justices of the
Supreme Court.

To understand the majority's position, it is necessary to examine the relationship between the parties and the property at issue.
Both have an interest in it. While Mitchell may have owned the property, state law gave Grant a *vendor's lien* until Mitchell had completed paying the purchase price. The balance due the Grant Co.
was $574.17. "Plainly enough," Justice White noted for the majority,
"this is not a case where the property sequestered by the court is ex-
clusively the property of the . . . debtor. The question is not whether
a debtor's property may be seized by his creditors [pending litiga-
tion], where they hold no present interest in the property sought to
be seized. The reality is that both seller and buyer had current, real
interests in the property, and the definition of property rights is a
matter of state law. Resolution of the due process question must take
account not only of the interests of the buyer of the property but
those of the seller as well."

Based on that analysis of the facts, the majority concluded that
the Louisiana procedure did not violate the due process clause. The
justices found some protection for the debtor in state law. The creditor
was required to convince a judge that it was entitled to seize the
property and was required to post a bond to protect the debtor in
case the sequestration was invalid. Furthermore, the debtor could
immediately seek to have the order reversed, at which time the
creditor must prove that there were grounds for the issuance of
the order. "We, [therefore]," Justice White insisted, "cannot accept
[Mitchell's] broad assertion that the Due Process Clause of the Fourteenth Amendment guaranteed to him the use and possession of the
goods until all issues in the case were judicially resolved after full
adversary proceedings had been completed."

The four justices who thought the Louisiana procedure violated
due process were concerned with the relative ease with which the
order to sequester could be secured from the court and the lack of

any prior notice to the debtor. Justice Stewart explained the dissenters' position.

> All that is required to support the issuance of the writ and seizure of the goods is the filing of a complaint and an affidavit containing *pro forma* allegations in support of the seller's purported entitlement to the goods in question. Since the procedure . . . is completely *ex parte*, the state official charged with issuing the writ [the judge] can do little more than determine the formal sufficiency of the [creditor's] allegations before ordering the state agents to take the goods from the [debtor's] possession.

Turning Off Gas and Lights May Require Due Process

> Utility service is a necessity of modern life; indeed, the discontinuance of water or heating for even short periods of time may threaten health and safety. And the risk of an erroneous deprivation, given the necessary reliance on computers, is not insubstantial.*

Willie and Mary Craft became involved in a controversy with the Memphis Light, Gas & Water Division not of their own making. The Light Division is part of the city of Memphis. When the Crafts moved into a residence, previously a duplex, they discovered that it had two gas and electric meters and one water meter. Although they assumed that one set of meters had been disconnected, they began to receive two monthly bills. They sought the help of a contractor to have the gas and electricity come through a separate meter for each. Although they did not realize it at the time, the contractor bungled the job, and the Crafts continued to receive two separate billings. They tried through phone calls and a personal visit to the division's offices to resolve the two-meter problem, but were unsuccessful. In the meantime, the division cut off their utility service five times. Finally the Crafts sought relief in the federal district court.

Judge Harry W. Welford found that if the utility bill is not paid within twenty days, the division sends a "final notice" warning the customer that if payment is not received in four more days, the service will be terminated. When payment is not forthcoming, the meter reader is instructed to cut off the service. Based upon this information, Judge Welford concluded that utility customers "had no property interest in continued utility service while a disputed bill remained unpaid."[48] He did, however, "on the basis of a very limited possible denial of due process," order that the Crafts to be reimbursed

*Memphis Light, Gas & Water Div. v. Craft, 436 U.S. 1, 18 (1978).

in the amount of $35 "for 'duplicate and unnecessary charges made and expenses incurred by [them].'" The court of appeals reversed. The Crafts had not received due process. A majority of the Supreme Court came to the same conclusion.

It was necessary for the justices first to determine whether the utility's customers had a property interest in the continuation of service. If such an interest did not exist, due process was not required. In searching the Tennessee law on the subject, the Court found that "if the public utility discontinues service for nonpayment of a disputed amount it does so at its peril and if the public utility was wrong (e.g., customer overcharged) it is liable for damages." Moreover, "an aggrieved customer may be able to enjoin a wrongful threat to terminate, or to bring a subsequent action for damages or a refund." From this the justices concluded that the state was giving recognition to "a protected interest" in continued utility service.

Having reached that conclusion, it was an easy step for the majority to find that the Crafts had not been given an adequate opportunity to be heard on why they were not paying their bills. "Notice in a case of this kind," Justice Powell explained, "does not comport with constitutional requirements when it does not advise the customer of the availability of a procedure for protesting a proposed termination of utility service as unjustified. As no such notice was given [the Crafts] — despite 'good faith efforts' on their part — they were deprived of the notice which was their due." The Court did not spell out in detail the kind of procedure due process required but suggested that "some administrative procedure for entertaining customer complaints prior to termination is required to afford reasonable assurance against erroneous or arbitrary withholding of essential services."

The three dissenting justices did not disagree with the majority's conclusion that under Tennessee law the Crafts had a protectable property interest in continued service but thought that the division's method of handling cutoffs adequately protected that interest.

Justice Requires a Fair Tribunal

> It is sufficiently clear from our cases that those with substantial pecuniary interest in legal proceedings should not adjudicate these disputes.*

*Gibson v. Berryhill, 411 U.S. 564, 579 (1973).

The facts of Mr. Tumey's case, as set forth by the Supreme Court, were as follows:

> Tumey ... was arrested and brought before Mayor Pugh, of the Village of North College Hill, charged with unlawfully possessing intoxicating liquor. He moved for his dismissal because of the disqualification of the Mayor to try him, under the Fourteenth Amendment. The Mayor denied the motion, proceeded to trial, convicted the defendant of unlawfully possessing intoxicating liquor within Hamilton County, as charged, fined him $100, and ordered that the be imprisoned until the fine and costs were paid.[49]

Tumey's reason for asserting that the mayor was disqualified to act as judge in his case was that in addition to his salary, the mayor was entitled to keep the fees and costs of each case in which a defendant was convicted. Furthermore, half the fines collected went to the village's treasury, from which the mayor's salary was paid.

In the Ohio appellate process, Tumey won one and lost two. The Hamilton County Court of Common Pleas concluded that the mayor was disqualified and reversed. The court of appeals held otherwise and affirmed the mayor. The Ohio Supreme Court dismissed Tumey's appeal, finding that there was no constitutional issue.

In an opinion joined by all justices, the U.S. Supreme Court reversed. Chief Justice William Howard Taft stated the general rule applicable in cases where the judge may have a pecuniary interest in the outcome. "It certainly violates the Fourteenth Amendment, and deprives a defendant in a criminal case of due process of law, to subject his liberty or property to the judgment of a court the judge of which has a direct, personal, substantial, pecuniary interest in reaching a conclusion against him in his case."

Counsel for the village argued that the general rule should not be applied in cases like this one, contending that the only way states could maintain a system of courts such as the mayor's court was to use funds generated by fees and costs. But the justices did not believe that that eliminated the due process issue "unless the costs usually imposed are so small that they may properly be ignored." In Tumey's case, Mayor Pugh was paid $12, and for handling other cases under the Prohibition Act he had received about $100 a month for seven months. "It is certainly not fair," the chief justice wrote, "to each defendant, brought before the Mayor for the careful and judicial consideration of his guilt or innocence, that the prospect of such a loss by the Mayor should weigh against his acquittal." The village's counsel also argued that the evidence showed that Tumey was guilty and that because he was fined the minimum amount, there really was no denial of due process. But the justices were not impressed. The bottom line: "No matter what the evidence against him, he had a right to have an impartial judge."

L. M. Berryhill and a number of other optometrists in Alabama found their fate in the hands of a biased tribunal when charges were brought against them for unprofessional conduct. Berryhill and the others were employed by Lee Optical Co. However, no provision of the Alabama statutes regulating the practice of optometry expressly permitted corporate entities to engage in the practice. The Alabama Optometric Association therefore brought charges against the Berryhill group before the Alabama Board of Optometry, asserting that they were practicing their profession illegally. The charges against the group included "aiding and abetting a corporation in the illegal practice of optometry; practicing optometry under a false name, that is, Lee Optical Co.; unlawfully soliciting the sale of glasses; lending their licenses to Lee Optical Co.; and splitting or dividing fees with Lee Optical."[50]

Before taking any action, the board brought suit against Lee Optical in a local Alabama court, asking the court to enjoin the company from practicing optometry, which the court odid. Following that victory, the board took up the charges against the Berryhill group, but before they could be heard, Berryhill and the others turned to the local federal district court for help. They sought an injunction against the hearings before the board, claiming that the Alabama procedure was unconstitutional because "the Board was biased and could not provide the [group] with a fair and impartial hearing in conformity with due process of law." The Berryhill group asserted two reasons why they would not recieve a fair hearing from the optometry board: (1) the members of the board were all optometrists engaged in the private practice of optometry; (2) the board itself, before conducting a hearing into the charges against the group, had brought the action seeking to enjoin Lee Optical and the individuals from the practice.

The district court agreed that the board was biased and that for it to conduct a hearing on the charges would be a violation of due process. District Judge Robert E. Varner, writing for himself and two other judges, declared: "Nonetheless, this Court is of the opinion that the statute places the fate of [the group], as practicing optometrists, in the hands of persons who have apparent personal interests in the matter in controversy. This invades the very core of due process of law."[51] A unanimous Supreme Court came to the same conclusion and in an opinion by Justice White emphasized the fact that "the financial stake need not be as direct or positive as it appeared in *Tumey*. It has also come to be the prevailing view that '[m]ost of the law concerning disqualification because of interest applies with equal force to . . . administrative adjudicators.'"[52]

Justice and the Justices

> Man's capacity for justice makes democracy possible, but man's inclination to injustice makes democracy necessary.[*]

In considering man's capacity for justice and injustice, one should not exclude the woman and men who serve and have served on the Supreme Court since 1789. Their capacity to do justice, and sometimes injustice, is chronicled in the reports of the cases that come before them.

Recognizing that justice, like beauty, may be in the eye of the beholder, what follows are a few cases in which to this beholder the justices' decisions indicate an "inclination to injustice."

Fleming v. Nestor[53] is one of those decisions. Justice Black, who dissented from the decisions, detailed the facts of Ephram V. Nestor's case.

> Nestor came to this country from Bulgaria in 1913 and lived here continuously for 43 years, until 1956. He was then deported from this country for having been a Communist from 1933 to 1939. At that time membership in the Communist Party as such was not illegal and was not even a statutory ground for deportation. From December 1936 to January 1955 Nestor and his employers made regular payments to the Government under the [Social Security laws.] These funds went to a special federal old-age and survivors insurance trust fund . . . in return for which Nestor, like millions of others, expected to receive payments when he reached statutory age. In 1954, 15 years after Nestor had last been a Communist, and 18 years after he began to make payments into the old-age security fund, Congress passed a law providing, among other things, that any person who had been deported from this country because of past Communist

[*]Reinhold Niebuhr, The Children of Light and the Children of Darkness (1944).

membership . . . should be wholly cut off from any benefits of the fund to which he had contributed under the law. After the government deported Nestor in 1956 it notified his wife, who had remained in this country, that he was cut off and no further payments would be made to him.

Judge Edward A. Tamm, who heard Nestor's case in the federal district court, concluded that the withholding of Nestor's social security benefits was a violation of due process of law. Five justices of the Supreme Court voted to reverse him, thus upholding the termination of Nestor's benefits. In an opinion written by Justice Harlan, the majority held that Congress had the power to make the decision to cut off benefits and that that decision would not violate due process unless it was "utterly lacking in rational justification." They then concluded that that was "not the case here."

Justice Black thought this was an outrageous decision. "The fact that the Court is sustaining this action," he insisted, "indicates the extent to which people are willing to go these days to overlook violations of the Constitution perpetrated against anyone who has ever even innocently belonged to the Communist Party." And for justices Brennan and Douglas and Chief Justice Warren, this decision was inconsistent with the spirit of the Constitution. "The Framers ordained," Justice Brennan declared, "that even the worst of men should not be punished for their past acts or for any conduct without adherence to the procedural safeguards written into the Constitution."

Clyde W. Summers's application for admission to practice law in Illinois was denied "on the ground of [his] inability to take in good faith the required oath to support the Constitution of Illinois."[54] The part of the Illinois Constitution with which Summers had difficulty required all men to serve in the state militia in time of war. He based his objection upon his religious beliefs.

> He is opposed to the use of force for either offensive or defensive purposes. The taking of human life under any circumstances he believes to be against the Law of God and contrary to the best interests of man. He would if he could, he told his examiners, obey to the letter these percepts of Christ: "Love your Enemies; Do good to those that hate you; Even though your enemy strike you on your right cheek, turn to him your left cheek also." The record of his evidence before us bears convincing marks of the deep sincerity of his convictions, and counsel for Illinois with commendable candor does not question the genuineness of his professions.

A majority of the Court held that denial of Summers's application for admission to the bar was not a violation of the free exercise
clause of the First Amendment. If the United States could deny
citizenship to one who refuses to pledge military service, the state
did not have to admit to the practice of law a person who could not
take the some pledge because of religious beliefs.

For dissenters Black, Douglas, Murphy, and Rutledge, the decision could not be squared with the Constitution. "I cannot agree,"
Justice Black insisted, "that a state can lawfully bar from a semi-
public position a well-qualified man of good character solely because
he entertains a religious belief which might prompt him at some time
in the future to violate a law which has not yet been and may never
be enacted."

A conflict between the estate succession laws of Louisiana and
Rita Nell Vincent found a majority of the justices upholding the laws
against Rita's claim as the surviving child of Ezra Vincent.

> In 1961, Ezra Vincent was 69 years old and Lou Bertha Patterson . . .
> was 41. . . . Soon after meeting each other in 1961, Mrs. Patterson
> moved in with Mr. Vincent. Although they did not marry, Mrs. Pat-
> terson had a daughter by Mr. Vincent on March 15, 1962. The child's
> birth certificate identified the father and mother by name. Within
> two months, Mr. Vincent and Mrs. Patterson appeared before a
> notary public and executed a form, in accordance with Louisiana
> law, acknowledging that Mr. Vincent was the father of the child. A
> month later, the child's birth certificate was changed to give the child
> Mr. Vincent's name, and she has always been known as Rita Nell
> Vincent. By acknowledging the child, Mr. Vincent became legally
> obligated under state law to support her. Mr. Vincent and Mrs. Pat-
> terson continued to live together and raise Rita Nell until Mr. Vin-
> cent died in 1968. He left no will.[55]

Despite the attempt of Rita's parents to have the record show
that Ezra was her father, in the eyes of the law she was an illegitimate
child because Ezra and Lou Bertha had never married. Under the
law, illegitimate children had no right of inheritance, and therefore
Mr. Vincent's estate passed to other relatives. In upholding this
result, the majority held that "the power to make rules to establish,
protect, and strengthen family life as well as to regulate the disposition of property left in Louisiana by a man dying there is committed by the Constitution of the United States and the people of
Louisiana to the legislature of that State. Absent specific constitutional

guarantee, it is for that legislature, not life-tenured judges of this Court, to select from among possible laws."

The "central reality of this case" for four dissenting justices was that "Louisiana punishes illegitimate children for the misdeeds of their parents." And because they could "find no rational basis to justify the distinction Louisiana creates between an acknowledged illegitimate child [as Rita was] and a legitimate one, that discrimination [was] clearly invidious."

As pointed out above, "The power to exclude or to expel aliens . . . is vested in the political departments of the government," the president and Congress. And because of this the Court has adopted a policy of generally deferring to their judgment in immigration cases. But sometimes that deference can have very unjust consequences. Such was the result in Ignatz Mezie's case.

> Mezei came to this country in 1923 and lived as a resident alien in Buffalo, New York, for twenty-five years. He made a trip to Europe in 1948 and was stopped at our shore on his return in 1950. Without charge of or conviction for any crime, he was for two years held a prisoner on Ellis Island by order of the Attorney General. Mezei sought habeas corpus in the District Court. He wanted to go to his wife and home in Buffalo. The Attorney General defended the imprisonment by alleging that it would be dangerous to the Nation's security to let Mezei go home even temporarily on bail. Asked for proof of this, the Attorney General answered the judge that all his information was "of confidential nature," so much so that telling any of it or even telling the names of any of his secret informers would jeopardize the safety of the Nation. Finding that Mezei's life as a resident then in Buffalo had been "unexceptionable" and that no facts had been proven to justify his continued imprisonment, the District court granted bail.[56]

The Court of Appeals agreed with this decision, but a majority of the Supreme Court upheld the detention of Mezei at Ellis Island, even though it appeared that other nations would not accept him. For the majority, this was not a difficult case. Even though Mezei had lived in this country for twenty-five years, upon his return from a trip abroad he was considered by the government an alien subject to exclusion. As such, he was not entitled to the protection of the Constitution, and therefore the decision of the attorney general to restrain him at Ellis Island was lawful.

But holding Mezei in limbo without giving him an opportunity to meet his accusers and to prove that he was not a threat to the

security of the country greatly disturbed four justices. "It is incon-
ceivable to me," Justice Jackson argues, "that this measure of simple
justice and fair dealing would menace the security of this country.
No one can make me believe that we are that far gone."

The Supreme Court has held that "enlisted military personnel
may not maintain a suit to recover damages from a superior officer
for alleged constitutional violations."[57] This, a majority of the justices
believed, was necessary because of "the unique disciplinary structure of the Military Establishment and Congress' activity in the
field." The majority applied that philosophy in the unusual case of
Master Sergeant James B. Stanley.

> In February 1958, James B. Stanley . . . volunteered to participate in
> a program ostensibly designed to test the effectiveness of protective
> clothing and equipment as defenses against chemical warfare. . . .
> Four times that month, Stanley was secretly administered doses of
> lysergic acid diethylamide (LSD), pursuant to an Army plan to study
> the effects of the drug on human subjects. . . . Stanley has suffered
> from hallucinations and periods of incoherence and memory loss,
> was impaired in his military performance, and would on occasion
> "awake from sleep at night and, without reason, violently beat his
> wife and children, later being unable to recall the entire incident."
> . . . He was discharged from the Army in 1969. One year later, his
> marriage dissolved because of the personality changes wrought by
> the LSD.

Stanley had no knowledge that he had received LSD until 1975 when
the army sought his cooperation in a study of the effects LSD on
"'volunteers who participated' in the 1958 tests."

By legal action, Stanley attempted to secure compensation for
his injuries, first from the government, which was denied, and then
from the officers involved in administering the drug to him. The
federal district court, Judge José A. Gonzalez, Jr., presiding, and the
court of appeals sustained his right to proceed against the officers,
but a majority of the Supreme Court disagreed. "A test for liability,"
Justice Scalia insisted, "that depends on the extent to which particular
suits would call into question military discipline and decisionmaking
would itself require judicial inquiry into, and hence intrusion upon,
military matters." Therefore, prohibiting any claim that arises 'incident to service' . . . provides a line that is relatively clear and that can
be discerned with less extensive inquiry into military matters."

Justice O'Connor accepted the majority's position that "civilian
courts [should] avoid entertaining a suit involving harm caused as a

result of military service." But this, she thought, was clearly an exceptional case. She wrote:

> In my view, conduct of the type alleged in this case is so far beyond the bounds of human decency that as a matter of law it simply cannot be considered a part of the military mission. [The Court's previously created rule prohibiting actions against superior officers] surely cannot insulate defendants from liability for deliberate and calculated exposure of otherwise healthy military personnel to medical experimentation without their consent, outside of any combat, combat training, or military exigency, and for no other reason than to gather information on the effect of lysergic acid diethylamide on human beings.

Two of the more infamous cases in which the Supreme Court allowed injustice to be done are *Dred Scott v. Sandford*[58] and *Korematsu v. United States*.[59]

In 1834 Dr. Emerson, an army surgeon, took his slave Dred Scott from Missouri to Rock Island, Illinois, and two years later to Fort Snelling, Minnesota. While at Fort Snelling, Scott married Harriet, another slave of Dr. Emerson's, and two children were born of that marriage. In 1838 Dr. Emerson moved back to Missouri and took the Scotts with him. Shortly thereafter, he sold the Scotts to John F. A. Sandford.

Some years later, Dred Scott brought an action against Sandford alleging that Sandford has assaulted him and his family. Scott commenced the suit in the federal court, arguing that the court had jurisdiction because he was a citizen of Missouri and Sandford was a citizen of New York. Sandford responded that because the Scotts were slaves, they were not citizens of Missouri and that therefore the federal court had no jurisdiction over the case. Scott's answer was that he and his family became free when they were taken from Missouri into Illinois, a part of the United States in which slavery was prohibited, and therefore were citizens of Missouri upon their return.

The Supreme Court agreed with Sandford and ordered the case dismissed. A majority of the justices concluded that Scott "acquired no title of freedom by being taken, by his owner, to Rock Island, in Illinois, and brought back to Missouri" because under the laws of Missouri, "a slave does not become entitled to his freedom, where the owner takes him to reside in a State where slavery is not permitted, and afterwards brings him back to Missouri."[60] On that basis the Court held that the Scotts were not citizens of Missouri and that the federal court therefore had no jurisdiction in the case. In addition, the Court held that even free Negroes were not citizens of the United States, a finding that was annulled by the Fourteenth Amendment, which provides: "All persons born or naturalized in the United States . . . are citizens of the United States and the State wherein they reside."

Justices John McLean and Benjamin Curtis dissented. In his dissent Justice McLean argued that "being born under our Constitution and laws, no naturalization is required, as one of foreign birth, to make him a citizen. The most general and appropriate definition of the term citizen is 'a freeman.' Being a freeman, and having his domicile in a State different from that of the defendant, he is a citizen within the act of Congress, and the courts of the Union are open to him."

During World War II, President Franklin D. Roosevelt issued an executive order giving the military authority to issue orders protecting the country from espionage and sabotage. Pursuant to that order, orders were issued by the military placing an 8 P.M. to 6 A.M. curfew upon persons of Japanese ancestry and excluding them from certain areas of the western United States. Toyosaburo Korematsu, an American citizen, was convicted of remaining in an area designated as off limits to those of Japanese descent. His conviction was upheld by a court of appeals and by a majority of the Supreme Court. In so doing, the Court acknowledged that Korematsu's loyalty was not questioned and that "exclusion from the area in which one's home is located is a far greater deprivation that constant confinement to the home from 8 P.M. to 6 A.M."[61] Furthermore, "all legal restrictions which curtail the civil rights of a single racial group are immediately suspect."

The majority believed, however, that under the circumstances, the exclusion order was necessary, even though it caused great hardship upon "a large group of American citizens." Justice Black declared for the majority:

> But hardships are part of war, and war is an aggregation of hardships. All citizens alike, both in and out of uniform, feel the impact of war in greater or lesser measure. Citizenship has its responsibilities as well as its privileges, and in time of war the burden is always heavier. Compulsory exclusion of large groups of citizens from their homes, except under circumstances of direst emergency and peril, is inconsistent with our basic governmental institutions.

But when under conditions of modern warfare our shores are threatened by hostile forces, the power to protect must be commensurate with the threatened danger.

But this did not satisfy Justice Frank Murphy, who thought that the exclusion of these American citizens was racism, pure and simple. "Such exclusion," he emphasized, "goes over 'the very brink of constitutional power' and falls into the ugly abyss of racism." It was the fall out that this judicial decision would have on liberty that concerned Justice Jackson.

Much is said of the danger to liberty from the Army program for deporting and detaining these citizens of Japanese extraction. But a judicial construction of the due process clause that will sustain this order is a far more subtle blow to liberty than the promulgation of the order itself. A military order, however unconstitutional, is not apt to last longer than the military emergency. . . . But once a judicial opinion rationalizes such an order to show that it conforms to the Constitution, or rather rationalizes the Constitution to show that the Constitution sanctions such an order, the Court for all time has validated the principle of racial discrimination in criminal procedure and of transplanting American citizens. The principle then lies about like a loaded weapon ready for the hand of any authority that can bring forward a plausible claim of an urgent need. Every repetition imbeds that principle more deeply in our law and thinking and expands it to new purposes.

For a more comprehensive review of cases I believe are lacking the spirit of the Constitution, see "Tinkling Cymbals and Sounding Brass: 'Liberty' and 'Justice' in Supreme Court Adjudication."[62]

CHAPTER 3

Equality

> Statutes create many classifications which do not deny
> equal protection; it is only "invidious discrimination"
> which offends the Constitution.
> —*Ferguson v. Skrupa*, 372 U.S. 726, 732 (1963)

In the Beginning

That people should be treated equally by government was a belief held by many during the settlement of the colonies. For example, the Massachusetts Body of Liberties (1641) contains this statement: "2. Every person within this Jurisdiction, whether Inhabitant or forreiner shall enjoy the same justice and law, that is generall for the plantation, which we constitute and execute one towards another without partialitie or delay."

The concept of equality can also be found in the first section of the Declaration of Rights of the colonies of Virginia, Pennsylvania, Massachusetts, Vermont, and New Hampshire. The Virginia Declaration of Rights (1776) expresses the idea this way: "1. That all men are by nature equally free and independent." And the first truth to be declared by the Declaration of Independence (1776) was "that all men are created equal."

It is, of course, paradoxical that notwithstanding these lofty pronouncements, real equality did not exist during this period in our history. Slavery existed in some of the colonies, and some declarations of rights therefore referred to "freemen" or "free inhabitants." We also know that the Constitution itself recognized and allowed the continuation of slavery, at least until 1808. Even the Supreme Court contributed to the maintenance of the status quo by its decision in *Dred Scott* where it held that a slave was not a citizen of the United States.

It was not until the adoption of the Thirteenth, Fourteenth, and Fifteenth Amendments after the Civil War that the ideal of equality became part of our constitutional system. The Thirteenth Amendment prohibits slavery. The Fourteenth makes citizens of all persons born or naturalized in the United States and guarantees to all persons the equal protection of the laws. The Fifteenth ensures that the right to vote shall not be denied because of race or color or because the person was a slave.

But even then it is clear that the guarantee of equal protection, does not mean that the government must treat all people equally under all circumstances. To the extent that at least five justices of the Supreme Court are willing to permit it, the government by its laws and its actions may affect some people differently than others.

Classifications by Race

> It [the Fourteenth Amendment] was designed to assure to the colored race the enjoyment of all the civil rights that under the law are enjoyed by white persons, and to give to that race the protection of the general government, in that enjoyment, whenever it should be denied by the States.*

Shortly after the adoption of the Fourteenth Amendment, Mr. Strauder, a black man, was tried and convicted of murder in Ohio County, West Virginia, before an all-white jury. The laws of the state at that time provided that "All white male persons who are twenty-one years of age and who are citizens of this State shall be liable to serve as jurors."[1] The West Virginia Supreme Court affirmed Strauder's conviction, but the U.S. Supreme Court reversed, two justices dissenting. In referring to the Fourteenth Amendment, Justice William Strong expressed the opinion for the majority that "the words of the amendment, it is true, are prohibitory, but they contain a necessary implication of a positive immunity, or right, most valuable to the colored race, — the right to exemption from unfriendly legislation against them distinctively as colored, — exemption from legal discriminations, implying inferiority in civil society, lessening the security of their enjoyment of the rights which others enjoy, and discriminations which are steps towards reducing them to the condition of a subject race." This led the majority to con-

*Strauder v. West Virginia, 100 U.S. 303, 306 (1880).

clude "that the statute of West Virginia, discriminating in the selection of jurors, as it does, against negroes because of their color, amounts to a denial of the equal protection of the laws to a colored man when he is put upon trial for an alleged offense against the State."

It would, of course, be erroneous to conclude that the equal protection clause protected only members of the black race. That it applies to other people as well was confirmed in *Yick Wo v. Hopkins, Sheriff*.[2] The facts of that case, as admitted on the record:

> That [Yick Wo] is a native of China and came to California in 1861, and is still a subject of the Emperor of China; that he has been engaged in the laundry business in the same premises and building for twenty-two years last past; that he had a license from the board of fire wardens, dated March 3, 1884, from which appeared "that the above described premises have been inspected by the board of fire wardens, and upon such inspection said board found all proper arrangements for carrying on the business; . . . that he [Yick Wo] had a certificate from the health officer that the same premises had been inspected by him, and that he found that . . . all proper arrangements for carrying on the business of a laundry, . . . had been complied with; that the city license of [Yick Wo's] was in force and expired October 1st 1885; and that [Yick Wo] applied to the board of supervisors, June 1st, 1885, for consent of said board to maintain and carry on his laundry, but that said board, on July 1st, 1885 refused said consent." It is also admitted to be true . . . that, on February 24, 1880, "there were about 320 laundries in the city and county of San Francisco, of which about 240 were owned and conducted by subjects of China, and of the whole number, viz., 320, about 310 were constructed of wood, the same material that constitutes nine-tenths of the houses in the city of San Francisco."
>
> . . . .
>
> It was also admitted "that [Yick Wo] and 200 of his countrymen similarly situated petitioned the board of supervisors for permission to continue their business in the various houses which they had been occupying and using for laundries for more than twenty years, and such petitions were denied, and all petitions of those who were not Chinese, with one exception of Mrs. Mary Meagles, were granted."

Yick Wo was in custody of the sheriff, having been convicted of conducting a laundry in a building not constructed of "either brick or stone." He sought release on a writ of habeas corpus, which was denied. A unanimous Supreme Court reversed and ordered Yick Wo released from custody.

Justice Stanley Matthews authored the opinion for the Court. He first pointed out that "though the law itself be fair on its face and impartial in appearance, yet, if it is applied and administered by public authority with an evil eye and an unequal hand, so as practically to make unjust and illegal discriminations between persons in similar circumstances, material to their rights, the denial of equal justice is still within the prohibition of the Constitution." The Court held that the otherwise neutral requirement that laundries be in "brick or stone" buildings was applied in this case with "an evil eye and an unequal hand" because "no reason for [the denial] exists except hostility to the race and nationality" of Yick Wo. "The discrimination is, therefore," Justice Matthews stressed, "illegal, and the public administration which enforces it is a denial of the equal protection of the laws and a violation of the Fourteenth Amendment of the Constitution."

The Court seemed to establish a strong commitment to equality of the races in *Strauder* and *Yick Wo*, but ten years later retreated from that position in *Plessy v. Ferguson*.[3] Plessy, who was seven-eighths Caucasian and one-eighth African, was arrested for taking a seat on a passenger train in Louisiana in a coach reserved for white passengers. Before he was tried, he petitioned the supreme court of Louisiana for an order prohibiting Judge John H. Ferguson of the Orleans Parish criminal court from proceeding with the case. Plessy argued that the state law which required separate but equal passenger coaches on trains was unconstitutional. The Louisiana Supreme Court denied Plessy's request, and he appealed to the U.S. Supreme Court, which upheld the decision, with only Justice Harlan dissenting. The issue before the Court, simply put, was whether a state government's requirement of separate but equal facilities for blacks and whites on passenger trains violated the equal protection clause.

In explaining why the separate but equal doctrine did not violate equal protection, Justice Brown wrote:

> The object of the [Fourteenth] amendment was undoubtedly to enforce the absolute equality of the two races before the law, but in the nature of things it could not have been intended to abolish distinctions based upon color, or to enforce social, as distinguished from political equality, or a commingling of the two races upon terms

unsatisfactory to either. Laws permitting, and even requiring, their separation in places where they are liable to be brought into contact do not necessarily imply the inferiority of either race to the other.

This decision greatly disturbed the first Justice Harlan. He did not believe that the government had any right to know the race of the people protected by the Constitution. "But in view of the Constitution, in the eye of the law," he proclaimed, "there is in this country no superior, dominant, ruling class of citizens. There is no caste here. Our Constitution is color-blind, and neither knows nor tolerates classes among citizens. In respect of civil rights, all citizens are equal before the law. The humblest is the peer of the most powerful.... It is, therefore, to be regretted that this high tribunal, the final expositor of the fundamental law of the land, has reached the conclusion that it is competent for a State to regulate the enjoyment by citizens of their civil rights soley upon the basis of race."

The separate but equal theory existed for almost sixty years before it was finally overruled in *Brown v. Board of Education*.[4] Oliver Brown, together with other parents in Topeka, Kansas, brought suit in the federal district court seeking an injunction preventing the board of education from maintaining separate schools for black and white students. A three-judge district court, in an opinion written by Circuit Judge Walter A. Huxman, found that "segregation in public education has a detrimental effect upon Negro children, but denied relief on the ground that the Negro and white schools were substantially equal with respect to buildings, transportation, curricula, and educational qualifications of teachers."

At the time the Supreme Court agreed to hear Brown's appeal, it also accepted cases from South Carolina, Virginia, and Delaware, which raised the same issue—whether separate but equal public schools violate equal protection. The justices unanimously responded that such schools were unconstitutional under the equal protection clause.

Before addressing the question before them, the justices, in an opinion written by Chief Justice Warren, set forth their thoughts on the part public education plays in our society.

Today, education is perhaps the most important function of state and local governments. Compulsory school attendance laws and the great expenditures for education both demonstrate our recognition of the importance of education to our democratic society. It is required in the performance of our most basic public responsibilities, even service in the armed forces. It is the very foundation of good citizenship. Today it is a principal instrument in awakening the child to cultural values, in preparing him for later professional training, and in helping him to adjust normally to his environment. In these days, it is doubtful that any child may reasonably be expected to succeed in life if he is denied the opportunity of an education. Such an opportunity, where the state has undertaken to provide it, is a right which must be made available to all on equal terms.

That brought the justices to the issue to be decided. "Does segregation of children in public schools solely on the basis of race, even though the physical facilities and other 'tangible' factors may be equal, deprive the children of the minority group of equal opportunities?" The answer: "We believe that it does." "We conclude," the chief justice declared, "that in the field of public education the doctrine of 'separate but equal' has no place. Separate educational facilities are inherently unequal."

The *Brown* decision required states to integrate public schools. In the years that followed, the Court also struck down segregation on buses, in public parks, airport restaurants, courtroom seating, municipal auditoriums, prison facilities, municipal golf courses, and public beaches. It also struck down a state law which prohibited integrated athletic contests.

In ordering that schools be integrated, the Court said that it should be done with "all deliberate speed." Such was not to be. Many school boards that were operating segregated schools fought the Court's order. Even the Court became aware of the delaying tactics being used. In 1971 Chief Justice Burger wrote:

> Over the 16 years since *Brown II*, many difficulties were encountered in implementation of the basic constitutional requirement that the State not discriminate between public school children on the basis of their race. Nothing in our national experience prior to 1955 prepared anyone for dealing with changes and adjustments of the magnitude and complexity encountered since then. Deliberate resistance of some to the Court's mandates has impeded the good-faith efforts of others to bring school systems into compliance. The detail and nature of these dilatory tactics have been noted frequently by this Court and other courts.[5]

Racial discrimination takes many forms. Sometimes it is blatantly discriminatory, but sometimes it can be found only by careful examination of the actions of those representing the government. Linda Sidoti Palmore was confronted with a straightforward case of racial discrimination when a court took her daughter from her and gave custody to the child's father. The Sidotis, both Caucasians, had been divorced, and Mrs. Palmore had been given custody of their three-year-old child. Some time thereafter, Anthony J. Sidoti, the father, sought to obtain custody of the daughter, arguing that the mother was then cohabiting with Clarence Palmore, Jr., a Negro, whom she later married.

Although the father also alleged that the mother was not taking proper care of the daughter, no evidence was found to support that claim. The only issue then before the court was whether the best interests of the child would be served by taking her from a home that now consisted of a black stepfather and the white mother and child. A court counselor recommended that custody be given to the father because the mother "has chosen for herself and for her child, a lifestyle unacceptable to the father *and to society.*"[6]

The court agreed that it would be in the child's best interests and gave custody to the father. The court expressed its reason: "'*This Court feels that despite the strides that have been made in bettering relations between the races in this country, it is inevitable that Melanie will, if allowed to remain in her present situation and attains school age and thus more vulnerable to peer pressures, suffer from the social stigmatization that is sure to come.*'" A Florida appellate court affirmed, but a unanimous Supreme Court did not.

"A core purpose of the Fourteenth Amendment," Chief Justice Burger explained, "was to do away with all governmentally imposed discrimination based on race. . . . Classifying persons according to their race is more likely to reflect racial prejudice than legitimate public concerns; the race, not the person, dictates the category. . . . Such classifications are subject to the most exacting scrutiny; to pass constitutional muster, they must be justified by a compelling governmental interest and must be 'necessary . . . to the accomplishment' of their legitimate purpose."

The Court was aware, of course, that protecting the interest of children is one of the highest priorities of a state. And the Court admitted that "it would ignore reality to suggest that racial and ethnic prejudices do not exist or that all manifestations of those prejudices have been eliminated." "There is a risk that a child living with a stepparent of a different race may be subject to a variety of pressures and stresses not present if the child were living with parents of the same racial or ethnic origin." But that will not justify the decision made by the trial court. "The effects of racial prejudice, however real," the chief justice noted, "cannot justify a racial classification removing an infant child from the custody of its natural mother found to be an appropriate person to have such custody."

Finding purposeful discrimination sometimes requires searching inquiry into motives. The case of Carmen Edwards, a black, and Victor Underwood, a white, required the justices to make that kind of investigation into the motivation behind the adoption of Section 182 of the Alabama Constitution of 1901, which disqualified from voting those convicted of any one of a long list of crimes, including any "crime involving moral turpitude."[7]

Edwards and Black were disenfranchised because each had been convicted of issuing a worthless check. Each sued his board of registrars in the federal district court and included "a claim that the misdemeanors encompassed within Section 182 were intentionally adopted to disenfranchise blacks on account of their race and that their inclusion in Section 182 has had the intended effect."

District Judge Frank H. McFadden found that the purpose for holding the constitutional convention in 1901 was to disenfranchise blacks but did not believe that there was any connection between that purpose and the adoption of Section 182. The court of appeals took issue with that conclusion and reversed. It found that "the crimes selected for inclusion in Section 182 were believed by the [convention] delegates to be more frequently committed by blacks." And the evidence seemed to bear out the delegates' beliefs, because during the two-year period following the adoption of the section, "approximately ten times as many black as whites," were stricken from the voting rolls.

All justices of the Supreme Court, except Justice Powell who did not participate in the case, voted to affirm the court of appeals. The Court found that "the delegates to the all-white convention were not secretive about their purpose, [and that] John B. Knox, president of the convention, stated in his opening address: 'And what is it that we want to do? Why it is within the limits imposed by the Federal Constitution, to establish white supremacy in this State.'" The justices, taking note that the evidence "demonstrates conclusively that Section 182 was enacted with the intent of disenfranchising blacks," concluded that the court of appeals was correct in declaring the section, as it applied to those committing misdemeanors, unconstitutional.

Sometimes racial discrimination can be so subtle that it is

difficult to recognize. But once discovered, it should be held a violation of the equal protection clause just like more obvious discrimination. That was the position of a majority of the justices in Larry Joe Powers's case. Powers, a white man, was being tried in Ohio for murder.

> In the jury selection process, Powers objected when the prosecutor exercised his first peremptory challenge to remove a black venireperson. Powers requested the trial court to compel the prosecutor to explain, on the record, his reasons for excluding a black person. The trial court denied the request and excused the juror. The state proceeded to use nine more peremptory challenges, six of which removed black venirepersons from the jury. Each time the prosecutor challenged a black prospective juror, Powers renewed his objections. . . . His objections were overruled.[8]

Powers was convicted. An Ohio appellate court affirmed, and the Ohio Supreme Court dismissed an appeal to that court, believing that the case did not present a substantial constitutional issue.

The U.S. Supreme Court, with seven justices concurring in the opinion, reversed. Although the Court had dealt with the discriminatory use of peremptory challenges in a number of cases since *Strauder*, this was the first time it was confronted with an objection by a person of one race to the exclusion from the jury of persons of another race.

To put the case in proper focus, Justice Kennedy, for the majority, pointed out that "for over a century, this Court has been unyielding in its position that a defendant is denied equal protection of the laws when tried before a jury from which members of his or her race have been excluded by the State's purposeful conduct." Also, "although a defendant has no right to a 'petit jury composed in whole or in part of persons of [the defendant's] own race,' . . . he or she does have the right to be tried by a jury whose members are selected by nondiscriminatory criteria." Further, "jury service preserves the democratic element of the law, as it guards the rights of the parties and insures continued acceptance of the laws by all of the people." The majority then held

> that the Equal Protection Clause prohibits a prosecutor from using the State's peremptory challenges to exclude otherwise qualified and unbiased persons from the petit jury solely by reason of their race, a practice that forecloses a significant opportunity to participate in civic life. An individual juror does not have a right to sit on any particular petit jury, but he or she does possess the right not to be excluded from one on account of race.

It is clear that the Court's principal objection to the exclusion of the blacks from the jury was that *they* are being discriminated against because of their race, and racial discrimination of any kind has no place in a trial. "The purpose of the jury system," Justice Kennedy insisted, "is to impress upon the criminal defendant and the community as a whole that a verdict of conviction or acquittal is given in accordance with the law by persons who are fair. The verdict will not be accepted or understood in these terms if the jury is chosen by unlawful means at the outset. Upon these considerations, we find that a criminal defendant suffers a real injury when the prosecutor excludes jurors at his or her own trial on account of race."

For Justice Scalia and Chief Justice Rehnquist, this decision was a "clear departure" from the Court's prior cases. Justice Scalia listed many of the cases which involved the exclusion of jurors because of their race and noted that "in *all* these cases, the basis for our decision was that the State had violated the *defendant's* right to equal protection, because it had excluded jurors of *his* race." And "we have *never* held, or even said, that a juror has an equal-protection right not to be excluded from a particular case through peremptory challenge; and the existence of such a right would call into question the continuing existence of a centuries-old system that has important beneficial effects." The dissenters read the Court's opinion as requiring "convictions . . . to be overturned, apparently, *whenever* 'race is implicated in the trial,'" "To me," Justice Scalia declared, "this makes no sense. Lofty aims do not justify every step intended to achieve them. Today's supposed blow against racism, while enormously self-satisfying, is unmeasured and misdirected."

Just because a state law may have the same effect upon a white person as it does upon a black person does not mean that the law is immune from attack as a racial classification under the equal protection clause. Under Virginia's antimiscegenation law, both the black and the white person were guilty of a crime if they intermarried. When Mildred Jeter, a black woman, married Richard Loving, a white man, both were convicted of violating the law and ordered to leave Virginia for twenty-five years.[9] In attacking their convictions, the Lovings argued that the law was a racial classification in violation of equal protection. A unanimous Supreme Court agreed.

In support of the law, Virginia argued that "because its miscegenation statutes punish equally both the white and the Negro participants in an interracial marriage, these statutes, despite their reliance on racial classifications, do not constitute an invidious discrimination based upon race." The justices were not convinced. Writing for the Court, Chief Justice Warren stated: "In the case at bar, however, we deal with statutes containing racial classifications, and the fact of equal application does not immunize the statute from the very heavy burden of justification which the Fourteenth Amendment has traditionally required of state statutes drawn according to race."

Not finding any legitimate reason for the classification, and concluding that the purpose of the law was to maintain white supremacy, the Court held that "there can be no doubt that restricting the freedom to marry solely because of racial classifications violates the central meaning of the Equal Protection Clause."

Aliens Have Equal Protection Rights Too

> But the Court's decisions have established that classifications based on alienage, like those based on nationality or race, are inherently suspect and subject to close judicial scrutiny. Aliens as a class are a prime example of a 'discrete and insular' minority . . . for whom such heightened judicial solicitude is appropriate.*

Carmen Richardson, sixty-four years old and a Mexican citizen, had lawfully resided in the United States for approximately thirteen years when she became totally disabled. She applied for benefits under the Social Security Act but was denied because she had not lived in Arizona for fifteen years. Under Arizona law a person must be a citizen of the United States or have lived in the state for fifteen years to receive general assistance.[10]

Elsie Mary Jane Leger, who was born in Scotland, came to the United States in 1965 and worked as a domestic in Havertown, Pennsylvania. Later she moved to Philadelphia, where she married. Both she and her husband became disabled and applied to the state for public assistance. Although Mr. Leger received some assistance, Mrs. Leger was turned down because she was an alien.

Beryl Jervis was born in Panama and came to Philadelphia in 1968 to work as a domestic. Illness forced her to retire, and she applied for general assistance, which was denied because she was not a citizen.

Richardson in Arizona and Leger and Jervis in Pennsylvania sought help from federal district courts. Both courts held that the denial of public assistance to the applicants because they were aliens

Graham v. Richardson, 403 U.S. 365, 371–372 (1971).

was a violation of the equal protection clause. Both Arizona and Pennsylvania appealed to the Supreme Court, but the justices unanimously agreed with the district courts and affirmed. As a starting point for analysis, the Court cited *Yick Wo* for the position that the word *person* in the Fourteenth Amendment includes aliens. Excluding aliens, therefore, from public assistance divided needy people into two classes, citizens and noncitizens. And while as a general rule government can treat persons differently if the reasons for doing so are reasonable, that does not apply to cases involving aliens. In such cases, the state bears a much heavier burden in justifying the discrimination. When it relegates aliens to a less favored class than citizens, its actions are "inherently suspect and subject to close judicial scrutiny." This means that the fifteen-year waiting period before aliens can qualify for assistance in Arizona, and the absolute prohibition against their participation in Pennsylvania could have been upheld only if the states had compelling reasons why they should be.

In these cases, the states' reason for not giving benefits to noncitizens were simply economic. The states "seek to justify their restrictions on the eligibility of aliens for public assistance," wrote Justice Blackmun for the Court, "solely on the basis of a State's 'special public interest' in favoring its own citizens over aliens in the distribution of limited resources such as welfare benefits." While this could well be considered a reasonable decision, it was not sufficient to overcome the presumption that alienage classifications are "inherently suspect." The justices therefore concluded that "a State's desire to preserve limited welfare benefits for its own citizens is inadequate to justify Pennsylvania's making noncitizens ineligible for public assistance, and Arizona's restricting benefits to citizens and longtime resident aliens." The Court pointed out that aliens pay taxes and are subject to being called into the armed forces. Furthermore, the federal government's immigration policy provides for favorable treatment for those who are here with our permission, and these state policies conflict with those national goals.

The decision in this case opened the door for aliens to question other state restrictions on noncitizens. Patrick Dougall, Esperanza Jorge, Teresa Vargas, and Sylvia Castro, for example, challenged a provision of the New York Civil Service Law that excluded noncitizens from civil service appointments. A federal district court struck down the citizenship requirement, and the Supreme Court affirmed, with only Justice Rehnquist dissenting. The majority acknowledged that "while the State has an interest in defining its political community, and a corresponding interest in establishing the qualifications for persons holding state elective and important nonelective executive, legislative, and judicial positions, the broad citizenship requirement established by [the law] cannot be justified on this basis."[11]

Fre Le Poole Griffiths challenged a requirement that only citizens could be members of the bar in Connecticut. She came to the United States from the Netherlands, married here, and graduated from law school. Her request to take the Connecticut bar examination was denied because she was not a citizen, and that decision was upheld by the Connecticut Supreme Court. Seven justices of the U.S. Supreme Court concluded that Griffiths had been denied equal protection of the laws and reversed. Here again, the question was whether the state's interest in high professional standards for its lawyers could overcome the "strict judicial scrutiny" demanded by the equal protection clause. The majority held that the state's interest could not withstand such examination.

> Classifications based on alienage, being inherently suspect, are subject to close judicial scrutiny, and here, the State through [its bar] committee has not met its burden of showing the classification to have been necessary to vindicate the State's undoubted interest in maintaining high professional standards.[12]

When the Court struck down New York's civil service requirement of citizenship in *Dougall*, it recognized that state interests might be of sufficient weight to justify excluding aliens from some governmental positions without running afoul of the equal protection clause. It was confronted with the question whether the position of a teacher was one of such positions in *Ambach v. Norwick*.[13]

> [Susan] Norwick was born in Scotland and is a subject of Great Britain. She has resided in this country since 1965 and is married to a United States citizen. [She] currently meets all of the educational requirements New York has set for certification as a public school teacher, but [she] consistently [has] refused to seek citizenship in spite of [her] eligibility to do so. Norwick applied in 1973 for a teaching certificate covering nursery school through sixth grade.

New York denied Norwick's application on the grounds of her alienage, and she brought suit in the federal district court. The court held that New York's law denied Norwick equal protection "because it excluded all resident aliens from all teaching jobs regardless of the subject sought to be taught, the alien's nationality, the nature of the alien's relationship to this country, and the alien's willingness to substitute some other sign of loyalty to this Nation's political values, such as an oath of allegiance."

The Supreme Court reversed, in a 5–4 decision, with Justice Powell authoring the opinion for the majority. Justice Powell's analysis started with the Court's acceptance in *Dougall* that "some functions are so bound up with the operation of the State as a governmental entity as to permit the exclusion from those functions of all persons who have not become part of the process of self-government." Further, "the exclusion of aliens from such governmental positions would not invite as demanding scrutiny from the Court." That being the case, the exclusion of aliens would be justified as long as the reasons for doing so were rational. The Court's problem then was twofold. First it had to decide whether the governmental position at issue was one in which citizenship was an important ingredient. Upon finding that it was, it remained to be determined whether the preference for citizens was rational as opposed to arbitrary and unreasonable.

By examining the role that education plays in our society and the "responsibility and discretion teachers possess in fulfilling that role," the majority concluded that "public school teachers may be regarded as performing a task 'that go[es] to the heart of representative government.'" "Public education," Justice Powell declared," . . . fulfills a most fundamental obligation of government to its constituency.' . . . The importance of public schools in the preparation of individuals for participation as citizens, and in the preservation of the values on which our society rests, long has been recognized by our decisions." Furthermore:

> A teacher serves as a role model for his students, exerting a subtle but important influence over their perceptions and values. Thus, through both the presentation of course materials and the example he sets, a teacher has an opportunity to influence the attitudes of students toward government, the political process, and a citizen's social responsibilities. This influence is crucial to the continued good health of a democracy.

The majority also pointed out that teachers, no matter what their specialty, may be called upon to teach political and social subjects, and the "State properly may regard all teachers as having an obligation to promote civic virtues and understanding in their classes, regardless of the subject taught." Because of this, the Court concluded, New York's decision to restrict the position of teacher to citizens was rationally related to the state's goals.

The majority's decision was challenged by justices Blackmun, Brennan, Marshall, and Stevens. These dissenters recognized that the Court had allowed states to discriminate against aliens in some important government positions but believed that teaching should not be one of those positions. To them, this case was more like the *Dougall* (civil servant) and *Griffiths* (lawyer) cases, and therefore New York should be required to meet the "strict judicial scrutiny test." For the dissenters, New York's law was not rational. First, it did not apply to private school teachers, and the state seemed not to be concerned that noncitizens might be teaching in those schools. Second, an alien who had declared his or her intention to become a citizen might be employed as a teacher pending the granting of citizenship. And third, the exclusion might result in the hiring of "a poor citizen teacher [rather] than an excellent resident alien teacher."

Justice Blackmun asked, "Is it preferable to have a citizen who has never seen Spain or a Latin American country teach Spanish to eighth graders and to deny that opportunity to a resident alien who may have lived for 20 years in the culture of Spain or Latin American?" The fourth reason why the law was irrational for the dissenters was that they could see no difference between requiring a state to admit aliens to the practice of law and allowing noncitizen teachers to teach. "If an attorney," argued Justice Blackmun, "has a constitutional right to take a bar examination and practice law, despite his being a resident alien, it is impossible for me to see why a resident alien, otherwise completely competent and qualified, [as Norwick is], is constitutionally disqualified from teaching in the public schools of the great State of New York."

The Court had previously applied the rationale of *Norwick* to uphold a New York law requiring members of the state police force to be citizens,[14] and after *Norwick* it upheld a California law prohibiting aliens from becoming peace officers, which included probation officers.[15] But when the Court heard that Efrem Bernal was denied the opportunity to become a notary public in Texas because he was a native of Mexico, it held that he was being denied equal protection. A majority did not believe that a notary's duties had anything to do with the "responsibilities that go to the heart of representative government."[16] Based on that conclusion, the Court carefully scrutinized the state's reasons for the requirement and found them wanting. The state had argued that the law served a "'legitimate concern that notaries be reasonably familiar with state law and institutions' and 'that notaries may be called upon years later to testify to acts they have performed.'" These arguments did not sway the Court. As Justice Marshall noted, the state had no requirement that applicants be familiar with state laws before they were commissioned, nor did it introduce any evidence showing that there was a problem because of unavailability of notaries.

Chief Justice Rehnquist's disagreement with the majority regarding classification of aliens is premised upon his belief that nothing in the Fourteenth Amendment suggests that aliens are entitled to heightened judicial scrutiny. "There is no language . . . in the [Fourteenth] Amendment," he insisted, "or any historical evidence as to the intent of the Framers, which would suggest to the slightest degree that it was intended to render alienage a 'suspect' classification, that it was designed in any way to protect 'discrete and insular minorities' other than racial minorities."[17]

All of the alien cases discussed above have examined *state* restrictions on noncitizens, and the Court has struck down many of them. But when the federal government restricts or prohibits aliens from receiving benefits available to citizens, the Court has generally approved. It did so when called upon to determine whether the government could deny enrollment in the Medicare Part B supplemental medical insurance program to aliens who had not resided in the United States for at least five years.[18] Mr. Espinosa, a resident alien, applied for such benefits but was found to be ineligible because he did not meet the five-year requirement.

The Court's respect for decisions made by the federal government concerning noncitizens is based upon Congress's power over immigration and naturalization. And even when the government provides benefits for some aliens (those who have resided here for five years) and not others (such as Espinosa), as long as the classification is reasonable, it is constitutional, and the Court will not substitute its judgment for that of Congress. Writing for a unanimous Court, Justice Stevens stated: "In this case, since [Espinosa has] not identified a principled basis for prescribing a different standard than the one selected by Congress, [he has] merely invited us to substitute our judgment for that of Congress in deciding which aliens shall be eligible to participate in the supplementary insurance program on the same conditions as citizens. We decline the invitation."

Restraints on the Right to Travel

> For all the great purposes for which the Federal Government was formed, we are one people, with one common country. We are all citizens of the United States; and, as members of the same community, must have the right to pass and repass through every part of it without interruption, as freely as in our own States.*

Vivian Marie Thompson, nineteen years old, was unwed with one child and pregnant with a second when she moved from Dorchester, Massachusetts, to Hartford, Connecticut. Unable to work because of the pregnancy, she applied to the state for AFDC assistance, which was denied because she had not lived in Connecticut for a year. She turned to the federal district court for help, and the court responded by declaring the state's one-year waiting period unconstitutional as a violation of Thompson's right to travel. The court also held that the law created two classes of people: one, those residents who had lived in the state for one year or more, the other, those who had recently moved there. This, the court held, was a violation of the equal protection clause, and six justices agreed.[19]

The state justified its denial of benefits to recent residents by several arguments. First it asserted that the waiting period was necessary to keep the program financially sound. This premise was based on the belief that if "people can be deferred from entering the jurisdiction by denying them welfare benefits during the first year, state programs to assist long-time residents will not be impaired by a substantial influx of indigent newcomers." The justices acknowledged that the one-year requirement would indeed discourage indigent persons from moving to another state. "An indigent," Justice Brennan declared in the majority's opinion, "who desires to migrate, resettle, find a new job, and start a new life will doubtless hesitate if he knows that he must risk making the move without the possibility of falling back on state welfare assistance during his first year of residence, when his need may be most acute. But the purpose of inhibiting migration by needy persons into the State is constitutionally impermissible." It is constitutionally impermissible because it infringes upon the person's right to travel, a right recognized by the Court more than 120 years before.

The state then argued that the law ought to be sustained because it was a method by which indigent persons would be

---

Passenger Cases, 48 U.S. 283, 492 (1849).

discouraged from moving to another state solely to receive benefits higher than those they were receiving in the state in which they were then residing. This argument did not impress the justices. Just because someone moves to another state for the purpose of receiving greater benefits does not mean that that person is any less deserving. Further, the law is not tailored to accomplish that goal. It bars all newcomers, regardless of their reason for moving into the state.

The state's next justification for the law related to administrative needs. It argued that "the requirement (1) facilitates the planning of the welfare budget; (2) provides an objective test of residency; (3) minimizes the opportunity for recipients fraudulently to receive payments from more than one jurisdiction; and (4) encourages early entry of new residents into the labor force." After examining these administrative needs, the majority concluded that taken together they did not justify the infringement on the right to travel. "Since the classification here touches on the fundamental right of interstate movement, its constitutionality must be judged by the stricter standard of whether it promotes a *compelling* state interest. Under this standard, the waiting-period requirement clearly violates the Equal Protection Clause."

Justice Harlan's dissent focused upon two points. He objected to the use of a "compelling state interest" test. He wrote: "I think . . . the 'compelling interest' doctrine is sound when applied to racial classifications, for historically the Equal Protection Clause was largely a product of the desire to eradicate legal distinctions founded upon race. However, I believe that the more recent extensions have been unwise." Secondly, while the justice acknowledged the existence of a right to travel, his disagreement with the majority was in its labeling that right as "fundamental" and giving it greater constitutional protection. "I must reiterate that I know of nothing which entitles this Court to pick out particular human activities, characterize them as 'fundamental,' and give them added protection under an unusually stringent equal protection test."

Justice Stewart, who concurred in the majority's decision, reacted to this criticism by noting that "the Court today does *not* 'pick out particular human activities, characterize them as "fundamental," and give them added protection. . . .' To the contrary, the Court simply recognizes, as it must, an established constitutional right, and gives to that right no less protection than the Constitution itself demands."

In most right to travel cases, the alleged restraint is indirect, as it was in *Thompson*; therefore, not everyone will agree that there is an infringement on the right. For example, in *Sosna v. Iowa*,[20] the Court upheld an Iowa law requiring a one-year residence before suing for divorce. This requirement created a class of people who could obtain divorces because they had lived in Iowa for more than one year and another who were required to wait the year. It was argued that some people would not move to Iowa because of this waiting period, thus restricting their right to travel.

The majority justified its decision by acknowledging the state's substantial interest in divorce proceedings. Such interests include concern for children, a desire to minimize the likelihood that the divorce decree might be attacked in proceedings outside the state, and ensuring that the decree will be given full faith and credit in another jurisdiction. The right to travel played no part in the decision, and that disturbed justices Marshall and Brennan, who dissented. They thought the case was controlled by *Thompson* and that the Iowa residency requirement should have been found a violation of equal protection because it infringed upon the right to travel and the state's reasons for the infringement were not compelling.

The case of Eduardo Soto-Lopez and Eliezer Baez-Hernandez also illustrates the difficulty in determining whether a government requirement is a restraint on traveling.

> Both Soto-Lopez and Baez-Hernandez passed New York City civil service examinations, but were denied the veterans' preference by the New York City Civil Service Commission because they were residents of Puerto Rico at the time they joined the military.[21]

By virtue of New York's civil service laws, honorably discharged veterans who had served during wartime and resided in New York when they entered service were entitled to five points additonal credit on examinations. Soto-Lopez and Baez-Hernandez sued the city, claiming that the law was unconstitutional as a violation of their right to travel. The district court dismissed the case, but the court of appeals reversed, agreeing with these veterans that the law made an unconstitutional classification affecting the right to travel.

Four justices of the Supreme Court were of the same opinion and voted to affirm. Two justices concluded that the state had no rational basis for preferring some veterans and concurred in the result.

Justice Brennan, for himself and justices Marshall, Blackmun, and Powell, found that "Soto-Lopez and Baez-Hernandez have been denied a significant benefit that is granted to all veterans similarly situated, except for state of residence at the time of their entry into the military," and that "such a permanent deprivation of a significant benefit, based only on the fact of nonresidence at a past point in time, clearly operates to penalize . . . [them] for exercising their rights to migrate."

Finding that the New York law was a constraint on traveling is not as apparent as the plurality deemed it. Nevertheless, one can conclude that the five-point advantage given to some veterans is an irrational distinction and therefore violates equal protection, and that was the position taken by Chief Justice Burger and Justice White. But for justices O'Connor, Rehnquist, and Stevens, "the modest scheme at issue here does not penalize in a constitutional sense veterans who joined the Armed Forces in other States for choosing to eventually settle in New York, and does not deny them equal protection."

Sometimes finding that a government requirement does not affect the right to travel comes easy for the justices. This was true when the Court was called upon to examine a city requirement that its employees live within the municipal boundaries. Those employees who moved beyond those boundaries were subject to termination. Such was the case of Francis McCarthy, who had worked for the Philadelphia Fire Department for sixteen years. When the city learned that he had moved to New Jersey, he was discharged. In his appeal, he argued that the city's requirement denied him the right to travel and therefore was a violation of equal protection. The lower courts all thought otherwise and dismissed the case. A majority of the justices reached the same conclusion. "In this case," the opinion states, "[McCarthy] claims a constitutional right to be employed by the city of Philadelphia *while* living elsewhere. There is no support in our cases for such a claim."[22]

Unequal Restraints on the Right to Vote

> Undeniably the Constitution of the United States protects the right of all qualified citizens to vote, in state as well as in federal elections. A consistent line of decision by the Court in cases involving attempts to deny or restrict the right of suffrage has made this indelibly clear.

It has been repeatedly recognized that all qualified voters have a constitutionally protected right to vote.*

No specific provision of the Constitution supports the above statement. It is clear that at the time of the adoption of the Constitution and for many years thereafter the right to vote was restricted to white males and in some cases only property owners. It took a constitutional amendment, the Fifteenth, to guarantee the right to vote to all races and another amendment, the Nineteenth, to give the same right to women. It was these amendments, together with many Supreme Court cases throughout our history that provided a foundation for the Court's declaration that "all qualified voters have a constitutionally protected right to vote."

Governments, of course, both federal and state, can and do place restrictions upon the exercise of the right, but when it is alleged that such constraints violate other provisions of the Constitution, the courts must decide their validity.

Herbert N. Carrington, an army sergeant, called upon the courts to do just that when he was denied the right to vote in Texas. The Texas Constitution provided that members of the military service could vote "only in the county in which he or she resided at the time of entering such service."[23] Sergeant Carrington had joined the army in Alabama but moved his family to Texas when he was assigned to duty at White Sands, New Mexico. He purchased a home in Texas, paid taxes there, was a proprietor of a small business, and had Texas license plates on his car, but could not vote.

Texas courts upheld the constitutional provision, but the Supreme Court found it unconstitutional as a violation of equal protection. In support of its constitution, Texas claimed that it protected against a "takeover" of a community where a large number of military personnel reside.

> A base commander, Texas suggests, who opposed local police administration or teaching policies in local schools, might influence his men to vote in conformity with his predilections. Local bond issues may fail, and property taxes stagnate at low levels because military personnel are unwilling to invest in the future of the area.

The justices found no fault with Texas's desire "that all military personnel enrolled to vote be bona fide residents of the community."

Reynolds v. Sims, 377 U.S. 533, 554 (1964).

Requiring all voters to be residents is one thing, but "'fencing out' from the franchise a sector of the population because of the way they may vote is constitutionally impermissible. '[T]he exercise of rights so vital to the maintenance of democratic institutions,' . . . cannot constitutionally be obliterated because of a fear of the political views of a particular group of bona fide residents."

Texas also maintained that protecting the integrity of the ballot box made the prohibition necessary because of the "transient nature of service in the Armed Forces." But Justice Stewart responded for the Court that of all transients in the state, only military personnel were totally excluded from voting. "Students at colleges and universities in Texas," he noted, "patients in hospitals and other institutions within the State, and civilian employees of the United States Government may be as transient as military personnel. But all of them are given at least an opportunity to show the elections officials that they are bona fide residents." Justice Stewart concluded the Court's opinion with a quotation from a message of Governor Ellis Arnall to the general assembly of Georgia: "[T]he uniform of our country [must not] be the badge of disfranchisement for the man or woman who wears it."

Only Justice Harlan dissented. He expressed grave concern for the "extension of federal power [in this case by the courts] into the political affairs of the States." Further, he did not think that the guarantee of equal protection was offended because, for him, the "voting eligibility requirements which Texas has made is founded on a rational classification."

If Texas cannot disenfranchise military personnel who are residents of the state, can New York prevent a bachelor who has no children in a public school from voting in a school election? When the school district prohibited bachelor Morris H. Kramer from voting in its election, he sued the district in federal district court.

> Morris H. Kramer, a college graduate, is a twenty-eight-year-old bachelor who resides in the private home of his parents located in Atlantic Beach, New York, within the confines of District No. 15. He has lived with his parents for many years, and he has voted in federal and state elections since 1959. He is not a property owner, a lessee or a parent with school-age children. On April 25, 1965, he attempted to register in the forthcoming school district election, but his application was rejected by [the district] on the ground that he failed to meet the special voter qualifications set forth in Section 2012.[24]

The "special voter qualifications" found in Section 2012 allow individuals to vote in school elections "only if they (1) own (or lease) taxable real property within the district, (2) are parents (or have custody of) children enrolled in the local public schools."[25]

The district court dismissed Kramer's complaint, and he appealed to the Supreme Court, which held that the restrictions were incompatible with the equal protection clause, and reversed, three justices dissenting. Chief Justice Warren wrote the opinion for the majority. The issue was whether the "requirements which prohibit some district residents who are otherwise qualified by age and citizenship from participating in district meetings and school board elections — violate the Fourteenth Amendment's command that no State shall deny persons equal protection of the laws." Because the fundamental right to vote was in question, it was necessary that the Court "carefully and meticulously" scrutinize Section 2012.

The state believed that only "those 'primarily interested in such elections'" should be qualified to vote. Persons with such interest were those who owned property and paid taxes, and parents with children in school. But the majority found the state's position suspect. The chief justice pointed out that people like Kramer were not the only ones disenfranchised.

> Besides [Kramer] and others who similarly live in their parents' homes, the statute also disenfranchises the following persons (unless they are parents or guardians of children enrolled in the district public school): senior citizens and others living with children or relatives; clergy, military personnel, and others who live on tax-exempt property; boarders and lodgers; parents who neither own nor lease qualifying property and whose children are too young to attend school; parents who neither own nor lease qualifying property and whose children attend private schools.

That the requirements are rationally related to the state's goals is not enough. "The issue," the chief justice declared, "is whether Section 2012 requirements do in fact sufficiently further a compelling state interest to justify denying the franchise to [Kramer] and members of his class." The majority believed that the state's interest did not meet that standard.

Dissenting justices Stewart, Black, and Harlan approached the issue differently, "So long as the classification is rationally related to a permissible legislative end, therefore — as are residence, literacy, and age requirements imposed with respect to voting — there is no denial of equal protection." Because the case did not involve any racial classification, there was no need to apply any "exacting" equal protection test.

Other restraints on voting the Court has struck down on the equal protection grounds include

> a $1.50 annual poll tax, because "to introduce wealth or payment of a fee as a measure of a voter's qualifications is to introduce a capricious or irrelevant factor"[26];
> a state law that permits only "property taxpayers" to vote on municipal utility bond issues because "certainly property owners are not alone in feeling the impact of bad utility service or high rates, or in reaping the benefits of good service and low rates"[27]; and
> a law requiring residence in the state for one year and in the county for three months before one can vote, because neither the desire to prevent fraud nor being assured that a voter is knowledgeable are compelling reasons to restrict the franchise when other less restrictive measures may accomplish the same results.[28]

On the other hand, the Court has found no equal protection violation and has upheld regualtions that

> disenfranchise convicted felons who have completed their sentences and paroles[29]; and
> set a fifty-day voter registration and residence requirement for state and local elections.[30]

Discrimination Affecting Marriage and Parental Rights

> We are dealing here with legislation which involves one of the basic civil rights of man. Marriage and procreation are fundamental to the very existence and survival of the race.*

In the *Skinner, Loving,* and *Zablocki* cases discussed in Chapter 1, the Court identified certain personal relationships encompassed with the word *liberty* which the government cannot take without due process of law. The issue in each of those cases was

---

*Skinner v. Oklahoma, 318 U.S. 535, 541 (1942).

whether states could treat some people differently than others with regard to those liberty interests.

For example, in *Skinner*, the Court was required to determine whether Oklahoma could sterilize some habitual criminals but not others. Habitual criminals were those who had been convicted of crimes involving moral turpitude two or more times. The law did not apply to embezzlers. The exemption for embezzlers created some anomalies, as pointed out be Justice Douglas for the Court. "A person who enters a chicken coop and steals chickens commits a felony; . . . and he may be sterilized if he is thrice convicted. If, however, he is a bailee of the property and fraudulently appropriates it, he is an embezzler. . . . Hence, no matter how habitual his proclivities for embezzlement are and no matter how often his conviction, he may not be sterilized."[31]

Because the Court was dealing with the fundamental liberty interest of procreation, it strictly scrutinized the law's classification and held that "the guaranty of 'equal protection of the laws is a pledge of the protection of equal laws.' . . . When the law lays an unequal hand on those who have committed intrinsically the same quality of offense and sterilizes one and not the other, it has made as invidious a discrimination as if it had selected a particular race or nationality for oppressive treatment." Although all justices concurred in the *Skinner* decision, Chief Justice Stone thought that the real issue was one of procedural due process. "A law," he insisted, "which condemns, without a hearing, all the individuals of a class to so harsh a measure as the present because some or even many merit condemnation, is lacking in the first principles of due process."

When Roger Redhail applied for a marriage license, it was refused by County Clerk Thomas E. Zablocki because Redhail was under a court order to support a child he had fathered. In refusing the license, the county clerk was acting under a Wisconsin law that required residents who had been ordered to support children to secure permission from a court before marrying.[32] The Wisconsin law created two classes of residents: those, like Redhail, who were required to secure court permission to marry and most others, who were not. This classification, he contended in an action against Zablocki, violated his rights to equal protection. The court accepted Redhail's position and ordered the clerk not to enforce the law thereafter. The clerk appealed to the Supreme Court where all justices except Justice Rehnquist voted to affirm.

Because the law placed a restraint upon the liberty interest in marriage, the majority said, a "'critical examination' of the state interests advanced in support of the classification is required." The state advanced two interests to justify the statute. Requiring applicants like Redhail to seek court permission provided an opportunity to counsel the applicant with regard to present and possible future support obligations. Second, the law acted as a "collection device"; it was an incentive to those required to do so to make their support payments.

The justices did not accept these as interests of sufficient magnitude to override a person's right to marry, particularly in view of the fact that the process would not guarantee that the support payments would be made. "The statute," Justice Marshall pointed out, "merely prevents the applicant from getting married, without delivering any money at all into the hands of the applicant's prior children." Furthermore, the state could use other means to enforce the support obligation that would be just as effective and "do not impinge upon the right to marry." Justice Stewart concurred in the judgment on the ground the the law infringed upon the liberty interest in marriage and thus violated due process. Of the equal protection argument, he wrote: "Like almost any law, the Wisconsin statute now before us affects some people and does not affect others. But to say that it thereby creates 'classifications' in the equal protection sense strikes me as little short of fantasy."

Because parents have a constitutional liberty interest in their children, proceedings for the termination of that interest must be conducted in accordance with the requirement of due process of law. And in those instances where the state gives preference to one parental group over another, equal protection requirements also come into play. That was the situation in *Quillion v. Walcott*.[33]

Ardell Williams had a child by Leon Webster Quillion in December 1964, Darrell Webster Quillion. The couple never lived together or married, and Quillion's support for the child was irregular. He had visited the mother and child once in a while, but according to the mother, these visits were a disrupting influence in the child's life. In 1967 Williams married Randall Walcott, and some years later she consented to Walcott's adopting Darrell. Georgia law required the consent of both parents for the adoption of a child born in wedlock, but only the consent of the mother was required for the adoption of illegitimate children. In response to Randall Walcott's petition for adoption of Darrell, Quillion sought to have the child legitimized. He also entered an objection to the adoption. Judge

Elmo Holt heard the case. The evidence included information concerning Quillion's contacts and irregular support for the child, and a statement from Darrell that he would like to be adopted by Walcott. This brought Judge Holt to the conclusion that it would be in Darrell's best interest to grant the adoption.

The Georgia Supreme Court affirmed, as did a unanimous U.S. Supreme Court. Quillion's argument was twofold. First, the adoption denied him due process in that it terminated his parental rights to Darrell; second the law which required parental consent for the adoption of a child born in wedlock, but only from the mother in cases of illegitimate children, denied him equal protection. With regard to the due process issue, the justices concluded that so long as Judge Holt's decision was made "in the best interests of Darrell," due process was not offended. Quillion argued that he should be treated no differently than the father of a child born in wedlock who is separated or divorced and not living with the child. The consent of that father under the law would have been necessary before the adoption could have been granted. The justices thought Quillion's situation was different. "He had never exercised actual or legal custody over his child, and thus had never shouldered any significant responsibility with respect to the daily supervision, education, protection, or care of the child," wrote Justice Marshall. This was sufficient to find that Quillion's equal protection rights were not violated.

Equal Justice under Law

> Providing equal justice for poor and rich, weak and powerful alike is an age-old problem. People have never ceased to hope and strive to move closer to that goal. . . . Both equal protection and due process emphasize the central aim of our entire judicial system — all people charged with crime must, so far as the law is concerned, "stand on an equality before the bar of justice in every American court."*

The Constitution does not require the federal or state governments to provide appellate courts or any other method of having a criminal conviction reviewed. However, once a right of review is provided, equal protection demands that it be available to rich and poor alike: there must be equal justice under law.[34] That is the message of *Griffin v. Illinois*.[35]

*Griffin v. Illinois, 351, U.S. 12, 16–17 (1956).

After Griffin and Crenshaw were convicted of robbery in Illinois, they asked the trial court to furnish them with a copy of the record of their trial, including a transcript of the proceedings, so they could appeal. Because they were without funds, they requested that the record be supplied without cost. Even though perfecting an appeal without the record is almost impossible, the request was denied without a hearing. A petition to review the trial court's decision was dismissed by the Illinois Supreme Court. Upon appeal to the U.S. Supreme Court, the decisions of the Illinois courts were reversed.

In an opinion in which Chief Justice Warren and justices Douglas and Tom Clark joined, Justice Black acknowledged that states were not required to provide for appellate review, but noted that all states did so because of "the importance of appellate review to a correct adjudication of guilt or innocence." But a state cannot, he asserted, "grant appellate review . . . in a way that discriminates against some convicted defendants on account of their poverty." "There can be no equal justice where the kind of trial a man gets depends on the amount of money he has. Destitute defendants must be afforded as adequate appellate review as defendants who have money enough to buy transcripts."

Justice Frankfurter concurred in the judgment, preferring to set forth his views in a separate opinion. "The State is not free," he insisted, "to produce such a squalid discrimination, [as in this case.] If it has a general policy of allowing criminal appeals, it cannot make lack of means an effective bar to the exercise of this opportunity." Four justices dissented. They thought that as long as Illinois granted the right to appeal to all, there was no denial of equal protection because "some may not be able to avail themselves of the full appeal because of their poverty."

Gideon v. Wainwright[36] is one of the landmark cases in our history. Clarence Gideon had his share of hard times — drinking, domestic troubles, and health problems — which caused him to resort to petty crime to survive. Gideon was arrested for breaking into a poolroom in Flordia and brought before a local judge. He asked that counsel be appointed for him, but the judge refused, telling him that under the law he could appoint counsel only for indigents in capital cases. Gideon replied that the Constitution of the United States allowed him to be represented by counsel. The trial, however, proceeded with Gideon attempting to represent himself and resulted in his being convicted. He appealed all the way to the U.S. Supreme

Court where all justices agreed with him, reversed, and ordered a new trial. At this trial, Gideon had a lawyer and was acquitted.

Gideon established the constitutional rule that not only the rich are entitled to have counsel represent them during a criminal trial and that if the accused cannot afford to pay counsel, the government must do so.

After William Douglas and Bennie Will Meyes were convicted in California of a number of crimes, including robbery and assault to commit murder, they sought review of their convictions in a appellate court. Although Douglas and Meyes were indigent, their request for assistance of counsel on appeal was denied, and their convictions were affirmed. Appointment of counsel on appeal in California was at the discretion of the appellate court, and appointment was made only if the court was of the opinion that it would be beneficial to the defendant and the court.

A divided Supreme Court, relying on *Griffin* , reversed, holding that not to appoint counsel for Douglas and Meyes violated their right to equal protection. Writing for the majority, Justice Douglas stated that the question was a very narrow one. "We are dealing," he declared, "only with the first appeal, granted as a matter of right [by California law] to rich and poor alike," and "where the merits of the one and only appeal an indigent has as of right are decided without benefit of counsel, we think an unconstitutional line has been drawn between rich and poor."[37]

Dissenting in this case, as he had in *Griffin*, Justice Harlan took issue with the majority's conclusion that the equal protection clause required the government to equalize the criminal justice system for rich and poor.

> The States, of course, are prohibited by the Equal Protection Clause from discriminating between "rich" and "poor" *as such* in the formulation and application of their laws. But it is a far different thing to suggest that this provision prevents the State from adopting a law of general applicability that may affect the poor more harshly than it does the rich, or, on the other hand, from making some effort to redress economic imbalances while not eliminating them entirely.

The inability of Willie E. Williams to pay a $500 fine plus $5 court costs created a real dilemma for him. Williams was convicted of petty theft and sentenced to a year in prison, a $500 fine, and $5 court costs, but he was unable to pay either. Illinois law provided that in addition to giving a sentence, a judge could order that if the fine is not paid, the defendant remain in prison beyond the time of the sentence until the fine is paid, at the rate of $5 a day for each day of imprisonment. Williams asked Judge Joseph R. Gill not to require him to stay in prison beyond the time of the sentence because he had no funds to pay the fine. Judge Gill refused. The Illinois Supreme Court held that there was no denial of equal protection in this case and affirmed. Seven justices of the U.S. Supreme Court voted to reverse on equal protection grounds. Justice Harlan also voted to reverse but thought that the Illinois procedure violated due process. Justice Blackmun did not participate in this case.[38]

In support of the constitutionality of its law, Illinois argued that is was a rational method of collecting the revenue that fines and costs produced and that the law should not be declared unconstitutional because the legislature has chosen this method of collection rather some others.

In addressing the issue before the Court, Chief Justice Burger reviewed a little history. "The custom of imprisoning a convicted defendant for nonpayment of fines," the chief justice recalled, "dates back to medieval England and has long been practiced in this country. At the present time almost all States and the Federal Government have statutes authorizing incarceration under such circumstances." But simply because something has been done for a long time does not make it constitutional. And this case called for a reexamination of the practice because the "increased use of fines as a criminal sanction has made nonpayment a major cause of incarceration in this country."

The majority acknowledged that judges are vested with a wide discretion in sentencing and that the Constitution does not require that persons convicted of the same offenses be given the same sentence. Sentencing requires the consideration of many factors. But requiring a person to serve a longer sentence because of his or her inability to pay a fine is not consistent with the Fourteenth Amendment. The chief justice summed up the Court's decision: "We hold only that the Equal Protection Clause of the Fourteenth Amendment requires that the statutory ceiling placed on imprisonment for any substantive offense be the same for all defendants irrespective of their economic status." "I concur in today's judgment," Justice Harlan wrote, "but in doing so wish to dissociate myself from the 'equal protection' rationale employed by the Court to justify its conclusions." For him, keeping a person in jail to pay a fine violated due process of law.

The appointment of counsel for indigent defendants costs tax-payers huge sums of money. States have therefore sought various methods to recoup some of those funds. David E. Strange became emeshed in Kansas's recoupment policy when counsel was appointed to defend him against a charge of first-degree robbery. When the charge against him was reduced to pickpocketing, he pleaded guilty and was sentenced. After paying Strange's appointed attorney $500, the state asked Strange for reimbursement. Under Kansas law, if a defendant did not reimburse the state within sixty days, judgment for the amount paid to his attorney was entered against him.[39] Unable to pay the amount demanded, Strange brought suit against James R. James, the administrator of the law, in a federal court, claiming that the recoupment law violated his right to counsel under the Sixth Amendment. The court agreed and held the law unconstitutional.

A unanimous Supreme Court upheld the lower court's decision but chose to do so on equal protection grounds rather than relying on the Sixth Amendment. The Court turned to an equal protection analysis because it found that Kansas treated indigent *defendant debtors* substantially differently than ordinary civil judgment debtors, who were given a long list of exemptions against levy under a judgment. The Court was particularly disturbed by the fact that the *defendant debtor* received no protection from garnishment of wages. "Of [all the] exemptions," the Court declared, "none is more important to a debtor than an exemption of his wages from unrestricted garnishment. The debtor's wages are his sustenance, with which he supports himself and his family. The average low income wage earner spends nearly nine-tenths of those wages for items of immediate consumption."

The Court pointed out that if Strange had hired an attorney but did not pay him, Strange would have been entitled to all exemptions provided by law against the collection of any judgment the attorney might secure against him. And that included some protection against garnishment of wages. Indigent defendants, therefore, the Court believed, were disfavored by the Kansas procedure. "A criminal conviction," Justice Powell declared, "usually limits employment opportunities. This is especially true where a prison sentence has been served. It is in the interest of society and the State that such a defendant, upon satisfaction of the criminal penalties imposed, be afforded a reasonable opportunity of employment, rehabilitation and return to useful citizenship." There was therefore only one conclusion to be drawn. "The statute before us embodies elements of punitiveness and discrimination which violate the rights of citizens to equal treatment under law."

Equality of the Sexes

> Since sex, like race and national origin, is an immutable character-istic determined solely by the accident of birth, the imposition of special disabilities upon the members of a particular sex because of their sex would seem to violate "the basic concept of our system that legal burdens should bear some relationship to individual respon-sibility."*

"A woman's place is in the home." That was the message Myra Bradwell received from three justices of the Supreme Court in 1873 when she applied for admission to practice law in Illinois. Except for the fact that she was a woman, Bradwell met all other qualifications. Furthermore, there was nothing in Illinois law that barred women from becoming members of the bar. However, when the Illinois Supreme Court considered her application, it concluded that to admit her would be an exercise of power not granted to them by the legislature. "If we were to admit them [women], we should be exercising the authority conferred upon us in a manner which, we are fully satisfied, was never contemplated by the legislature."[40]

When Bradwell appealed to the U.S. Supreme Court, she argued that as a citizen of the United States, she was entitled by the Fourteenth Amendment to the "privileges or immunities of citizens of the United States." Eight justices did not think so. Only Chief Justice Salmon P. Chase dissented. Five of the justices, in an opinion written by Justice Samuel F. Miller, held that "the right to admission to practice in the courts of a State is not one [of the privileges and immunities belonging to citizens of the United States]. This right [to practice law] in no sense depends on citizenship of the United States."

Justices Bradley, Swayne, and Field, while concurring in the judgment, did so because it was the legislature that had the power to prescribe qualifications for the practice of law, and furthermore, the legal field was no place for a woman. "The paramount destiny and mission of woman," Justice Bradley claimed, "are to fulfill the noble and benign offices of wife and mother. This is the law of the Creator. And the rules of civil society must be adapted to the general constitution of things, and cannot be based upon exceptional cases."

*Frontiero v. Richardson, 411 U.S. 677, 686 (1973).

Being a U.S. citizen did not help Myra Bradwell become a lawyer in Illinois, nor did it help Virginia Minor secure the right to vote in Missouri.

> Mrs. Virginia Minor, a native born, free, white citizen of the United States, and of the State of Missouri, over the age of twenty-one years, wishing to vote for electors for President and Vice-President of the United States, and for a representative in Congress, and for other officers, at the general election held in November, 1872, applied to one Happersett, the registrar of voters, to register her as a lawful voter, which he refused to do, assigning for cause that she was not a "male citizen of the United States," but a woman. She thereupon sued him in one of the inferior State courts of Missouri, for willfully refusing to place her name upon the list of registered voters, by which refusal she was deprived of her right to vote.[41]

After the courts of Missouri refused to order Happersett to register her, Mrs. Minor brought her case to the Supreme Court. But she received no help there either. A unamimous court found that as a woman, she had no right to vote in Missouri. After reviewing the history of citizenship, the Court concluded: "Other proof of like character might be found, but certainly more cannot be necessary to establish the fact that sex has never been made one of the elements of citizenship in the United States. In this respect men have never had an advantage over women." They both can be citizens.

This brought the Court to the question of whether U.S. citizenship automatically conferred the right to vote on all people. In seeking an answer, the Court made an extensive review of the qualifications of voters at the time of the adoption of the Constitution. It found that "in no state were all citizens permitted to vote." And in many, only male citizens were given the franchise. Summing up the Court's research, Chief Justice Morrison R. Waite expressed the view that "in this condition of the law in respect to suffrage in the several States it cannot for a moment be doubted that if it had been intended to make all citizens of the United States voters, the framers of the Constitution would not have left it to implication. So important a change in the condition of citizenship as it actually existed, if intended, would have been expressly declared." Finding that voting was not a "privilege" or "immunity" of citizenship, the justices concluded that "the constitution and laws of the several States which commit that important trust [voting] to men alone are not necessarily void."

At the end of a long and hard-fought battle, the *Minor* decision was nullified by the adoption of the Nineteenth Amendment in 1920. That amendment provides: "The right of citizens of the United States to vote shall not be denied or abridged by the United States or by any State on account of sex."

Changes in deeply ingrained attitudes in society are not easy to come by. Even as recently as 1948 the Court upheld a Michigan law which prohibited females from becoming bartenders "unless she be 'the wife or daughter of the male owner' of a licensed liquor establishment."[42] To sustain their decision, a majority of the justices hearkened back to the "good old days." Recalling those days, Justice Frankfurter wrote: "We are, to be sure dealing with a historic calling. We meet the alewife, sprightly and ribald, in Shakespeare, but centuries before him she played a role in the social life of England." Nevertheless, neither history nor the equal protection clause prevents a legislature from controlling the sale of liquor. "The Fourteenth Amendment did not tear history up by the roots, and the regulation of the liquor traffic is one of the oldest and most untrammeled of legislative powers." Three justices dissented. They found that the law discriminated against female bar owners, who "may neither work as a barmaid herself nor employ her daughter in that position, even if a man is always present in the establishment to keep order."

But times change, society changes, and so does the Supreme Court. And finally in 1971 the Court unanimously held that discrimination on the basis of gender violated equal protection. The case involved the question whether a father was more qualified to be administrator of a son's estate than the mother.

> Richard Lynn Reed, a minor, died intestate in Ada County, Idaho, on March 29, 1967. . . . Approximately seven months after Richard's death, his mother, . . . Sally Reed, filed a petition in the Probate Court of Ada County, seeking appointment as administratrix of her son's estate. Prior to the date set for a hearing on the mother's petition, . . . Cecil Reed, the father of the decedent, filed a competing petition seeking to have himself appointed administrator of the son's estate. [The Reeds had separated prior to Richard's death.][43]

The probate judge appointed the father, Cecil Reed, as administrator because of an Idaho law which provided, "Of several persons claiming and equally entitled . . . to administer [estates], males must be preferred to females."

Sally Reed won an appeal from a district court in Idaho, which returned the case to the probate court to determine which of the Reeds was the best qualified to do the job. The Idaho Supreme Court reversed, holding that the law did not give the probate judge any discretion in matter and that the law did not violate the equal protection clause. The justices of the U.S. Supreme Court unanimously reversed.

The Court, in an opinion by Chief Justice Burger, first acknowledged that the law "provides that different treatment be accorded to the applicants on the basis of their sex; it thus establishes a classification subject to scrutiny under the Equal Protection Clause." Such classifications have traditionally been examined to determine whether they are "reasonable, not arbitrary." Idaho attempted to sustain the law by arguing that it reduced the workload of its courts by making it unnecessary for a judge to hold a hearing on the question of who shall be appointed administrator. The Court accepted this as legitimate but concluded that "to give a mandatory preference to members of either sex over members of the other, merely to accomplish the elimination of hearings on the merits, is to make the very kind of arbitrary legislative choice forbidden by the Equal Protection Clause."

Although all justices joined the opinion in *Reed* where the chief justice found the Idaho law to be arbitrary, less than two years later it became apparent that all justices were not satisfied with that approach. Their differences were revealed in *Frontiero v. Richardson*,[44] a case involving the validity of quarters allowances for married military personnel.

When air force Lieutenant Sharron Frontiero requested quarters allowance and benefits for her husband, Joseph, they were denied because she had not shown that he was dependent upon her for more than half his support. Had the situation been reversed—if Joseph Frontiero had requested allowances and benefits for his wife, Sharron—they would have been automatically granted on the assumption that she was his dependent, even though she might not have been monetarily dependent upon him at all.

The Frontieros sued the secretary of defense, claiming this disparity in treatment of male and female members of the armed forces violated equal protection. Because the equal protection clause of the Fourteenth Amendment requires only *states* to give equal protection, the Court had read into the due process clause of the Fifth Amendment an equal protection requirement which applied to actions of the federal government. The federal district court where the case was brought held that the law was not a violation of equal protection and dismissed the action. The Supreme Court, with only Justice Rehnquist dissenting, reversed. The other eight justices, although agreeing on the result, could not agree on a majority opinion.

Four justices, in an opinion written by Justice Brennan, rejected the traditional equal protection analysis, which holds that classifications which are not rationally related to a legitimate governmental interest violate equal protection. For them, gender-based classifications were just as suspect as racial ones and therefore should be subject to the same strict judicial scrutiny. This was necessary, Justice Brennan declared, because

> there can be no doubt that our Nation has had a long and unfortunate history of sex discrimination. Traditionally, such discrimination was rationalized by an attitude of "romantic paternalism" which, in practical effect, put women, not on a pedestal, but in a cage.... As a result of notions such as these, our statute books gradually became laden with gross, stereotyped distinctions between the sexes and indeed, throughout much of the 19th century the position of women in our society was, in many respects, comparable to that of blacks under the pre–Civil War slave codes.

Having reached that conclusion, the plurality turned to the examination of the government's reason for treating female members of the service differently than male members. The government argued that Congress "might reasonably have concluded that it would be both cheaper and easier simply conclusively to presume that wives of male members are financially dependent upon their husbands, while burdening female members with the task of establishing dependency in fact."

That was simply not acceptable to the plurality and led them to the conclusion that "by according differential treatment to male and female members of the uniformed services for the sole purpose of achieving administrative convenience, the challenged statutes violate the Due Process Clause of the Fifth Amendment insofar as they require a female member to prove the dependency of her husband."

It was not necessary, according to three concurring justices, to equate sex classifications with racial classifications and characterize them as suspect. These statutes were unconstitutional for the same reason that the Idaho law was in *Reed*, and there was no reason to go further at this time. This was especially true in view of the fact that the Equal Rights Amendment had just been submitted to the states for ratification. Justice Rehnquist based his dissent on the district court's opinion, which upheld the statutes, believing that not requiring married servicemen to prove dependency was a rational method of eliminating a great administrative burden on the services.

The Court's attempt to eliminate discrimination based on gender, of course, can be a two-edged sword. For the sexes to be treated equally, the sword must sometimes cut against women. That was the decision of the Court in William and Lillian Orr's divorce case. William Orr had been ordered by Judge G. H. Wright, Jr., to pay Lillian Orr alimony in the amount of $1,240 per month. When he fell behind in payments, Mrs. Orr bought contempt proceedings against him. He responded that the Alabama statutes that authorized courts to require only husbands to pay alimony were unconstitutional. Judge Wright upheld the statutes and entered judgment against Mr. Orr for back alimony payments. The appellate courts in Alabama affirmed, but the Supreme Court reversed.

Although the justices could not agree in *Frontiero* on just what standard of review should be applied to gender classifications, in a subsequent case they discarded the rational-basis standard and held that "to withstand constitutional challenge, previous cases establish that classifications by gender must serve important governmental objectives and must be substantially related to achievement of those objectives."[45] This standard is somewhere between the strict-scrutiny standard applied to racial classifications and the traditional rational-basis standard applied in most other equal protection cases. These standards place a different degree of burden upon the government to justify dissimilar treatment of people. While the strict-scrutiny standard makes it almost impossible for the government to justify a racial classification, most other categorizations are upheld when the court applies the rational-basis rule.

Having determined that gender-based discriminations must be carefully scrutinized, the Court examined the state's reasons for requiring only husbands to pay alimony. The state's interests appeared to be twofold.

> One is a legislative purpose to provide help for needy spouses, using sex as a proxy for need. The other is a goal of compensating women for past discrimination during marriage, which assertedly has left them unprepared to fend for themselves in the working world following divorce.[46]

But the justices did not believe that the laws were necessary to meet these state's interests because individualized hearings by the court in each case could determine where the need was and who had the ability to pay. The majority therefore found that "where, as here, the State's compensatory and ameliorative purposes are as well served by a gender-neutral classification as one that gender classifies and therefore carries with it the baggage of sexual stereotypes, the State cannot be permitted to classify on the basis of sex."

This decision was not unanimous. The dissenters, however, focused on whether William Orr was the proper person to raise the constitutional issue in this case because they doubted that he was really injured by the statutes. Even if the law was changed to allow a court to order a wife to pay alimony to a husband, that might or might not benefit him. It would depend upon his and his wife's financial conditions.

Joe Hogan's desire to become a nurse brought him to the Supreme court, where Justice O'Connor set forth the problem he encountered on the way: "This case," she stated, "presents the narrow issue of whether a state statute that excludes males from enrolling in a state-supported professional nursing school violates the Equal Protection Clause of the Fourteenth Amendment."[47] Hogan had been working as a nursing supervisor but desired to obtain a degree in nursing and therefore applied to the Mississippi University for Women School of Nursing. His application was denied because the school admitted only women. There was a coeducational nursing school some distance from his home.

Hogan brought an action against the University in the federal district court seeking admission to the nursing program and damages. Judge L. T. Senter, Jr., refused to grant his request, being of the opinion that the single-sex admissions policy of the nursing school was "not arbitrary because providing single-sex schools is consistent with a respected, though by no means universally accepted, educational theory that single-sex education affords unique benefits to students." The court of appeals reversed, concluding that Judge Senter had used the wrong standard to evaluate this discrimination against males: "The proper test is whether the State has carried the heavier burden of showing that the gender-based classification is substantially related to an important governmental objective." The state had not met that test here. In a 5–4 decision, the Supreme Court sustained the court of appeals decision. The fact that males are being discriminated against does not change the standard of

Gordon thereafter supported Deta Mona in accordance with the paternity order and openly acknowledged her as his child.

When Sherman Gordon's estate was probated, Deta Mona was excluded from the list of heirs by an order of the probate court. The court acted pursuant to an Illinois law which made an illegitimate child the heir only of the mother unless the parents had married and the father had acknowledged the child as his. Deta Mona, acting through her mother, appealed the order to the Illinois appellate courts but was not successful in having it reversed. She then appealed to the Supreme Court, where five justices held that her exclusion as an heir of Gordon's because she was illegitimate was a violation of equal protection.

Illinois asserted that one of its interests in excluding illegitimate children from inheritance was "in 'the promotion of [legitimate] family relationships.'" To this the justices responded, "We have expressly considered and rejected the argument that a State may attempt to influence the actions of men and women by imposing sanctions on the children born of their illegitimate relationships." Another interest asserted by the state was the need for a reliable system for disposition of a decedent's property. This, of course, is a substantial interest and may well have been accepted by the majority had there been no alternative methods of protecting that interest. "For at least some significant categories of illegitimate children of intestate men," Justice Powell declared, "inheritance rights can be recognized without jeopardizing the orderly settlement of estates or the dependability of titles to property passing under intestacy laws." And this case was one where property interests would not be jeopardized because Shermon Gordon, determined by a court to be the father of Deta Mona had accepted her into his family as his child.

Because of a strong belief that the Court's use of equal protection as a means of striking down some state laws was flawed, Justice Rehnquist dissented. "Unfortunately," he insisted, "more than a century of decisions under this Clause of the Fourteenth Amendmen' have produced . . . a syndrome wherein this Court seems to rega' have produced the Equal Protection Clause as a cat-o-nine-tails to be kept in judicial closet as a threat to legislatures which may, in the vie' the judiciary, get out of hand and pass 'arbitrary,' 'illogica 'unreasonable' laws." Furthermore, he argued, the framers Constitution did not intend for "the federal judiciary . . . t a council of revision and veto which it considered unwise."

review in sex discrimination cases. "If the State's objective is legitimate and important," Justice O'Connor emphasized, "we next determine whether the requisite direct, substantial relationship between objective and means is present."

Mississippi argued that not admitting men to the nursing program at MUW was to compensate women for past discrimination against them. But the majority did not buy that argument because there had never been discrimination against women in the nursing profession in Mississippi. Justice O'Connor pointed out that "Mississippi has made no showing that women lacked opportunities to obtain training in the field of nursing or to attain positions of leadership in that field when the MUW School of Nursing opened its door or that women currently are deprived of such opportunities." Thus, while the objective of compensating women for past discrimination is surely a worthy one, there was little or no relationship between that objective and the means chosen to accomplish it. The law, therefore, was invalid.

That this decision might place in "jeopardy any state-supported educational institution that confines its student body in any area to members of one sex" disturbed Justice Blackmun. He wrote: "I hope that we do not lose all values that some think are worthwhile (and are not based on differences of race or religion) and relegate ourselves to needless conformity. The ringing words of the Equal Protection Clause of the Fourteenth Amendment—what Justice Powell aptly describes as its 'liberating spirit,' . . . do not demand that price."

Justices Powell and Rehnquist also thought that the decision did not bode well for the "honored tradition" of single-sex education in this country.

> A distinctive feature of America's tradition has been respect for diversity. This has been characteristic of the people from numerous lands who have built our country. It is the essence of our democratic system. At stake in this case as I see it is the preservation of a small aspect of this diversity. But that aspect is by no means insignificant, given our heritage of available choice between single-sex and coeducational institutions of higher learning.

In adopting the Social Security system, Congress included some gender-based rules for payment of benefits. For example, death benefits from the earnings of a husband and father were payable to his widow and children, but such benefits from a deceased mother were available only to the children. The Court found this to be a violation of equal protection because "it unjustly discriminates against female wage earners required to pay social security taxes by affording them less protection for their survivors than is provided for male wage earners."[48]

The Court found unconstitutional part of the Social Security Act which provided that "benefits to families whose dependent children have been deprived of parental support because of the unemployment of the father, but does not provide such benefits when the mother becomes unemployed."[49] They believed this law was "part of the 'baggage of sexual stereotypes' . . . that presumes the father has the 'primary responsibility to provide a home and its essentials,' . . . while the mother is the 'center of home and family life.' Legislation that rests on such presumptions, without more, cannot survive scrutiny under the Due Process Clause of the Fifth Amendment."

Despite those protestations, however, sexual stereotypes do exist, and the Court has recognized some of them. In 1981 a majority of the justices upheld California's statutory rape law, which punishes males who have sexual intercourse with a female under the age of eighteen, even though California had no similar law applicable to females.[50] And shortly thereafter, the Court approved President Jimmy Carter's reactivation of draft registration, even though only males were required to register.[51] A majority of the justices found no equal protection violation because "the fact that Congress and the Executive have decided that women should not serve in combat fully justifies Congress in not authorizing their registration, since the purpose of registration is to develop a pool of potential combat troops." But that was not reason enough to perpetuate the conventional image of women according to justices Marshall and Brennan. "The Court today," insisted Justice Marshall, "places its imprimatur on one of the most potent remaining public expressions of 'ancient canards about the proper role of women.'"

Illegitimate Children Need Equal Protection

> We start from the premise that illegitimate children are not "nonpersons." They are humans, live, and have their being. They are clearly "persons" within the meaning of the Equal Protection Clause of the Fourteenth Amendment.*

*Levy v. Louisiana, 391 U.S. 68, 70 (1968).

The five illegitimate children of Louise Levy brought a wrongful death action in Louisiana against a doctor who treated their mother prior to her death. Although Louisiana law gave children a right to sue for wrongful death of their mother, the court dismissed the action. An appellate court affirmed, "holding that 'child' in [the law] means 'legitimate child,' the denial to illegitimate children of 'the right to recover' being 'based on morals and general welfare because it discourages bringing children into the world out of wedlock.'"[52]

> Louise Levy . . . gave birth to these five illegitimate children and . . . they lived with her; . . . she treated them as a parent would treat any other child; . . . she worked as a domestic servant to support them, taking them to church every Sunday and enrolling them, at her own expense, in a parochial school.

In an opinion reversing the Louisiana courts, Justice Douglas wrote: "When the child's claim of damage for loss of his mother is in issue, why, in terms of 'equal protection,' should the tortfeasors go free merely because the child is illegitimate? Why should the illegitimate child be denied rights merely because of his birth out of wedlock? He certainly is subject to all the responsibilities of a citizen, including the payment of taxes and conscription under the Selective Service Act. How under our constitutional regime can he be denied correlative rights which other citizens enjoy?" The answer provided by the majority was that to deny the illegitimate child rights similar to those enjoyed by other children was an invidious discrimination and unconstitutional. Three dissenting justices viewed this case entirely differently. They believed that it was entirely rational for the state to limit recovery for wrongful death to legitimate members of a family. They therefore would have held that the law did not violate equal protection.

The question of the inheritance rights of illegitimate children discussed in the *Vincent* case in Chapter 2, came to the Court again in *Trimble v. Gordon.*[53]

> Deta Mona Trimble [was] the illegitimate daughter of . . . Jessie Trimble and Sherman Gordon. Trimble and Gordon lived in Chicago with Deta Mona from 1970 until Gordon died in 1974, the victim of a homicide. On January 2, 1973, the Circuit Court of Cook County, Ill. had entered a paternity order finding Gordon to be the father of Deta Mona and ordering him to pay $15 per week for her support.

Fourteenth Amendment was not intended to give them that power either. That amendment was intended to eliminate classifications by race, which the Court later extended to include classifications of aliens. "But when the Court has been required to adjudicate equal protection claims not based on race or national origin, it has faced a much more difficult task." Justice Rehnquist, therefore, would not engage in the kind of analysis the majority did. He would accept the legislature's classification unless it was irrational, and he did not believe that the legislature's decision to exclude illegitimate children from inheritance was "mindless [or] patently irrational."

About a year and a half after, *Trimble* the Court upheld a New York law which allowed an illegitimate child to "inherit from his father if a court of competent jurisdiction has, during the lifetime of the father, made an order of filiation declaring paternity in a proceeding instituted during the pregnancy of the mother or within two years from the birth of the child."[54]

Requiring a paternity action to be commenced within two years of the child's birth may no longer be valid. Recently the Court struck down a Pennsylvania law prohibiting an illegitimate child from obtaining support from an alleged father unless the paternity suit is instituted within six years of the birth and paternity is established.[55] In finding the six year limitation too restricting on the rights of illegitimate children, the Court placed illegitimacy classifications on the same plane as sex classifications. To sustain discrimination between the sexes and between legitimate and illegitimate children, the government must show that its classification is "substantially related to an important governmental objective." Pennsylvania argued that the purpose of the law was to prevent stale and fraudulent claims. The justices, however, noted that "in a number of circumstances, Pennsylvania permits the issue of paternity to be litigated more than six years after the birth of an illegitimate child." That being true, the statute at issue was simply not substantially related to the state's goals.

Traditional Equal Protection

The general rule is that legislation is presumed to be valid and will be sustained if the classification drawn by the statute is rationally related to a legitimate state interest.... When social or economic legislation is at issue the Equal Protection Clause allows the states

wide latitude, . . . and the Constitution presumes that even improvident [legislative] decisions will eventually be rectified by the democratic processes.*

It is no exaggeration to say that most laws that deal with economic and social legislation classify in some respects.some, because
of their age, are allowed to drive automobiles, and others are not.
There is also an age limit for purchasing alcoholic beverages and
voting. Many occupations are restricted to those who hold licenses,
and by our zoning laws we allow property to be used for some purposes but not others. We tax most real property but exempt property
owned by a charitable or religious organization. And the list goes on.
    Social and economic classifications, like other categorizations
that treat similarly situated people differently, trigger the equal protection clause. That is not to say that such disparate treatment is
necessarily unconstitutional. Only social and economic distinctions
that a court finds not rationally related to a legitimate governmental
goal are struck down. And more than fifty years ago, Justice Jackson
expressed the opinion that "while claims of denial of equal protection are frequently asserted, they are rarely sustained."[56]
    Justice Jackson made that statement concurring in a decision
which upheld a New York City traffic regulation that banned from
city streets any vehicle having advertising on it. The city had apparently concluded that advertising on vehicles constituted a dis-
traction which led to accidents and therefore enacted the regulation
for safety purposes. The regulation, however, permitted advertising
on vehicles used by the owner of the business being advertised.
    Railway Express, which sold space on the sides of its delivery
trucks, was convicted of violating the law and appealed through
New York courts to the Supreme Court. It argued that not allowing
businesses to carry advertising for others but permitting businesses
to advertise on their own trucks was a classification in violation of
equal protection. The Court disagreed and affirmed the conviction.
The Court accepted the argument "that those who advertise their
own wares on their trucks do not present the same traffic problem
in view of the nature or extent of the advertising which they use."
This made the classification rational and constitutional. Justice Jackson was skeptical that there was less hazard to traffic from business
messages on an owner's vehicle than from advertising on rented

*City of Cleburne v. Cleburne Living Center, 473 U.S. 432, 440 (1985).

space on other vehicles, but concluded that that was not his business and voted to affirm.

Grandfather clauses in laws and regulations have the effect of favoring those exempted from compliance and discriminating against those who must obey. That was the situation when New Orleans enacted an ordinance prohibiting vendors "selling . . . foodstuffs from pushcarts in the Vieux Carré, or French Quarter."[57] Vendors who had operated pushcarts in the French Quarter for more than eight years were allowed to continue. Two vendors, one who sold hot dogs and another who sold ice cream, had operated their push-carts for more than twenty years and were therefore exempt from the law. Nancy Dukes, who had operated a pushcart business selling hot dogs, drinks, confections, and novelties in the French Quarter for only two years, sued the city, asserting that the regulation was discriminatory and therefore a violation of equal protection.

District Court Judge Jack M. Gordon granted judgment for the city. The court of appeals upheld Duke's equal protection claim and reversed. A unanimous Supreme Court, however, concluded that the grandfather clause did not violate the equal protection clause and set aside the court of appeals decision. Recognizing that they were dealing with an economic regulation, the justices set forth the constitutional rule relating to such classifications.

> Unless a classification trammels fundamental personal rights or is drawn upon inherently suspect distinctions such as race, religion, or alienage, our decisions presume the constitutionality of the statutory discriminations and require only that the classification challenged be rationally related to a legitimate state interest. States are accorded wide latitude in the regulation of their local economies under their police powers, and rational distinctions may be made with substantially less than mathematical exactitude.

The city asserted that the purpose of the ordinance was to "preserve the appearance and custom valued by the Quarter's residents and attractive to tourists." Dukes countered that allowing some vendors to operate and not others was arbitrary and irrational. But the justices accepted the city's position. "The city," the opinion stated, "could reasonably decide that newer businesses were less likely to have built up substantial reliance interests in continued operation in the Vieux Carré and that the two vendors who qualified under the 'grandfather clause'—both of whom had operated in the area for over 20 years rather than only eight—had themselves become part of the distinctive character and charm that distinguishes the Vieux Carré. We cannot say that these judgments so lack rationality that they constitute a constitutionally impermissible denial of equal protection."

Sometimes government regulations, while not affecting fundamental rights, touch such sensitive areas of society that finding them arbitrary and unreasonable, and therefore unconstitutional, is not difficult for the courts. Jacinta Moreno, Sheilah Hejny, and Victoria Keppler brought this kind of a case to the courts when they sued the Department of Argiculture for excluding them from the food stamp program.[58]

> Jacinta Moreno . . . is a 56-year-old diabetic who lives with Ermina Sanchez and the latter's three children. They share common living expenses, and Mrs. Sanchez helps to care for [Moreno]. [Moreno's] monthly income, derived from public assistance, is $75; Mrs. Sanchez receives $133 per month from public assistance. [After paying her share of utilities, her transportation, etc., Moreno is left with] $10 per month for food and other necessities. Despite her poverty, [she] has been denied federal food assistance solely because she is unrelated to the other members of her household.
>
> . . . .
>
> Sheilah Hejny is married and has three children. Although the Hejnys are indigent, they took in a 20-year-old girl, who is unrelated to them, because [they] "felt she had emotional problems." The Hejnys receive $144 worth of food stamps each month for $14. If they allow the 20-year-old girl to continue to live with them, they will be denied food stamps [because they too will have an unrelated person living with them].
>
> . . . .
>
> Victoria Keppler has a daughter with an acute hearing deficiency. The daughter requires special instruction in a school for the deaf. . . . In order to make the most of her limited resources, [Keppler] agreed to share an apartment near the school with a woman who, like [Keppler,] is on public assistance. Since [Keppler] is not related to the woman, [her] food stamps have been, and will continue to be, cut off if they continue to live together.

The reason these women are unable to receive food stamps was that the law specifically excluded "households containing one or more members who are unrelated to the rest."

Moreno, Keppler, and Hejny, together with other plaintiffs,

instituted a class action against the Department of Agriculture" alleging that the law created an "irrational classification in violation of the equal protection component of the Due Process Clause of the Fifth Amendment." Seven justices of the Supreme Court accepted their argument and held the law unconstitutional. In reaching their decision, the justices examined the purpose of the food stamp program and found that Congress wanted to eliminate hunger and malnutrition among low-income people and at the same time utilize surplus agricultural products. The Court could find no connection between those goals and excluding unrelated households from the program.

Searching for some other governmental interests that might justify the classification, the justices found that the legislative history of the law indicated that it "was intended to prevent so-called 'hippies' and 'hippie communes' from participating in the food stamp program." "The challenged classification," declared Justice Brennan for the majority, "clearly cannot be sustained by reference to this congressional purpose. For if the constitutional conception of 'equal protection of the laws' means anything, it must at the very least mean that a bare congressional desire to harm a politically unpopular group cannot constitute a *legitimate* governmental interest." The government then contended that the purpose of the law was to minimize fraud in the food stamp program. The answer to that was that even if the goal was accepted as valid, the exclusion of "*all* otherwise eligible households containing unrelated members [was not] a rational effort to deal with these concerns." This brought the majority to the conclusion that the law was "wholly without any rational basis," therefore invalid.

In an extensive concurring opinion, Justice Douglas stressed the fact that these people were being penalized for exercising their right to freedom of association. "We deal here, however," he maintained, "with the right of association, protected by the First Amendment. People who are desperately poor but unrelated come together and join hands with the aim better to combat the crises of poverty. The need of those living together better to meet those crises is denied, while the need of households made up of relatives that is no more acute is serviced."

Although Justice Rehnquist and Chief Justice Burger may have agreed that Congress used the wrong method to accomplish its goals, they thought that the judiciary should not interfere and dissented. Justice Rehnquist declared:

> Undoubtedly, Congress attacked the problem with a rather blunt in-
> strument and, just as undoubtedly, persuasive arguments may be
> made that what we conceive to be its purpose will not be significantly
> advanced by the enactment of the limitation. But questions such as
> this are for Congress, rather than for this Court; our role is limited
> to the determination of whether there is any rational basis on which
> Congress could decide that public funds made available under the
> food stamp program should not go to a household containing an in-
> dividual who is unrelated to any other member of the household.

They were of the opinion that even though "the limitation will have
unfortunate and perhaps unintended consequences, . . . this does
not make it unconstitutional."

When the Massachusetts Board of Retirement forced Robert
Murgia to retire as a state policeman at the age of fifty, he went to
court to get his job back. Murgia claimed that the state's mandatory
retirement age for police officers discriminated against those who
like him, were in excellent physical and mental condition and therefore violated equal protection. A three-judge district court concluded
that "'a classification based on age 50 alone lacks a rational basis in
furthering any substantial state interest,' and enjoined enforcement
of the statute."[59]

The Supreme Court reversed, with only Justice Marshall dissenting. The majority was of the opinion that the district court's application of the rational-basis standard was correct but disagreed
that the retirement age lacked a "rational basis." Despite the fact that
Murgia was in good health and that testimony indicated that some
individuals over fifty could perform well as a police officer, the
justices seemed impressed with the testimony of what the aging process does to people generally.

> The testimony clearly established that the risk of physical failure,
> particularly in the cardiovascular system, increases with age, and
> that the number of individuals in a given age group incapable of per-
> forming stress functions increases with the age of the group.

In response to the argument that the Court should apply the strict-
scrutiny standard, the opinion stated: "Equal protection analysis requires strict scrutiny of a legislative classification only when the
classification impermissibly interferes with the exercise of a fundamental right or operates to the peculiar disadvantage of a suspect
class." And neither was involved in this case.

The justices then turned to an examination of the state's goal for the retirement age of its police officers. That goal was protection of the public by being assured that its police officers were physically fit to do their job. Because the evidence indicated that as individuals grow older, their abilities decrease, mandatory retirement at age fifty was a rational method of protecting the public from officers who might not be fully capable of doing their work. But this left unanswered the question whether the state could achieve its goal by individualized testing. The justices answered that "the State chooses not to determine fitness more precisely through individualized testing after age 50 is not to say that the objective of assuring physical fitness is not rationally furthered by a maximum-age limitation. It is only to say that with regard to the interest of all concerned, the State perhaps has not chosen the best means to accomplish this purpose. But where rationality is the test, a State, 'does not violate the Equal Protection Clause merely because the classifications made by its laws are imperfect.'"

This case created an aberration for Justice Marshall. He pointed out that the Court had heretofore "called the right to work 'of the very essence of the personal freedom and opportunity that it was the purpose of the (Fourteenth) Amendment to secure.'" He then assailed the Court for rigidly adhering to a two-tiered analysis — strict scrutiny and rational relationship — in equal protection cases and argued that "there is simply no reason why a statute that tells able-bodied police officers, ready and willing to work, that they no longer have the right to earn a living in their chosen profession merely because they are 50 years old should be judged by the same minimal standards of rationality that we use to test economic legislation that discriminates against business interests." Justice Marshall argued for a more flexible approach to equal protection issues. He would require the state in this case to "show a reasonably substantial interest and a scheme reasonably closely tailored to achieving that interest." He pointed out that that is similar to the approach the Court took in *Reed* when it struck down an Idaho law which required the appointment of a male rather than a female as the administrator of an estate.

In reality, the justices have used a multitiered approach to equal protection cases, and Justice Marshall acknowledged this. In cases involving gender and illegitimacy classifications, the Court has required states to show that the reason for the discrimination is "substantially related to an important governmental objective."[60]

The use of the multitiered approach to discrimination cases finds the justices sometimes at odds as to which tier is appropriate, and that was true in Jan Hannah's case.

> In July 1980, Jan Hannah purchased a house at 201 Featherston Street in Cleburne, Texas. Hannah is the Vice President and part owner of Cleburne Living Centers, Inc. ("CLC"), a Texas corporation organized for the purpose of establishing and operating supervised group homes for the mentally retarded.... [The Featherston Street house was to be leased by Hannah to CLC and used for that purpose.]
>
> . . . .
>
> The home would house thirteen men and women who are mildly or moderately retarded. They would receive twenty-four hour supervision from CLC staff members, working eight-hour shifts. In addition to handling some cooking and cleaning, the staff would work with the mentally retarded residents to train them in such skills as "kitchen management, maintenance, personal budgeting, meat preparation, academics related to independent living (such as how to read classified advertisements for jobs and housing), and the use and enjoyment of leisure time activities."[61]

The city denied CLC a special-use permit to operate the home. Special-use permits were "required for the construction of '(h)ospitals for the insane or feeble-minded, or alcoholic . . . or drug addicts, or penal or correctional institutions.'"[62] And this home was a "hospital for the feeble-minded."

CLC brought suit in a federal district court, asserting that the city was discriminating against the mentally retarded. Judge Robert W. Porter, "concluding that no fundamental right was implicated and that mental retardation was neither a suspect nor a quasi-suspect classification,... employed the minimum level of judicial scrutiny applicable to equal protection claims. The court deemed the ordinance, as written and applied to be rationally related to the City's legitimate interests in the 'legal responsibility of CLC and its residents, . . . the safety and fears of residents in the adjoining neighborhood,' and the number of people in the home." A court of appeals reversed, basing its decision on a determination that classifications affecting mental retardation should be examined under the intermediate level of scrutiny, and therefore, not only was the ordinance invalid, but it was invalidly applied.

The Supreme Court affirmed. There was, however, disagreement among the justices as to which equal protection standard should be applied. In an extensive discussion of mental retardation, the majority noted that the mentally retarded "are not all cut from the same pattern: as the testimony in this record indicates, they range from those whose disability is not immediately evident to those who must be constantly cared for." Further, lawmakers have recognized the needs of the mentally retarded and enacted laws extending special treatment to them. Some of these laws may be viewed as a disadvantage to the mentally retarded, but "given the wide variation in the abilities and needs of the retarded themselves, governmental bodies must have a certain amount of flexibility and freedom from judicial oversight in shaping and limiting their remedial efforts." Therefore, the majority concluded, "to withstand equal protection review, legislation that distinguishes between mentally retarded and others must be rationally related to a legitimate governmental purpose."

The majority examined four reasons given by the city for denying the permits to CLC. First, the city was concerned about the negative attitude of those living near the home. The justices brushed this aside as not a valid reason to deny the permit. Second, the city saw a problem with the location of the property, across from a junior high school. "It feared that the students might harass the occupants of the Featherston home." But the Court noted that about thirty mentally retarded students were attending that school and there didn't seem to be a problem. Then the city argued that the home was located in a "five hundred year flood plain." That didn't impress the justices either; the law would have allowed the existence of nursing homes, convalescent homes, homes for the aged, sanitariums, and hospitals in this area.

Finally the city expressed concern whether the size of the home could accommodate the number of people CLC expected to house there. Judge Porter, however, had found that "(i)f the potential residents of the Featherston Street home were not mentally retarded, but the home was the same in all other respects, its use would be permitted under the city's zoning ordinance." Justice White, for the majority, then declared: "The short of it is that requiring the permit in this case appears to us to rest on an irrational prejudice against the mentally retarded, including those who would occupy the Featherston facility, and who would live under the closely supervised and highly regulated conditions expressly provided for by state and federal law."

Justice Stevens and Chief Justice Burger concurred but found it difficult to accept the majority's multitiered approach. "Our cases,"

Justice Stevens insisted. "have not delineated three—or even one or two—such well-defined standards. Rather, our cases reflect a continuum of judgmental responses to differing classifications which have been explained in opinions by terms ranging from 'strict scrutiny' at one extreme to 'rational basis' at the other. I have never been persuaded that these so-called 'standards' adequately explain the decisional process."

Concurring with the majority in the decision but disagreeing with them on the standard use, Justice Marshall, for himself and justices Brennan and Blackmun, took the majority to task. Despite the majority's assertion that they were using a rational-basis test, the scrutiny given the classification was "most assuredly not the rational-basis test" of old. These concurring justices would have used a heightened level of scrutiny and gotten to the same result. Their principal concern was that generally most classifications tested under the rational-basis test were found to be valid. Using that test in cases like this, where personal rights were involved, could lead lower courts to follow the same pattern and sustain those kinds of classifications. Requiring lower courts to apply a higher level of scrutiny would make it more difficult for governments to discriminate.

CHAPTER 4

The Search for Liberty

> Striving to assure itself and the public that announcing
> rights not readily identifiable in the Constitution's text
> involves much more than the imposition of the Justices'
> own choice of values on the States and Federal Govern-
> ment, the Court has sought to identify the nature of the
> rights qualifying for heightened judicial protection. . . . It
> was said that this category includes those fundamental
> liberties that are "implicit in the concept of ordered lib-
> erty," such that "neither liberty nor justice would exist if
> [they] were sacrificed."
> —*Bowers v. Hardwick, 478 U.S. 186, 191–192 (1986).*

The Founding Fathers and Others

It is clear that people living in the colonies prior to the adoption
of the Bill of Rights assumed that they had many rights, although
they may not have agreed on just what those rights were. George
Mason, a delegate to the Constitutional Convention, for example,
expressed concern that the proposed Constitution did not contain a
bill of rights and moved that one be prepared and adopted. The motion failed. He therefore specifically refused to sign the Constitution,
giving as one of the reasons the lack of protection for the unnamed
rights of the people.
He wrote:

> There is no declaration of rights: and the laws of the general govern-
> ment being paramount to the laws and constitutions of the several
> states, the declarations of rights, in the separate states, are not security.[1]

The lack of protection for rights in the proposed constitution,
became the battle cry of the Anti-federalists, who opposed ratification. One of those who opposed the Constitution was Hugh Henry
Brackenridge, who eloquently expressed his concern this way:

The want of a bill of rights is a great evil. There was no occasion for a bill of wrongs; for there will be wrongs enough. But oh! a bill of rights. What is the nature of a bill of rights? "It is a schedule or inventory of those powers which Congress do[es] not possess." But if it is clearly ascertained what powers they have, what need of a catalogue of those powers they have, what need of a catalogue of those powers they have not? Ah! there is the mistake. A minister preaching, undertook, first, to show what was in his text; second, what was not in it. When it is specified what powers are given, why not also what powers are not given? A bill of rights is wanting, and all those things which are usually secured under it — .[2]

Neither Mason nor Brackenridge gave us a list of the rights they were concerned about. They probably would not have been able to agree on what the list would contain, but it is clear that they believed that some rights did exist.

Even the Federalists, strong supporters of the proposed Constitution, which did not contain a bill of rights, were concerned about people's rights. Federalist Alexander Hamilton argued that the inclusion of a bill of rights in the constitution would be dangerous because it would leave the implication that those enumerated were all there were. "I go further, and affirm that bills of rights in the sense and in the extent in which they are contended for, are not only unnecessary in the proposed constitution, but would even be dangerous. They would contain various exceptions to powers which are not granted; and on this very account, would afford a colourable pretext to claim more than were granted. For why declare that things shall not be done which there is no power to do?"[3]

James Madison acknowledged the validity of Hamilton's argument and expressed his own concern.

It has been objected also against a bill of rights, that, by enumerating particular exceptions to the grant of power, it would disagree those rights which were not placed in that enumeration; and it might follow by implication, that those rights which were not singled out, were intended to be assigned into the hands of the General Government, and were consequently insecure. This is one of the most plausible arguments I have heard against admission of a bill of rights into this system; but, I conceive, that it may be guarded against. I have attempted it, as gentlemen may see by turning to the last clause of the fourth resolution.[4]

The last clause of Madison's fourth resolution read: "The exceptions here or elsewhere in the constitution, made in favor of particular rights, shall not be so construed as to diminish the just importance of other rights retained by the people."[5] That clause eventually became the Ninth Amendment: "The enumeration in the Constitution, of certain rights, shall not be construed to deny or disparage others retained by the people."

Despite the fact that this forthright statement indicates that the people had rights the Constitution did not take away, it has not played an important role in defining those rights. Justice Goldberg, however, in voting to recognize a right of privacy, made a strong argument that the Ninth Amendment was intended to preserve rights not specifically guaranteed in the other amendments. "Rather," he declared, "as the Ninth Amendment expressly recognizes, there are fundamental personal rights such as this one [the right to marital privacy] which are protected from abridgment by the Government though not specifically mentioned in the Constitution."[6] This view has not been adopted by a majority of the justices.

If the Ninth Amendment is not the source of rights retained by the people, where else in the Constitution might one look? Justice Harlan [the grandson] suggested that such rights can be found in the word *liberty* of the due process clause.

> The full scope of the liberty guaranteed by the Due Process Clause cannot be found in or limited by the precise terms of the specific guarantees elsewhere provided in the Constitution. This "liberty" is not a series of isolated points pricked out in terms of the taking of property; the freedom of speech, press, and religion; the right to keep and bear arms; the freedom from unreasonable searches and seizures; and so on. It is a rational continuum which, broadly speaking, includes a freedom from all substantial arbitrary impositions and purposeless restraints, . . . and which also recognizes, what a reasonable and sensitive judgment must, that certain interests require particularly careful scrutiny of the state needs asserted to justify their abridgement.[7]

The idea that there were unnamed rights the Court could and would reveal as time went on did not go unchallenged. For Justice Black, this approach was totally unacceptable. He saw the argument as a resort to "natural justice," which did not belong in the judicial decision-making process. "If these formulas based on 'natural justice,'" he insisted, "or others which mean the same thing, are to prevail, they require judges to determine what is or what is not constitutional on the basis of their own appraisal of what laws are unwise or unnecessary. The power to make such decisions is of course that of a legislative body."[8]

Picking and Choosing Rights

> The Court today does not "pick out particular human activities, characterize them as 'fundamental,' and give them added protection. . . ." To the contrary, the Court simply recognizes, as it must, an established constitutional right, and gives to that right no less protection than the Constitution itself demands.*

When the justices began to identify those human activities that were fundamental and therefore entitled to constitutional protection, there were no signposts to guide them in their search. And they were therefore forced to "pick out particular human activities, and characterize them as 'fundamental.'"

For example, in 1915 the justices found a right to work in a case brought by Mike Raich, an alien, who had been discharged from his job as a cook. Raich was fired because an Arizona law required that any work force in excess of five workers must be composed of 80 percent "qualified electors or native-born citizens of the United States."[9] Citing several cases in which the Court had previously referred to a right to earn a living, the majority specifically held: "It requires no argument to show that the right to work for a living in the common occupations of the community is the very essence of the personal freedom and opportunity that it was the purpose of the [Fourteenth] Amendment to secure."[10]

The justices took the same approach in recognizing certain parental rights in *Meyer* and *Society of Sisters*, discussed in Chapter 1. Writing for a unanimous Court, Justice McReynolds declared in *Sisters*, "We think it entirely plain that the [Oregon law requiring all children to attend public schools] unreasonably interferes with the liberty of parents and guardians to direct the upbringing and education of children under their control."[11]

In the 1920s and 1930s lawyers began to argue to the Court that states should be required to follow the guarantees of the First Amendment, and the justices agreed. But again, there was no beacon of light which led directly to that conclusion. When it accepted the argument that states are bound by the free speech provision, the justices could find nothing more definitive to say than "for present purpose we may and do assume that freedom of speech and of the press — which are protected by the First Amendment from abridgment by Congress — are among the fundamental personal rights and 'liberties' protected by the due process clause of the Fourteenth Amendment from impairment by the States."[12]

In holding that the states were bound to recognize the right of the people peaceably to assemble, Chief Justice Hughes sought in a general way to establish the criteria which made the right fundamental. "For the right is one," he explained, "that cannot be denied without violating those fundamental principles of liberty and justice which lie at the base of all civil and political institutions — principles which the Fourteenth Amendment embodies in the general terms of the due process clause."[13]

It fell to Justice Cardozo, however, to define in only slightly more definitive terms just how fundamental rights were to be identified. He declared:

> In these and other situations immunities [in the Bill of Rights] that are valid as against the federal government by force of the specific pledges of particular amendments have been found to by *implicit in the concept of ordered liberty,* and thus, through the Fourteenth Amendment, become valid as against the states.[14]

The Concept of Ordered Liberty

> I do agree that the concept of liberty protects those personal rights that are fundamental, and is not confined to the specific terms of the Bill of Rights.*

The above statement is from the concurring opinion of justices Goldberg and Brennan and Chief Justice Warren in the right to privacy case *Griswold v. Connecticut.* These justices also pointed out that "the Court stated many years ago that the Due Process Clause protects those liberties that are 'so rooted in the traditions and conscience of our people as to be ranked fundamental.'"

As pointed out in Chapter 1, the justices have found many liberties not listed in the Bill of Rights that are fundamental because they are deeply "rooted in the traditions and conscience of our people." Among the rights deemed fundamental and within the concept of

Griswold v. Connecticut, 381 U.S. 479, 486 (1965).

ordered liberty are parental rights, rights affecting marriage and family relationships, the right to be let alone, and protection for the mentally ill, minors, and prisoners. And the process continues, as evidenced by the justices' recent acknowledgment that Nancy Cruzan had a "right to die," and that Walter Harper had "a significant liberty interest in avoiding the unwanted administration of antipsychotic drugs."

The acknowledgment that these rights exist and that there may be others not yet identified is in the best tradition of our country, as declared by those who signed the Declaration of Independence:

> We hold these truths to be self-evident, that all men are created equal, that they are endowed by their Creator with certain unalienable rights, that among these are life, liberty and the pursuit of happiness.

Notes

A note regarding citations of court cases: "X v. Y, 25 U.S. 372, 376 (19nn)" means that the X v. Y opinion appears in volume 25 of the *United States* reporter at page 372, that the quotation appears at page 376, and that the case was decided in 19nn.

Preface

1. Address at the Sanitary Fair, Baltimore [April 18, 1864]. See *Bartlett's Familiar Quotations*, p. 523.7.
2. *On Liberty* [1859]. See *Bartlett's Familiar Quotations*, p. 508.13, .15.
3. McNabb v. United States, 318 U.S. 332, 347 (1943).
4. Olmstead v. United States, 277 U.S. 438, 478 (1928).
5. *Bartlett's Familiar Quotations*, p. 134.8.
6. Solesbee v. Balkcom, 339 U.S. 9, 16 (1950).
7. "Chief Justice Warren's Fair Question," 58 *Georgetown Law Journal* 1, 4–5 (1969).
8. *Le Lys Rouge* [1894], ch. 7. See *Bartlett's Familiar Quotations*, p. 655.14.
9. Louisville Gas Co. v. Coleman, 277 U.S. 32, 37 (1928).
10. New Orleans v. Dukes, 427 U.S. 297, 303 (1976).
11. *Speech upon the Right of Election of the Lord Mayor of Dublin* [July 10, 1790]. See *Bartlett's Familiar Quotations*, p. 397.21.

Chapter 1.

1. Diogenes Laertius, *Lives of Eminent Philosophers*, bk. 6, sec. 2.
2. Speech in Virginia Convention, Richmond, March 23, 1775.
3. *Historical Review of Pennsylvania* (1759).
4. J. W. Ehrlich, *Ehrlich's Blackstone* (San Carlos, CA, Nourse, 1959), p. 49.
5. In re Gault, 387 U.S. 1, 20 (1967).
6. Munn v. Illinois, 94 U.S. 113, 142 (1877).
7. James Madison, 1 *Annals of Congress* 439 (1789).
8. L. Hand, *The Spirit of Liberty: Papers and Addresses of Learned Hand*, (Dillard ed., 1959), 144.
9. Meyer v. Nebraska, 262 U.S. 390 (1923).
10. Society of the Sisters of the Holy Name of Jesus and Mary v. Pierce, 296 Fed. Rep. 928, 929 (1924).
11. Pierce v. Society of Sisters, 268 U.S. 510, 534–535 (1925).

12. Commonwealth v. Prince, 46 N.E.2d 755, 756 (1943).
13. Prince v. Massachusetts, 321 U.S. 158, 164 (1944).
14. Wisconsin v. Yoder, 406 U.S. 205, 209 (1972).
15. 405 U.S. 645 (1972).
16. Lehr v. Robertson, 463 U.S. 248, 249 (1983).
17. Loving v. Virginia, 388 U.S. 1, 3 (1967).
18. Zablocki v. Redhail, 434 U.S. 374, 383 (1978).
19. Skinner v. Oklahoma, 316 U.S. 535, 541 (1942).
20. Cleveland Board of Education v. La. Fleur, 414 U.S. 632, 639–640 (1974).
21. Moore v. East Cleveland, 431 U.S. 494, 506 (1977).
22. Jacobson v. Massachusetts, 197 U.S. 11, 14 (1905).
23. 381 U.S. 479 (1965).
24. 410 U.S. 113 (1973).
25. 106 L. Ed. 2d 410 (1989).
26. Planned Parenthood of Missouri v. Danforth, 428 U.S. 52, 70 (1976).
27. 60 LW 4795 (1992).
28. Cruzan v. Director, Missouri Dept. of Health, 110 S. Ct. 2841, 2845 (1990).
29. Kelley v. Johnson, 425 U.S. 238, 239–240 (1976).
30. Hardwick v. Bowers, 760 F.2d 1202, 1204 (1985).
31. Bowers v. Hardwick, 478 U.S. 186, 190 (1986).
32. In re Gault, 387 U.S. 1, 4 (1967).
33. Ingraham v. Wright, 430 U.S. 651, 657 (1977).
34. 428 U.S. at 74.
35. Planned Parenthood Assn. v. Ashcroft, 462 U.S. 476, 479 (1983).
36. 450 U.S. 398 (1981).
37. Ohio v. Akron Center for Reproductive Health, 110 S. Ct. 2972, 2984 (1990).
38. Parham v. J.R., 442 U.S. 584, 600 (1979).
39. Ibid, at 599.
40. 274 U.S. 200 (1927). In Foucha v. Louisiana, 112 S. Ct. 1780 (1992) the Court held that when a person is found not guilty by reason of insanity a state cannot continue to hold the person if he is no longer mentally ill. If the state desires to continue to confine the person, it can do so only by complying with the procedural due process standards discussed at pages 90–95.
41. Jackson v. Indiana, 406 U.S. 715, 717 (1972).
42. O'Connor v. Donaldson, 422 U.S. 563, 565 (1975).
43. 457 U.S. 307 (1982).
44. Wolff v. McDonnell, 418 U.S. 539, 546 (1974).
45. Meachum v. Fano, 427 U.S. 215, 216 (1976).
46. Vitek v. Jones, 445 U.S. 480, 484 (1980).
47. Morrissey v. Brewer, 408 U.S. 471, 472–473 (1972). In Riggins v. Nevada, 112 S. Ct. 1810 (1992) a majority of the Court held that the forced administration of antipsychotic drugs during the course of the defendant's trial for murder violated his right to a fair trial.
48. 110 S. Ct. 1028 (1990).
49. Board of Pardons v. Allen, 107 S. Ct. 2415, 2420 (1987).
50. Slaughter-House Cases, 83 U.S. 36 (1873).
51. See Munn v. Illinois, 94 U.S. 113 (1877), elevators; Barbier v. Connolly, 113 U.S. 27 (1885), laundries; Mugler v. Kansas, 123 U.S. 623 (1887) liquor; Powell v. Pennsylvania, 127 U.S. 678 (1888), margarine; Dent v. West Virginia, 129 U.S. 114 (1889), physician's license; Frisbie v. United States, 157 U.S. 160 (1895), attorney's fees.
52. Dent v. West Virginia, 129 U.S. 114, 128 (1889).
53. Holden v. Hardy, 169 U.S. 366, 367 (1898).
54. Lochner v. New York, 198 U.S. 45, 46 (1905).

55. Muller v. Oregon, 208 U.S. 412, 416 (1908). See also Riley v. Massachusetts, 232 U.S. 671 (1914); Miller v. Wilson, 236 U.S. 373 (1915).
56. Radice v. New York, 264 U.S. 292 (1924).
57. Adkins v. Children's Hospital, 261 U.S. 525, 542 (1923).
58. 300 U.S. 379 (1937).
59. Williamson v. Lee Optical Co., 348 U.S. 483, 485 (1955).
60. Ferguson v. Skrupa, 372 U.S. 726–727 (1963).
61. New Motor Vehicle Board v. Orrin W. Fox Co., 439 U.S. 96, 107 (1978).
62. Di Martini v. Ferrin, 906 F. 2d 465, 466 (1990).
63. Barron v. Mayor and City Council of Baltimore, 32 U.S. 243, 246 (1833).
64. Gitlow v. New York, 268 U.S. 652 (1925).
65. Benton v. Maryland, 395 U.S. 784, 795 (1969).
66. Adamson v. California, 332 U.S. 46, 71–72 (1947).
67. Ibid. at 124, Justice Murphy; See also Justice Douglas dissenting in Poe v. Ullman, 367 U.S. 497, 515 (1961).
68. Duncan v. Louisiana, 391 U.S. 145, 177 (1968).

Chapter 2

1. Board of Regents v. Roth, 408 U.S. 564, 567 (1972).
2. Kelly v. Wyman, 294 F. Supp. 893, 904 (1968).
3. Goldberg v. Kelly, 397 U.S. 254 (1970).
4. Eldridge v. Weinberger, 361 F. Supp. 520, 522 (1973).
5. Mathews v. Eldridge, 424 U.S. 319, 323 (1976).
6. 397 U.S. at 262–263.
7. Ibid. at 268–269.
8. Armstrong v. Manzo, 380 U.S. 545, 550 (1965).
9. Santosky v. Kramer, 455 U.S. 745, 755 (1982).
10. Lassiter v. Dept. of Social Services, 452 U.S. 18, 21 (1981).
11. Little v. Streater, 452 U.S. 1, 3 (1981).
12. 483 U.S. 574 (1987).
13. 105 L. Ed. 2d 91 (1989).
14. In re Winship, 397 U.S. 358, 360 (1970).
15. McKeiver v. Pennsylvania, 403 U.S. 528, 536 (1971).
16. McNeil v. Director, Patuxent Institution, 407 U.S. 245, 246 (1972).
17. Addington v. Texas, 441 U.S. 418, 419–420 (1979).
18. 442 U.S. at 606.
19. 445 U.S. at 494–495.
20. 408 U.S. at 485.
21. 411 U.S. 778 (1973).
22. Ng Fung Ho. v. White, 259 U.S. 276, 282 (1922).
23. Chaunt v. United States, 364 U.S. 350, 353 (1960).
24. 387 U.S. 253 (1967).
25. Vance v. Terrazas, 444 U.S. 252 (1980).
26. Constitution, art. I, sect. 8, cl. 4.
27. Fong Yue Ting v. United States, 149 U.S. 698, 713 (1893).
28. Ibid, at 703.
29. United States v. Colding, 97 F. Supp. 592–593 (1951).
30. Kwong Hai Chew v. Colding, et al. 344 U.S. 590, 591 (1953).
31. 459 U.S. 21 (1982).
32. Lopez v. Williams, 372 F. Supp. 1279, 1285 (1973).
33. Goss v. Lopez, 419 U.S. 565, 572 (1975).

34. Board of Curators, U. of Missouri v. Horowitz, 435 U.S. 78, 87 (1978).
35. Perry v. Sindermann, 408 U.S. 593, 600 (1972).
36. 424 U.S. at 333.
37. 470 U.S. 532 (1985).
38. Loudermill v. Cleveland Bd. of Educ., 721 F.2d 550, 552 (1983).
39. 470 U.S. at 532.
40. Bell v. Burson, 402 U.S. 535, 537 (1971).
41. Mackey v. Montrym, 443 U.S. 1, 4–5 (1979).
42. Barry v. Barchi, 443 U.S. 55, 59 (1979).
43. 390 U.S. 544 (1968).
44. Ibid, at 550.
45. Willner v. Committee on Character, 373 U.S. 96, 102 (1963).
46. Sniadach v. Family Finance Corp., 395 U.S. 337, 338–339 (1969).
47. Mitchell v. W. T. Grant Co., 416 U.S. 600, 602–603 (1974).
48. Memphis Light, Gas & Water Div. v. Craft, 436 U.S. 1, 5 (1978).
49. Tumey v. Ohio, 273 U.S. 510, 515 (1927).
50. Gibson v. Berryhill. 411 U.S. 564, 568 (1973).
51. Berryhill v. Gibson, 331 F. Supp. 122, 126 (1971).
52. 411 U.S. at 579.
53. 363 U.S. 603 (1960).
54. In re Summers, 325 U.S. 561, 569 (1945).
55. Labine v. Vincent, 401 U.S. 532, 542 (1971).
56. Shaughnessy v. Mezei, 345 U.S. 206, 216–217 (1953).
57. United States v. Stanley, 483 U.S. 669, 674 (1987).
58. 60 U.S. 393 (1857).
59. 323 U.S. 214 (1944).
60. 60 U.S. at 396
61. Korematsu v. United States, 323 U.S. 214, 218 (1944).
62. 8 *California Western Law Review* 189 (1972).

Chapter 3

1. Strauder v. West Virginia, 100 U.S. 303, 305 (1880). See also Hernandez v. Texas, 347 U.S. 475 (1954) where the Court held that "the systematic exclusion of persons of Mexican descent from service" as jurors violated equal protection.
2. 118 U.S. 356 (1886).
3. 163 U.S. 537 (1896).
4. 347 U.S. 483 (1954).
5. Swann v. Board of Education, 402 U.S. 1, 13 (1971). The Court heard the *Brown* case again in 1955 and ordered desegregation "with all deliberate speed." The Court, however, had to decide a desegregation case as recently at 1990; see Missouri v. Jenkins, 110 S. Ct. 1651 (1990).
6. Palmore v. Sidoti, 466 U.S. 429, 431 (1984).
7. Hunter v. Underwood, 471 U.S. 222, 223 (1985).
8. Powers v. Ohio, 50 LW 4268, 4269 (1991). "A premeptory challenge is a challenge to a juror to be exercised by a party to a civil action or prosecution without assignment of reason or cause." (*Ballentine's Law Dictionary*, 3d ed., p. 933). In Georgia v. McCollum 60 LW 4574 (1992) the Court held that a criminal defendant cannot exercise his/her peremptory challenges in a racially discriminatory manner just as the prosecutor was prohibited from doing so in the Powers Case.
9. Loving v. Virginia, 388 U.S. 1 (1967). This case is discussed in Chapter 1 under "Marriage and Family Life."
10. Graham v. Richardson, 403 U.S. 365, 367 (1971).

11. Sugarman v. Dougall, 413 U.S. 634 (1973).
12. In re Griffiths, 413 U.S. 717 (1973).
13. 441 U.S. 68 (1979).
14. Foley v. Connelie, 435 U.S. 291 (1978).
15. Cabell v. Chavez-Salido, 454 U.S. 432 (1982).
16. Bernal v. Fainter, 467 U.S. 216, 225 (1984).
17. 413 U.S. at 649–650.
18. Mathews v. Diaz, 426 U.S. 67 (1976).
19. Shapiro v. Thompson, 394 U.S. 618 (1969).
20. 419 U.S. 393 (1975).
21. Attorney General of N.Y. v. Soto-Lopez, 476 U.S. 898, 900–901 (1986).
22. McCarthy v. Philadelphia Civil Ser. Comm'n., 424 U.S. 645, 646–647 (1976).
23. Carrington v. Rash, 380 U.S. 89 (1965).
24. Kramer v. Union Free School Dist., No. 15, 282 F. Supp. 70, 71 (1968).
25. Kramer v. Union Free School Dist., No. 15, 395 U.S. 621, 622 (1969).
26. Harper v. Virginia Bd. of Elections, 383 U.S. 663 (1966).
27. Cipriano v. City of Houma, 395 U.S. 701, 705 (1969).
28. Dunn v. Blumstein, 405 U.S. 330 (1972).
29. Richardson v. Ramirez, 418 U.S. 24 (1974).
30. Marston v. Lewis, 410 U.S. 679 (1973).
31. Skinner v. Oklahoma, 316 U.S. 535, 539 (1942).
32. Zablocki v. Redhail, 434 U.S. 374 (1978). See discussion of this case in Chapter 1 under "Marriage and Family Life."
33. 434 U.S. 246 (1978).
34. These words are etched in stone above the entrance to the Supreme Court Building in Washington, D.C.
35. 351 U.S. 12 (1956).
36. 372 U.S. 335 (1963).
37. Douglas v. California, 372 U.S. 353, 356 (1963).
38. Williams v. Illinois, 399 U.S. 235 (1970).
39. James v. Strange, 407 U.S. 128 (1972).
40. Bradwell v. The State, 83 U.S. 130, 132 (1873).
41. Minor v. Happersett, 88 U.S. 162, 163–164 (1875).
42. Goesaert v. Cleary, 335 U.S. 464, 465 (1948).
43. Reed v. Reed, 404 U.S. 71, 71–72 (1971).
44. 411 U.S. 677 (1973).
45. Craig v. Boren, 429 U.S. 190, 197 (1976).
46. Orr v. Orr, 440 U.S. 268, 280 (1979).
47. Mississippi University for Women v. Hogan, 458 U.S. 718, 719 (1982).
48. Weinberger v. Weisenfeld, 420 U.S. 636 (1975).
49. Califano v. Westcott, 443 U.S. 76 (1979).
50. Michael M. v. Sonoma County Superior Court, 450 U.S. 464 (1981).
51. Rostker v. Goldberg, 453 U.S. 57 (1981).
52. Levy v. Louisiana, 391 U.S. 68, 70 (1968).
53. 430 U.S. 762 (1977).
54. Lalli v. Lalli, 439 U.S. 259, 262 (1978).
55. Clark v. Jeter, 486 U.S. 456 (1988).
56. Railway Express v. New York, 336 U.S. 106, 111 (1949). In Nordlinger v. Hahn, 60 LW 4563 (1992) the Court upheld California's real property tax scheme, commonly known as Proposition 13. This law required real estate to be reassessed for tax purposes each time it was sold. Thus the new owner could be paying more taxes than his neighbor, who had purchased his home many years before. A majority of the Court upheld this unequal treatment concluding that it was rationally related to the state's interest in discouraging "rapid turnover of homes and businesses."

57. New Orleans v. Dukes, 427 U.S. 297, 298 (1976). "Grandfather clause. A clause in a licensing statute which exempts persons already engaged in the regulated business or occupation" (*Ballentine's Law Dictionary*, p. 532.)

58. U.S. Dept. of Agriculture v. Moreno, et al., 413 U.S. 528 (1973).

59. Massachusetts Bd. of Retirement v. Murgia, 427 U.S. 307, 310 (1976).

60. 486 U.S. at 461.

61. Cleburne Living Center v. City of Cleburne, Tex., 726 F.2d 191, 193 (1984).

62. Cleburne v. Cleburne Living Center, Inc., 473 U.S. 432, 436 (1985).

Chapter 4

1. Schwartz, *The Roots of the Bill of Rights*, vol. 2, p. 444.

2. Ibid, vol. 3, p. 522.

3. Ibid, vol. 3, p. 581.

4. 1 *Annals of Congress* 439 (1789).

5. Ibid., Schwartz, vol. 5, p. 1027.

6. Griswold v. Connecticut, 381 U.S. 479, 496 (1965).

7. Poe v. Ullman, 367 U.S. 497, 543 (1961).

8. 381 U.S. at 511–512.

9. Truax v. Raich, 239 U.S. 33, 35 (1915).

10. Ibid, at 41.

11. Pierce v. Society of Sisters, 268 U.S. 510, 535 (1925).

12. Gitlow v. New York, 268 U.S. 652, 666 (1925).

13. De Jonge v. Oregon, 299 U.S. 353, 364 (1937).

14. Palko v. Connecticut, 302 U.S. 319, 324–325 (1937). Italics supplied.

Index